# Street noises

Mon Dieu, mon Dieu, la vie est là
  Simple et tranquille!
Cette paisible rumeur-là
  Vient de la ville.   (Paul Verlaine, *D'une prison*)

# STREET NOISES

## Parisian pleasure, 1900–40

### ADRIAN RIFKIN

with a Foreword by George Melly

MANCHESTER UNIVERSITY PRESS

Manchester and New York

distributed exclusively in the USA and Canada by St. Martin's Press

Copyright © Adrian Rifkin, 1993. 1995

*Published by* Manchester University Press
Oxford Road, Manchester M13 9NR, UK
*and* Room 400, 175 Fifth Avenue, New York, NY 10010, USA

*Distributed exclusively in the USA and Canada*
*by* St. Martin's Press, Inc., 175 Fifth Avenue, New York, NY 10010, USA

*British Library Cataloguing-in-Publication Data*
A catalogue record for this book is available from the British Library

*Library of Congresss Cataloging-in-Publication Data*
Rifkin, Adrian.
    Street noises : Parisian pleasure, 1900-1940 / Adrian Rifkin
        p.      cm.
    Includes bibliographical references and index.
    ISBN 0-7190-3835-9 (hbk)
    1. Paris (France)—Social life and customs—20th century.
    I. Title.
    DC715.R56     1993
    944'.36081—dc20        92-29425

Paperback edition published 1995

ISBN 0 7190 4589 4 *paperback*

Typeset in Monotype Dante
with ITC Serif Gothic display
by Koinonia Limited, Manchester
Printed in Great Britain
by Biddles Ltd, Guildford and King's Lynn

# Foreword

The origins of this lively, original and provocative book were not immediately encouraging, and could have produced a dense yet boring, well-researched but lifeless tome. Adrian Rifkin has woven together several themes, not in themselves immediately related, and gradually created a coherent thesis; an image of Paris, not long ago intact, but now under threat from Macdonalds and Disneyland, from the universal threat of the sanitised theme-park, and of monuments 'scraped clean of history'. He admits, almost at the start, of coming towards his subject matter at a 'slight angle', but I don't believe that this works against the book, on the contrary. Indeed the effect is not unlike that of a cubist still-life; the solidity of his imagery is the more convincing for its prismatic viewpoints, its interlocking opaque planes. His aim is clearly stated; 'to release some of the repressed materials of the mythologies of Paris, to free them from those conventions that conscript them in the cruel objectivity of glamour'. In this he has succeeded triumphantly.

Although there are references to both ancient and modern Paris, most of the author's attention is focussed on the period between the turn of the century and the closing down of Les Halles. It would have been possible to have defined the city politically, but while politics play their part in explaining certain aspects of the story, they have a minor role. Equally the dazzling parade of art and literature is more or less intentionally pushed to the margins. Proust remains enclosed in his cork-lined room. The only reference to Lautrec is to warn us in advance that he won't be making an appearance. For all we hear of him, Picasso might have stayed in Spain. the Surrealists are to be spotted occasionally rooting about in the flea market, but their mythologising of the city (here I naturally disagree with him) is dismissed as marginal. The cinema on the other hand features widely, and in particular that great masterpiece *Les Enfants du Paradis*. The analysis of its meaning: the fact it was conceived and produced under the German occupation, the central importance of Jéricho, the treacherous old clothes man, and the interplay between theatre and reality, is both precise and at the same time suggestive. For all its historical accuracy, it acts as a metaphor.

Equally it points to what is certainly the main theme of the book; the tradition of the cabaret and variety artist as the emblem of working-class Paris, their links with the world of the criminal and the prostitute, and with the middle-class *flâneur* who raided this territory in the pursuit of vice and pleasure.

Piaf and Maurice Chevalier (with the ghost of Aristide Bruant rasping over their shoulders) are at the heart of the argument. In fact this large book grew from a short story of Parisian popular song called *Musical Moments* published by Yale University in 1987, and in itself the basis of a BBC series of programmes *City of Light*. Yet for all the diverse and exhaustive material which has accumulated around them, Piaf and Chevalier remain the cornerstone of this elaborate literary arch.

Chevalier was born in the inner working-class suburb of Ménilmontant and celebrated its virtues (at a distance) his whole life. Ménilmontant, and its older and dodgier neighbour Belleville, stand for many different aspects of Parisian life; revolutionary, respectable, immoral, coarse, honest, depending on the viewpoint of the observer. It was 'down into Paris' that those with talent brought to the cabarets of Montmartre the image of 'rough, spontaneous and libidinous working-class life' to entertain the middle classes. All this is given the closest attention.

In pointing out that the author has pragmatically, and possibly justifiably in this context, purposefully omitted most of the great writers who imposed their own image of Paris, he has drawn in contrast on a vast treasure trove of more humble material, journalists, popular novelists and the like. In particular he has assigned much significance to the photomontage orientated magazine *Détective*, which he contrasts to the less disinterested viewpoint of the great Parisian photographers, in that it 'maps onto a market for the literature of excitement, of prurience and of shock.' He compares it with another more or less constant presence in his documented mythology, the would-be repressive Père de Famille, the other side of the Parisian medal, aiming to conceal what *Détective* reveals.

It is in fact through such clashes of interest; social interplay, filth and glamour, cruelty and pity, light and darkness that Paris emerges so clearly from these kaleidoscopic pages. Its title is well-chosen. The streetcries are silenced finally by mechanical means. The human voice, rooted in reality, is smothered in universal blandness. Genet seems as distant a figure as Baudelaire. This book is a monument and worthy one.

**George Melly**, May 1992

# Contents

# Illustrations

# Preface

*Street Noises* started quite by chance back in 1983. I had gone to Paris to do some work in the holdings on religion of the Archives Nationales. My intention was to prepare a paper, in the event never to be written, on methods of insulting priests at the end of the Second Empire in France. The project was abruptly terminated by the combination of a religious examination that kept the archive in question closed to public access, and an unusually violent allergic reaction to the springtime chestnut trees of Paris, that kept me indoors. Alone, unable to read for days on end, I had nothing but some early recordings of Edith Piaf to assuage me. My attention drifted to *matelots* and *légionnaires*, my empathy to their sundry emotional victims. The outcome was 'Musical Moments', published in the 'Everyday Life' number of *Yale French Studies* in 1987 and the BBC Radio programmes *City of Light*, also 1987. They are the germ of this book.

It has, then, been a long time in the making. It is also a late first book. As a consequence, *Street Noises* is a debt-ridden text and though, like so many other consumers, I cannot repay all my debts, I am going to acknowledge them. The reader will accommodate these paragraphs that give me so much pleasure to write.

Alice Kaplan and Kristin Ross, who insisted that I write 'Musical Moments', are the 'onlie begetters' of *Street Noises*. David Perry sustained it in commissioning *City of Light* for the BBC. Molly Nesbit's work on Atget and Paris is a sine qua non of my own, a point of reference in method and research as, in a different way, is the writing of Jacques Rancière. Steve Edwards and Tony Dunne read one draft after another with patience, while Jill Forbes and Marcia Pointon offered terminal advice. Malcolm Imrie read more than every word. Talking with Carol Duncan and Muriel Dimen about and in the gendered spaces of New York made Paris seem quite simple, while Alex Potts enabled me to frame my *légionnaires* within a long-term aesthetic of the ideal man. Many colleagues assisted with invitations to give seminars, treating me to their and their students' invaluable critique – Griselda Pollock, Fred Orton, Lisa Tickner, Annie Coombes, Tamar Garb, Jon Bird, Barry Curtis, Martin Gaughan. Frank Mort, Rosi Huhn and Michael Orwicz were supportive in all kinds of ways. Ginette Vincendeau's advice on cinema was invaluable, Jean-Claude Freiermuth enabled me to re-read the *marché aux puces*, Alain Cottereau and Marie-Noélle Chamoux took me to the music-hall. The cover photo is the generous gift of its author, the photographic artist Hélène Hourmat.

I must thank the Director of the Archives Nationales, Paris, for permission to research into the Series BB/18 for the period still under restricted access. The reader will note that I have respected the requirement not to mention any name from these dossiers. The Faculty of Environmental Studies Research Committee at Portsmouth Polytechnic has not been ungenerous with grants and I have been given sabbatical time to research and write.

Many of the translations from French texts are my own. I have made them as literal as possible, but in some cases I have modified an existing translation or paired it with words from the original French where the sound has seemed important. John Moore kindly did the prose translations of verse and song. As the rhythm of the text develops pace, I have tried to spare the reader the need to turn too often to the notes, which are concentrated in the introduction and opening chapters. As far as possible I have tried to make some kind of reference to important works that have appeared since this manuscript was effectively completed – about two years ago. Obvious omissions may be attributed to my indolence. The illustrations are from my own collection.

**A.R.**, *Southsea, February 1992*

For my late grandmother, Rose
my mother Iris
and my sister Frances

# Introduction

La forme d'une ville change plus vite, on le sait, que le coeur d'un mortel. Mais avant de le laisser derrière elle en proie à ses souvenirs – saisie qu'elle est, comme le sont toutes les villes, par le vertige de métamorphose qui est la marque de la seconde moitié de notre siècle – il arrive aussi, il arrive plus d'une fois que, ce coeur, elle l'ait changé à sa manière.   (Julien Gracq, *La Forme d'une ville*, 1985, p. 1)

For my own part, I have never set foot in Alexandria. I neither can, nor try to imagine it, the texture of its buildings, the shapes and angles of its streets, the gestures and movement of its people. By one of those twists of chance and inevitability that mark the Jewish migrations of the twentieth century, I was born and brought up in Manchester – Salford, to be quite precise. But for two children growing up there, my sister and myself, Alexandria seemed like one possible origin among several. We glimpsed it in family photographs and old postcards, but above all in the marvellously detailed and endlessly overlapping narratives of our grandmother's own childhood and youth – which she insinuated into ours. Egypt became as vivid as Salford with its clustered houses, its grey-green parks, its heavy-paved and iron-railed staircases. As they threaded through the living archaeologies of the last century, as much in the ageing factories as in the memories of the people, they criss-crossed with long-made distant journeys from Alexandria to Damascus.[1] Salford and Alexandria. The one was as ordinary as the other, each an everyday. Except for this, of course – that memories of the city that never was are more perfect than those of a city lived but changing. Old Salford is gone. Yet even today, on a wet November evening, the centre of Manchester, in the little streets behind the Arndale Centre, is more apt to evoke a certain form of the urban poetic than any *quartier* of modern Paris.

Paris too came into the picture, and if, maybe, it was Manchester that eventually equipped me with a certain sympathy for the city-vision of a Baudelaire, it was, rather, once again my grand-mother's stories that led me into fascination. It is they that underlie this book. After settling in

England in 1923 she made occasional visits to Paris to stay with a cousin of her own age, who, like her, was living out an arranged marriage to a much older man. Left alone from time to time, they went out into the City of Light to amuse themselves, to the *thé-dansant* at Le Dôme in Montparnasse, the Concert Mayol, the boulevards, cafés, *grands magasins* and the Levantine groceries of the Rues Bleue and Lamartine. In her last years, when I went through boxes of her old books, I started reading what she had read at that time – the novels of Maurice Dekobra, Clément Vautel and Pierre Mac Orlan, Colette and the 'lighter' classics of the last century. Then it was that I realised how literary her stories had been, how a type of narrative, a poetic viewpoint and an experience of life might interweave to imagine a utopia, and envision Paris as a sign for happiness and the pleasure of escape. She was not, so to speak, a reader of the city. She was one of its writers.

It seems to me today that the tone of her stories shares something with gramophone recordings of the same period, from the popular hits like 'Parlez-moi d'amour' to a classic performance of Jules Massenet's opera *Manon*.[2] In this composition of the 1880s too, Paris is represented as the identity of love and the freedom of anonymity. Manon and her lover, des Grieux, escape the strictures of provincial family life, seclusion in a convent – 'nous irons à Paris tous les deux … nous vivrons à Paris tous les deux', the voices of the fated lovers exchange and harmonise the phrases. The singing of the principals in 1928 has something of the excitement of more popular cultures of the moment, their lyrical conventions and rhetorics of passion. Paris blurs boundaries, pulling place and time, the Opéra-Comique and café-concert, the popular pleasures of two centuries, into a single, complex warp. But it is only now that I can hear this, and when I first went to Paris at the age of fourteen, I did not know that the knowledge I already had of it was a woman's, nor that what I would come by, from books or for myself, would be that of men. *Street Noises* turns out to be structured by this irony, and also undermined.

In 1959, then, fascination began its long condensation into decades of work. *The Pied de Cochon* was still a meat porters' café in Les Halles, where middle-class people might slip in, even with their teenage offspring, to hear some bawdy singing and eat onion soup. On the other side of the table to us an elderly businessman was sliding oysters down the throat of his young companion. I counted the diamonds on her ring and tried to make out the words of the porters' songs that my mother omitted to translate for me. (It was only when I had been transcribing the words of some 1930s songs for this project that I found out how many of them *she* had known.) We were taken to the Marais to eat in an old Jewish restaurant. In 1960 John Russell described the Marais like this:

The MARAIS is more often talked about than visited. Most people know by now that it contains as many beautiful houses, yard for square yard, as may be found in any city in Europe ... Often, therefore, a luncheon party of enlightened foreign visitors has got up from the table at a quarter to four with the object of 'taking a look at the Marais' ... But this marvellous and contradictory quarter does not lend itself to improvisation. Foresight and a compass are essential, if the visitor is not to get lost in the souks; some form of sociological sextant should also, if possible, form part of the perambulator's equipment.(*Paris*, p. 94)

Indeed, despite the disastrous effects of the Nazi Occupation on its people, it was still a place of migrant and refugee communities. It had few obvious riches to flaunt, except the peeling monuments so dear to the historians of *Vieux Paris* – almost all today scraped clean of history. Perhaps the Marais was then more like one of Georges Simenon's depictions of the 1930s:

The name of the place, displayed in ceramic letters, was Au Roi de Sicile.
Below it were inscriptions in Hebrew, Polish, and other incomprehensible languages, probably including Russian ...
The shops were selling goods unknown to French people even by name.
Less than a hundred yards away were the Rue de Rivoli and the Rue Saint-Antoine – wide and well lit, with their buses, their shops, and their police. (*Pietr le Letton*, 1931)

I dislike these words, both for their barely veiled racism and because I need them to picture something I cannot quite remember. Even the look of the Plateau Beaubourg before the Pompidou Centre went up in the 1970s already escapes me. My own confessional, then, will have to be made up of words not wholly unlike Simenon's, but that is the risk of living at a 'slight angle' to one's own experience of a place, of coming to meditate on the myth of Paris and its living out from viewpoints that are never quite my own. Anyway, in these illiberal times, I seek only to release some of the repressed materials of the mythologies of Paris, to free them from those conventions that constrict them in the cruel objectivity of glamour.

Baudelaire's poem 'Le Cygne' has fed the imagination of urban space for nearly a century and a half. Crossing the Carrousel at the end of the 1850s the poet saw the transformations of Second Empire Paris as ruin, the blocks carved for its future embellishment only as the rain-soaked fragments of a lost past.[3]

Le vieux Paris n'est plus (la forme d'une ville
Change plus vite, hélas, que le coeur d'un mortel.)

As I have said, it is in Manchester, not Paris, that I feel with Baudelaire and can trace some effective metonym for his *anomie*. And, habituated as

I am to the split between memory and my experience of its materials, Julien Gracq's reformulation of Baudelaire, which heads this chapter, comes as something of a relief. The city and the human heart may, after all, shape each other in the banality of mortal form. Gracq's substitution of the phrase 'as we know' for the poet's 'alas' opens up the city for a reading that need be neither doleful in its sense of loss nor feverish only for the future.

For how can a city – Paris – be understood to change, when its images are so complexly made in overlapping histories, some not its own? Commonly Paris is imagined as *the* City of the People. At the same time it 'procures pleasures' for the rich.[4] This duality feeds a dream of multiple alterities, one that draws tourists and writers, historians and revolutionaries, demographers and urbanists – each to pursue their end in unravelling the possibilities that Paris yields up to them. Saturated as it is with such an excess of social values, this relation of the People and the City is continually worked, inflected and appropriated as the material for contending interests. It's difficult either to find in it any fixed and singular meanings or to endow it with a general sense that can be specified as any other than the effect of a moment.

To take but two appropriate examples. First, Kozintzev's and Trauberg's 1929 commemoration of the Paris Commune, the film *New Babylon*. Its polar images of bourgeois department store and crumbling workers' slum are the site of a class struggle to the death that represents the poor of Zola's Paris as the heroic bedrock of Russia's future. It re-enacts this classic episode in the history of revolutionary Paris at the inception of the first Soviet five-year-plan. The defeat of the Commune by Thiers's 'rural' army warns against the dire consequences of failing to achieve the worker–peasant alliance in Russia. Second, its near contemporary was Maurice Chevalier's first Hollywood film, *The Innocents of Paris*. This works a sentimental and maudlin stereotype of the self-same working class as pathos for the amusement of the capitalist masses of the West. *The Innocents of Paris* inaugurated a period of thirty years and more, culminating with *Gigi* in 1958, throughout which Maurice was to inscribe and reinscribe an increasingly atavistic image of popular Parisianism in the imaginary worlds of American cinema – though perhaps for television audiences in the USA this had already reached a point of orgiastic sentimentality in a film he made in 1956 called *Maurice Chevalier's Paris*. Here Maurice traces the vanishing life-forms of the city centre, the human types and dying industries, and between the iteration of so many sad exemplars of the effects of change, he introduces lively little commercials for 'Chicken of the Sea Tuna', cooked up with a variety of French effects.[5] These American and Soviet models of Parisianism, incompatible though they might be, equally take hold of the city's history and shape it in the image of their different needs.

My need is for a starting point, an access to the myth. So here is a People/Paris story published in 1951. It's from a book by the journalist J.-M.Campagne, entitled *Les Week-Ends de Saint-Ouen*, a luxury edition crafted on fine paper, with an elegant typeface and colour lithographs. It recounts a scene at a café in the fleamarkets of Saint-Ouen, a typical Sunday resort for all kinds of Parisian.[6] Amongst them are Campagne, his friends René Clair and Georges van Parys, and a party of firemen, who 'quench their inner fire with beaujolais.'

> a singer on the comeback, and verging on the ridiculous, sings 'Nini peau d'chien', and then some other songs. She really asked for it! The firemen are hugely amused and don't spare their witticisms. With all her strength and her courage, she carries on. And now, overcome, the firemen hum in melancholy – lo-o-ove.
>
> See, said René Clair, 'that's Paris. You start laughing, and you always end up tender. I don't think there's any other city in the world where you see that kindness, those subtleties.' (p. 115)

Or here, in the same vein, is a portrait of someone – of something – this time by Jules Bertaut, writing in 1920 in his study of the modern novel. During the first third of this century Bertaut was one of the most accomplished and versatile chroniclers of all things Parisian, covering the entire gamut from anecdotal history to moral enquiry, romance and theatre. He is presenting the novelist Henri Duvernois, author of such pre-war successes as *Popote* (1905):

> That talent, it's a pretty, Parisian smile, roguish, cheeky, cocky, and, at the same time, tender and moist … It's the smile of a pitiless observer, ready, you can say, openly to poke fun at imbeciles, yet who ends up warming to them … To have that talent and that smile is a French, and nothing but a French state of grace, it's something from our country, and better than that, from Paris.[7]

These two passages contain many of the key elements of what seems to be a timeless dream of the popular, deeply worked in the unconscious of social relations. There is the narrator's look, distant yet fascinated, which crosses the spaces of class and dissembles his watcher's expertise in the image of the people, even as he assumes their character. Campagne, for one, had been part of the pre-war scene of literary journalism, a friend of the most eminent popular musicians of the day like van Parys, and of illustrators like Dignimont who headed a whole fraternity of artists and poets who repeated and reworked the images of the people.[8] Later Campagne set himself up in the fleamarket as a kind of dealer–*flâneur*, and here he is taking his lunch in very much the same company as he would have found in a fashionable Parisian studio of the 1930s. Georges van Parys was the acme of the most sophisticated night-club pianist and composer, but also a fastidious Adorno of the entertainment industries.

He knew a phoney when he saw one, and heartily disliked the post-war Edith Piaf. The firemen are for real. Clair's conversation is that of a great film-maker, the author of such populist social utopias as *Le Million* and *À nous la liberté*. But Campagne is at pains to insist that his language is still *gavroche* (cheeky) and *gouaille* (cocky) – the intellectual with the common touch. All three of them are at ease in singing along with the firemen, and identify with their authenticity.

In assuming the character of the popular they expand the network of looks and narratives that Bertaut so skilfully overlays as he looks at himself, looking at Duvernois (*gouaille*, *gavroche*), who in turn recounts the people of Paris. Indeed Duvernois's tragicomic romance of drugs and prostitution, *Faubourg Montmartre*, was to provide one of the most appealing fabrics of Parisianism for the French cinema of the 1920s. This expert's look, then, is the ethnocentric look of the literary professional, trained and equipped to recognise the people through a hard-worked heritage of skills that dates back to Eugène Suè's *Mystères de Paris* in the 1840s, and before that to Balzac. 'Paris' is the word that secures his bonding with the people, and also the name for a special kind of masculine self-expression; and in Campagne's description the accretions of this history work his every word. The place itself, the fleamarket, is the repository of the imaginary margins of the city's history, made up of curiosities and detritus, patrolled alike by Surrealists, antique dealers and the urban poor. The singer herself is a predicate of such margins, of the scrap-heap of spaces that were the pavement and the cheaper fringes of the entertainment industries. The lineage of the song-writer is present in 'Nini peau d'chien', a classic of Aristide Bruant's from the 1880s, a music of which van Parys is an heir. And Campagne hides his controlling skill in a story as artless as the *faits divers* of a weekly magazine.

As with Bertaut's text, the lunchtime scene is terribly overdetermined and, at the same time, reveals our problem. For the city, even in upheaval or change – and neither 1920 nor 1951 were moments of calm or continuity – is disclosed through the cultural habits that frame each moment of its experience. This is both obvious and obscure. One purpose of my book is to unravel some of the senses and nonsenses of this timeless popular, the orders of reality that it weaves together as it drifts through the Parisian entertainment industries and beyond. Sociology and song-writing, demography and cinema, political utopias and criminal statistics are each contaminated by, and in turn contaminate each other with, its image.[9] There is no place to sidestep, no ideal, separate or unmoving master-viewpoint. To understand the motions of the figural and linguistic histories of the City of the People, it is as well to take it as it goes.

Walter Benjamin did just that. His work more than any other occupies the space between disparate forms of analysis and representation.

Whether operating in the mode of literary exegesis and philology, socio-logical enquiry or philosophical speculation, he describes an image of Paris, a 'dialectical image' – the gambler's gestures at the table, the rag-picker's limp, the prostitute. He breaks down and names its parts, traces its lineages and the sites of its occurrence. But even as he seeks to synthesise the relation between his findings, he accumulates new data from the inexhaustible city that will undo each theoretical discovery to prepare its next development. Nothing is left unquestioned or at rest, each sign is a warning of its own complexity. The *Passagen-Werk* and the *Baudelaire* can well be called, to borrow a formulation from Susan Buck-Morss, 'a utopian language which would transmit critical messages across the generations … [the] constructions of words that had the power to awaken the political consciousness of the readers of his time'.[10]

Yet Benjamin's words may seem to co-exist almost too comfortably with their objects. His arduous process of demystifying Paris has turned into a part of its mystery, and sometimes it looks as if the word Benjamin is just another name for the *anomie* of modernity, or for its equivocal pleasures – its fascination if anything intensified through his interven-tions.[11] For if he saw the popular literature of the nineteenth century – the typologies, the detective stories as producing a pleasure that was absent from the realities of the street-life of the crowds and of the poor, this pleasure was none the less produced. It still has its allure, remade in the conditions of modern mass cultures. Massenet had realised the power of the gambler's image forty years before the disaffected theorist. One of the crucial scenes of *Manon*, the one leading to the heroine's arrest and opening the spiral down to death, takes place in a gambling party. Manon lures the still socially innocent des Grieux to risk the tables, and as he must have the money to keep her, he does so and he wins. Quite sud-denly, love turns into money and money into love, sexual passion into the repetition of the game: good collector that he was, Benjamin in-vented nothing. No, he discovered back in the last century a scene that was regularly played out at the Opéra-Comique in his own day. Such pleasure in the city, this frenzied cycling of identity and commodity the one into the other, necessarily flickers like fashion, with all those forms of fashionable consumption that make it up, and yet it also seems not to change. As we have already seen, its tropes are remarkably stable over a long period of time, controlling and coding the representation of change as a succession of mere appearances and nostalgias.

In a sense it is Benjamin's very historicity that opens his work to becoming the object of a sentimental cult. The 'utopian language' is trapped in the life of his materials, which finally overflow his ability to control them. If the language were really to survive the problems that it was wrought to deal with – the mechanisation of art and urban life, the rise of fascist 'man' – it would have to evade all those words of pleasure that in the first place secure the continuity of meaning. To be recognised in the future, such a language may run the risk of seeming no more than just one of the flavours of an epoch, a trace amongst others, a resemblance of the falsity it reveals. Worse still; if, on account of this, utopia does forgo recognition, then it lends its own allure to the present with which it once stood at odds, offering it to the future with a utopian fascination it would otherwise have lacked. Benjamin and the 1930s become each other.

Pondering this problem is another dimension of my book. Is it open to me to rescue some utopia from Benjamin's nightmare, some traces of a semiotic paradise that the 1930s were, before the repressions of *post-war* France? I will return to this theme in the conclusion. But here I need to explain yet more about the origins of *Street Noises*.

More or less it is about Paris, as its material is largely drawn from Parisian entertainment industries, or from sources that deal with the regulation and definition of the pleasures and sociability of Paris between about 1900 and quite recent times. More than being about Paris it is concerned with trying to secure relations between its different materials. These include the archives of the Parisian judiciary, the 'Dossiers Banaux' that accumulate discussions on the legal niceties of prosecuting day-to-day offences for crimes of pleasure. A more specialised record of desire is the dossier in the Archives Nationales concerning the surveillance of homosexual and communist sailors, accumulated by the Naval Prefect in Toulon between 1928 and 1933.[12] Then there are literary ventures of the Goncourt school of writers in the lower depths and margins of Paris, which spill over into the photographic montages and special reports of *Détective Magazine*, one of the most successful of all illustrated weeklies from 1928 to1940. The narrative forms of popular romances and night-club songs, together with the autobiographies of music-hall stars, brush against sentences of Walter Benjamin and Theodor Adorno, turning their discussions around the way in which Paris can be understood as a sytem of aural imagery. Their debates over historical method are sited in the context of passages from Gustave Charpentier's opera *Louise* – if for no better reason than that Adorno advised his colleague to check up Charpentier's image of a rag-picker in preference to Baudelaire's.[13] And Marcel Carné's and Jacques Prévert's film *Les Enfants du Paradis*, with its central figure of Jéricho, the old second-hand clothes seller, offers a natural extension of this terrain. I use published memoirs and records of the Parisian Zone and fleamarkets, and unpublished snapshots of unknown women and men. Sometimes modern art movements like Surrealism get a look in from the edges.

The historiographical problems that I have had to deal with are largely quite traditional, for example those of structure, series and duration in the ordering themes elicited from archival materials, taken in relation to their analogous or homologous appearance in literary and sociological sources. I have almost completely sidestepped the highly troped reading of 'Paris-as-Modernity' which passes from a combination such as 'Baudelaire–Poe–Haussman' to that of 'Surrealism–Brassaï–Corbusier'.[14] These terms may be extended or shuffled, but, one way or another, they typify a species of narrative that will appear only at the margins of my own. As I understand them, such narratives are inflected by a greater complexity than can be revealed in even the wildest of their dreams. I work from the primacy of the 'underside', not as mystery to be revealed but as the substantive detail of the dream.

Within the limits of a given, relatively unitary urban context, even a bipartite relation such as that of the evolution of morals on the one hand, and of the social, legal and administrative structures that concern them on the other, may be extremely complicated. Each part of the relation is made up of separately developing and interrelating elements. In the first, for example, one can trace a gallant culture dating to the Directoire or the Restoration. By the mid nineteenth century this is represented predominantly through the trope of 'male *flâneur*', and it develops through and codes a range of culturally differentiated institutions from café society to the artistic cabaret, from the art of slumming to the touristic music-hall.[15] As a cultural field, the gallant encompasses a representation of women as protected onlookers, prostitutes or performers – almost any role except that of the *flâneur*. As a cultural field it is made by a range of professional and amateur producers, who may belong to the literary bohemia, the hack-world of the music industries or to the ministries of state – Willemetz, the author of Mistinguett's 'Mon homme', for one, was at the Interior. It is both assisted in its development and problematised by new technologies like the gramophone and the radio, which break down the edges of its institutional spaces, expanding its market but disturbing the composition of its public.[16] And, at the same time, it is tightly contained within informal institutional structures and social groupings like that of the Académie Goncourt, over which Lucien Descaves presided from his house in the working-class Thirteenth Arrondissement.

After the slaughter of the 1914–1918 war this culture turns out to provide the outlines for an altogether different city experience – that of a new stratum of single women, who learn their own circuits in the rounds of work and pleasure. They are represented in the writing of Colette and Victor Margueritte, and hide, so as to speak, in this man-made space, while their pleasures represent a real displacement of its values.[17] This can be glimpsed in the emergence of a whole gamut of gallant magazines and illustrated weeklies whose imagery and address is structured through the experience of the *flâneur*, but whose public is now female. And this new phenomenom maps itself in an uneven way on to already existing social and moral confrontations over the gallant and the pornographic, confrontations in which this new turn of events had neither been foreseen, nor could be seen as it unfolded.

Because the image of woman is so crucial in the systems of representation, whether moralising or gallant, all these elements enter into reaction both with the general evolution of the image of woman and with one of its special forms, the man in drag. And so there enters homosexuality – which has a higher and more privileged profile in the high life of literary society – Gide, Cocteau – than it does in more humdrum lives. For them, rather like the gallant literature for women, it hides inside alien images, both feeding off them and, at the same time, corrupting them with an untoward complexity of meaning. Its voices and images represent the return of more than one repressed. Amongst them, the repressed *politics* of social otherness. For why should the aspirations of the Commune sublimate themselves only in twentieth-century communist politics? Are Verlaine's *Hombres*, his erotic poems to working boys, any less a register of the deepest desires for a utopian transformation of social relations?[18]

On the other side, there is the evolution of the law and the private institutions of moral behaviour. There are the public prosecutors at the Parisian court and legal experts of the Interior Ministry. Very often this personnel is made up of worldly men, who form a bedrock of gallant culture, even while they are responsible for the understanding and implementation of the laws that control and limit it. The social spaces opened up by their interaction with the evolution of morals on the one hand, and their work on the other profoundly affects the implementation of the law.[19] Their perception of significant events, whether legal judgements or major explosions of political and social tension, or of new forms of technology, all of which may challenge or rework the formal legalities of pleasure, offers a particular insight into the perplexing symbiosis of political and moral change with the industrialisation of popular amusements. In apposition to these officials, now working with them, now against them, are the moralists, their private but powerful groupings of leagues and associations, immersed in their own objectives and social temporality.

These are all classic problems of the *moyenne durée*, in so far as they are phenomena that shape the social over long-term periods, but are at different states of change and evolution, different in their interaction with moments of catastrophe, which might undo or reorganise their relations and their differences altogether. The Occupation after 1940 is a case of an 'event', the evolution of attitudes to brothels or to homosexuality a good example of a long evolution of moral values with which it interacts.[20] The complicated form of chapter 3 is justified by the need to represent these questions, handling them like a walk through the city. I find that it is necessary to take on the form of a truly long-running

Parisianism, the memoir that is shaped as a *trajet*, – which has often been adopted and occasionally theorised.[21]

But this complexity is rather like what the *Vocabulary of Psychoanalysis* calls overdetermination, and so unravelling it marks the site of the congruence of psychoanalysis and history – here at a structural level, rather than through psychoanalytically generated theoretical insights such as 'gaze theory' – though these will play a crucial role at the level of language tools.[22] I try, then, to leave my narrative open to the randomising effects of overdetermination, which anyway, once they are allowed enough space, turn out to be rather like the form of the nineteenth-century serial novels that were then so characteristic of Parisian culture. These juxtapose series of materials with each other in such a way that their overlapping and repetitions secure different, if specific, meanings at each point of their resolution into event. Hence their frisson, their suspense and their modernity[23]

The selection of the materials in this book, then, poses its own problems of typicality and exceptionality. This is crucial in establishing their value within series and their character as series, especially where there is a very great discrepancy and overlapping in their modes of production, authorship and consumption. Texts, images and songs have been chosen from the many thousands available either because they are typical or because they are exceptional – as far as I can judge. Without resort to a statistical recension, I will not pretend to establish a set of indubitable 'sociological facts'.[24] However I do implicitly take a position in favour of the idea that, as Chombart de Lauwe puts it, 'social life is one ... we attach a particular importance to the "total social phenomenom" such as Marcel Mauss envisaged it, or to the unity of "all these deep strata" that "interpenetrate each other and form an indissoluble ensemble" ...' The book is emphatically, therefore, not about 'subculture'. At the same time I accept that 'indissoluble' can never be an alibi for the play of *différance*, and that neither the 'total social phenomenom' nor, for that matter, Benjamin's 'dialectical image', may be read as other than an effect of this play.[25]

As a result of this *Street Noises* can only claim to be one possible *trajet* through the city. My readers will find no trace of Toulouse-Lautrec, nor any of Henry Miller, Gertrude Stein or other Americans-in-Paris. There are some films, but no cinema as such.[26] Baudelaire himself is present only as a sign in the languages of memory and identity. Only occasionally are Jean Genet or Colette allowed to frame my materials. No such major absences are unintended.

But to return to the ideal of Parisian pleasure as a paradigm of social freedom, it is an attractive and a cruel mythology. This is because it is so deeply rooted in the criss-crossings of different forms of social objectification that almost no type of human life emerges unscathed from it. Its forms of expression are more than simply appealing, they are the substance of pleasure and identity. The voice of a Louis Chevalier or a Maurice Chevalier, the tone of the Goncourt *littérateurs* and the bohemian poets, override or give words to many other kinds of voice, shape them, give them sound and representation. Thus Parisian pleasures become the type-form of a semi-official masculinity that fills the entertainment industries with its 'I' as if this were alterity. Hence their power to provide image and self- image offers an important instance of what Henri Lefèbvre writes of as the difference between the 'everyday' and the 'lived'. My chapter on homosexuality especially deals with the ways in which understanding this can enable us to subvert the received images of Paris.

At the same time, subjectification of pleasure and the processes of self-recognition that occur in such a highly objectified cultural field not only exemplifies Lefèbvre's concept of the everyday but may well be one of its sources, part of the deeper cultural stimuli to his thinking.[27] This poses the conflict of the lived and the everyday as a topic for speculative discussion. Speculative not least because the quantification of pleasures, especially the pleasures taken in spectacle, and the qualities of pleasures, are difficult to assess.

Yet the project began far from all this, in puzzling over the significance of the image of the 'good worker' in the historiography of the Paris Commune of 1871. At that point I was trying to evolve an adequate critical taxonomy of the political caricature of the end of the Second Empire. I had set out to do this in terms of a social linguistics of popular cultures, hoping, amongst other things, to establish an exhaustive lexicon of difference in the meaning of the words 'people' and 'popular' in their many repetitions. Here Jacques Rancière's critique of the idea of the 'popular' and the ideology of the 'artisan', turned out to be of enormous value.

Beginning with his 1978 essay 'Good Times, or Pleasure at the Barriers',[28] I found that his writing suggested a starting point for reflection on these kinds of problem: the relation between the 'popular' in politics and in entertainment; the effects of the division of labour, economic and cultural, of professionalisation and amateurism, on work and leisure; and the refraction of social questions through these relations. A starting point, I believe, that enables us to go behind the debates on 'high' versus 'low' cultures into a more subtle understanding of the instability of cultural identity that comes from the complexity of the desire for social otherness. Rancière's argument against rooting our understanding of the popular in a singular class identity is philosophical rather than quantitative. It is not an issue of how many workers did or did not conform to the ideal artisan but of how the popular is thought and lived as a social relation by all of its participants.[29]

So I set about the question of how the imaging of the people and of the popular provided common subjectivities for the languages of politically and methodologically different histories and sociologies of the Parisian working classes. For example, there is an image of the good worker, clean, sober and restrained, which is exemplified by the militant Communard Eugène Varlin. Because of Varlin's sobriety, his complex and thoughtful politics, his image was beloved in the communist construction of working-class history. But abstracted from an individual, the same sets of attributes are equally relevant to a counter-revolutionary ideal of labour: the model, submissive artisan of Denis Poulot's *Sublime* (1870): or, with Georges Duveau, in his *La Vie ouvrière en France* (1946) for a Catholic humanist conception of the virtuous proletarian.[30] This respectable worker, wherever he appears, stakes a claim to political legitimacy for one or another of the varieties of the social *imaginaire*. What are the grounds for the survival of such contradictory uses of a single figure? Finally, I took the field of entertainment as the possible common system of unconscious, everyday links between them, and I elaborate this throughout chapters 1 and 5.

Throughout my book the writer Lucien Descaves will appear as a crucial figure. Little read today, a journalist, novelist, playwright, historian and, for forty years, president of the Académie Goncourt, he was one of those men who exercised enormous power in Parisian literary life. A man who worked what you might call the psychological and institutional frameworks of social identity and otherness. It is worth making a detour around him before coming to Chapter 1.

In 1913, Descaves published *Philémon vieux de la vieille*, a work that was to become one of the the most respected source-books for the history of the Paris Commune and its exiles in Switzerland. The author derives his story from the witness of two ex-Communards, an ageing artisan and his wife.[31] This old revolutionary, the Philémon of the title, entrusts his story to Lucien Descaves, the narrator-author, who speaks it for him. Descaves is an outsider, an intellectual, who has come to live in Philémon's quartier in search of an older, better Paris. This he finds when he first visits the couple in their humble workers' abode, where, as it happens, there is the image of Varlin on the mantelpiece, in sacred pride of place. Yet listening to the old people, we can detect a slightly prim and supercilious tone when they talk of their less refined comrades; we sense an atavistic belief in the integrity of a self-regarding, working-class culture that is ever respectful of a Hugo or a Courbet. Fiercely independent, it none the less knows its place. Philémon himself is something of a 'good worker', the figure for a deep-running, popular conservatism rooted in the stasis of revolutionary memory. Indeed Descaves emphasises the couple's narrowness. Before he gets to know them he comments on the starling they keep caged at their window, sensing not only that it is jealous of the free birds that he feeds on his balcony but that its owners resent him for making their pet discontented:

> But these old folk are like parents who persuade their daughter not to marry, because she will nowhere be more happy than by their hearth … but who are really frightened of being lonely together. (*Philémon*, p. 17)

He will learn from the wife, Baucis/Phonsine, that they do indeed have a daughter, who has left home and of whom they never speak. This appears to confirm his guess, and the couple he imagines seem to conform to a stereotype of repressive parenthood that had wide currency in the early 1900s. Before he uncovers their revolutionary past, Philémon–Baucis resemble the Father and Mother in Gustave Charpentier's *Louise*, those epigones of a long suffering, working-class respectability, whose resentment against their status forces them to refuse any and every alternative to it. And nothing more arouses their fear and hatred than the possibility of a love marriage between their daughter and Julien, a poet of Montmartre. It is to escape their refusal of her happiness that Louise flees her home, to follow her own alternative, to be a freewoman of a free city, with her poet–lover, who rewrites its ciphers in his verse.

But Philémon and Baucis turn out to be nothing less than a model for the ideal equivalence of revolutionary virtue and hard yet highly skilled, artisanal labour – they make jewellery. Descaves's set-up is carefully contrived. His faithful narration of authenticity veils a projection into authenticity of a liberal republicanism that is seeking to integrate the Parisian working class of the early 1900s, and its revolutionary history into the hegemonic structures of the Third Republic: to envisage its revolutionary tradition and sense of justice as being as French as French can be, a valuable expression of a national nostalgia.[32] The couple's conservatism is particularly apparant in any discussion that touches on matters of popular culture, and especially song. Very early Descaves overhears how his neighbours conduct their relationship through popular song, and admires their unusual knowledge of song, even of entire songs. But these days, he muses, no one really does sing in front of others, they shut themselves in, and it is only a few building workers who conserve the habit of song in public earshot:

> But perhaps, also, it is that living conditions and new forms of work have discouraged singers … One more reason to welcome this one, who outfaces ridicule and soothes me with reminiscences … (*ibid.*, p. 9).

As Rancière shows, and I follow him here, this reflection is confirmed by Philémon's own memories of the good old days, when 'a worker could still greet the product of his own hands with a song'. In a later passage Descaves writes of how summer Sundays in the courtyard are made insupportable by the sound of musicians practising pianos and violins. In a moment of peace from the cacophony, the old couple take up their singing, but a worse fate is yet to befall their hard-pressed autonomy:

> Suddenly, from an invisible noise-box came a kind of stuffed-up, buffoon-like voice, that eructated a sort of announcement – unintelligible at that distance from me. Then the popular tune 'Viens Poupoule' – every single verse of it, boiling and sizzling on a full heat. (*ibid.*, p. 114)

And then a polka, a monologue, an air from Faust, and finally a pot-pourri of 'La Charge' and the 'Marseillaise' with all the sounds of a whole battle, as if made up by 'a mad stage manager in the wings of the Ambigu':

> Progress – it was no longer there to fill the hearts of citizens with with heroism as they gathered around a music-kiosk, but to carry this heroism home to their hearth, just like errand-boys carry chops in sauce, in a container that keeps them hot. (*ibid.*, p. 115)

This 'progress', of course, is the gramophone, and by the following summer it has become an epidemic. Progress is the unfolding of cultural corruption, the latest technology of entertainment, which stops the people singing for themselves. The taylorising of amusement accompanies that of working life. Maybe some of Adorno's strictures on the consumer culture of jazz can be heard as a backgound whisper, in the not-too-distant future? At the same time, does not this space between the rhythms of work and of amusement give space to entertainment as the birthright of the good worker, to the possibility of the very idea of leisure? It was Maurice Chevalier's belief that it is they, the honest workers, who enjoy 'Viens Poupoule'. And will not the gramophone become the fetish-treasure of a new perception of the popular? Pierre Mac Orlan, the novelist, reporter, song-writer and poet who is one of my leading characters, was to think so, and to elaborate a global geography of the popular around its sounds. Even one of his North African novels, *Dans le quartier réservé* (1932), unfolds around a decaying record shop, whose owner, an unsuccessful song-writer, has chosen exile from Paris because he can no longer 'speak the arbitrary and changing language of the street'. Out in Africa, least among 'the dark pleasures of the flesh', in the heart of the colonial brothel, he will deal in the diffusion of a culture at whose creation he has failed.[33] But for Descaves, all in all, the contrast between the gramophone and the atavistic cultural identity of the couple works for his narrative. Philémon's and Baucis's narcissistic independence structures their politics as nostalgia, leaving the present free from their revolutionary ideal, or working it around the absent and impossible ideal of the artisan. Rancière comments, 'What merits our attention is the actual formation of this semi-real, semi-imaginary representation of songs as "things of the past" ...'(*Voices*, p.85). In the end, tired and without a future, the old couple die by their own hand, leaving Lucien Descaves, liberal journalist and President of the Académie Goncourt, as their sole executor.

The image of this respectability is a complex sign, whose presence can tell us much about its user. If we follow Descaves out on to the Parisian Zone, which I will do in chapter 5, we shall see how great was his fear of the people when they become the unrespectable and disinherited under classes, and how this deeply equivocal emotion was central to the imaging of Parisian pleasures, their histories and values. Through their cognitive and expressive nature, such signs of the popular are equipped to play their role in many different types of discourse, not least in those of the entertainment industries, and their imagery of Paris. In *Philémon* the old couple's exile from France meant first and foremost exile from Paris. The city frames their memory, its changes register loss, its stability the presence of an imaginary past. And its diversity makes possible and mediates their relationship with Descaves himself. For him, in his turn, street plans and buildings become metaphors for his states of mind as he broods on the sad fatality of working life. Descaves opens his book with an elegiac description of the Thirteenth Arrondissement, its linking, walled pathways between the wine-shop, the prison, the hospital and the mad-house. It is a stage set, a decor of the overlapping institutions of control that frame the tragedy of an impossible past and a lost future.

Descaves's work consolidates a particular connection between decor and historical narrative, the exploration of which plays an important role in my book. He evokes the figures of writers, artists, photographers, ciné-astes: Pierre Mac Orlan, Francis Carco, Utrillo, Brassaï, Colette and Carné. And he points forward to the sociology of Louis Chevalier, whose work on the popular classes has made a decisive contribution to consolidating their image as an object of academic attention. Amongst sociologists of the popular he is the one who has most artfully combined a highly bourgeois, voyeuristic and masculine subjectivity with sociological typologies that are typical of the networks of the popular that I examine, and nowhere more so than in his *Montmartre du plaisir et du crime*.[34] Here, as in his seminal *Labouring Classes and Dangerous Classes*, Chevalier takes his Paris from an astonishing range of nineteenth-century literature and demographic sources. Yet he seems unaware that the more recent culture in which he is immersed, and which he deploys in *Montmartre*, the bohemia of Mac Orlan or Auguste le Breton, lives in a complex relation to its own history, reworking its decors in the cognition of the present. When he asserts that Francis Carco's novel *Jésus la Caille* (1914) – one of the most admired sources of populist Parisianism – was only another of the *faits divers* of Paris, he really undermines the realist status of his entire apparatus of description. Carco's sentimental *récit* of a ruffi-an's life is no more authentic than Poulbot's contemporary prints of of big-eyed ragamuffins.

Chevalier's text suggests how sociology might be no more 'accurate' a representation of the city than the poet's song in *Louise*, or a music-hall hit like Mistinguett's 'Mon homme'. A sociology may be determined by the kinds of images articulated in crime fiction, in opera or in song, in bohemian fantasies of *déclassement*, and compounded in the failure to realise a difference between these representations and other orders of reality. Chevalier belongs to a line of twentieth-century bohemian *flâneurs* like Francis Carco and Pierre Mac Orlan. Unlike them he lives neither self-consciously nor ironically in the space that separates the intellectual, songwriter or novelist from the *populaire* that they represent and confect for public gaze. This, as we shall see, is a crucial space of entertainment – and of historical narrative, as we have already seen with Descaves.

### Notes

1 For a fine fictional representation of this kind of emotional ellipsis see Paula Jacques's novel, *L'Héritage de Tante Carlotta*, Paris, Mercure de France, 1987. Jacques confronts the Parisian suburbs of our day, the narrator's mother and her aunts' life there with their lost Alexandria as the tragicomic intertwining of unfinishable histories. Edgar Morin, in his autobiographical study of his father – *Vidal et les siens*, Paris, Seuil, 1989 – gives an account of a migrant Rhodes Jew in whom I can perfectly recognise the cultural hybrid of Levantine manners expressed through catches of popular and commercial French music of the 1920s and 1930s.

2 Cezar Vezzani and Jeanne Guyla on 'César Vezzani chante Massenet', compact disc, collection Music Memoria, 1928/1988. Jules Massenet, *Manon*, opera in five acts, book by Meilhac and Gille after the novel of L'Abbé Prévost, first performed 19 January, 1884 at the Opéra-Comique, Paris.

3 Marcel Roncayolo, in the recent re-edition of his *La Ville et ses territoires*, Paris, Folio, 1990, has drawn attention to the importance of literary representation in developing an understanding of the city, specifically citing Gracq, *La Forme d'une ville*, Paris, José Corti, 1985. My quotation at the head of this introduction is from p. 1 of Gracq. While *La Forme d'une ville* concerns the city of Nantes, it seems to me as near as perfect a rendering of the city as memory and identity as Walter Benjamin's essays on Berlin. Charles Baudelaire, 'le Cygne', from *Les Fleurs du mal*, Paris, Le Livre de Poche, 1972, p. 211. 'The old Paris is gone (the form of a city / changes faster, alas, than does the mortal heart!)'

4 Interviewed in the monthly magazine, *Actuel*, 108, June 1988, in the context of an article by Paul Rambali and Philippe Vandel, 'Le Java contre Le Pen' (a report on the development of a movement of popular retro-culture against Le Pen and modern fascism), the current master of French detective fiction, Didier Daeninckx, put it like this: 'In the 1920s all classes came into contact with each other. This provoked revolts and pleasures. Since Chirac more than half of Parisians are management and yuppies. Where are we going?' The article suggests both the power of an old myth and the desire to rework it as a new political reality. Daeninckx's answer to his own question is 'in the suburbs'. See his *Le Bourreau et son double*, Paris, Gallimard – Série Noire, 1986. Throughout the book I use both the terms 'other(ness)' and 'alterity', which is the less common but also the less loaded of the two terms. For a useful discussion of alterity, see Jean-Pierre Vernant, *La Mort dans les yeux, figures de l'autre en Grèce ancienne – Artémis, Gorgô* Paris, Hachette, 1990.

5 *The New Babylon*, a film by G. Kozintzev and L. Trauberg about the Communard uprising of 1871, works from and reinvents Zola's Paris as an allegory for the 1920s,

bringing together an implicit critique of the period of the New Economic Policy with a glorification of the origins of socialist organisation that the Commune was seen to represent – it was common in Russia in the early 1920s to invite aged Communards to meetings of the Third International. It is not without interest that the sets presage those of Trauner and Barsacq for *Les Enfants du Paradis*. Chevalier's film was more of a launchpad for his career in the USA than a real success, see *New York Times Film Reviews, 1913–1968*, Vol. 1, New York, New York Times and Arno, 1970 (6 vols). *Maurice Chevalier's Paris* is to be found in the CBS archives in New York.

6  J.-M. Campagne, *Les Week-Ends de Saint-Ouen*, Paris, 1951, p. 115. See also Georges van Parys, *Mémoires, Les jours comme ils viennent*, Paris, 1967, for insights into the sociability of these men in the 1930s.

7  Jules Bertaut, *Le Roman nouveau*, Paris, 1920, p. 7. *'Gouaille'* also has the sense of a form or tone of speech and song. For an interesting commentary on *'gavroche'* as an adjective – it is, of course, the name of Hugo's child hero in *Les Misérables*, see W. Benjamin in *Paris, capitale du xix siècle*, Paris, Cerf, 1989, p. 749, quoting Abel Bonnard on the history of the stereotype of the 'dubious man'. For Bonnard, Gavroche is a tarnished type of noble, the 'marquis of the gutter'. From now on I will shorten this edition of the *Passagen-Werk Paris capitale*.

8  On the relation between book illustration, cartoon and other images of Paris, see Molly Nesbit, *Atget's Six Albums*, New Haven, Yale University Press,1992. For Mac Orlan on illustration see, for example, his introductions for the series *Les Artistes du livre*. No. 2 is *Charles Martin*, chez Henri Babou, éditeur à Paris, with a preface by Pierre Mac Orlan, text by Marcel Valotaire and a portrait by Dignimont.

9  See Pierre Sansot, *Poétique de la ville*, Paris, Klincksieck, 1984, for an important attempt to construct an informal sociology of urban space and its multiple experiences, yet one that is none the less sadly uncritical of its method of procedure. On the contrary, for two instances of the city used as the object of theoretical critique, see Marc Augé, *Un Ethnologue dans le métro*, Paris, Hachette, 1986, and Anne Cauquelin, *La Ville la nuit*, Paris, PUF, 1977.

10 For Benjamin, I refer to *Paris capitale*, or to citations from the German edition to be found in other sources, especially Irving Wohlfarth, 'Et Cetera? The Historian as Chiffonnier' in *New German Critique*, 39, 1986, pp. 143–168, originally in Passages, Walter Benjamin et Paris, ed. H. Wismann, Paris, Cerf, 1986, pp. 559–610, and Susan Buck-Morss, both her *The Dialectics of Seeing*, Cambridge, MIT, 1989, and her essay 'The Flâneur, the Sandwichman and the Whore – the Politics of Loitering', in *New German Critique*, as above. For the earlier version, from which this quotation is translated, see Wismann, *Passages*, p. 361. ff. For Baudelaire, see Walter Benjamin, *Charles Baudelaire: A Lyric Poet in the Era of High Capitalism*, London, NLB, 1973.

11 See Buck-Morss, *The Dialectics...*, for a discussion of the de-politicised Benjamin industries, pp. 222ff.

12 In the central chapters of this book, in particular chapters 3 and 4, I engage in a literary-historical reading of two sets of archival material from the Archives Nationales in Paris. One of these is a selection of several hundred folders from the Dossiers Banaux of the sous-séries BB18 of the Ministry of Justice. These consist largely of letters, ministerial notes and exchanges between the Republican prosecutors in Paris and the provinces, the Garde des Sceaux and the Minister himself, letters between the authorities and moralising social groups and plaintiffs, concerning the state of current prosecutions for a whole range of offences to public morals and order, and legal problems arising from them, as well as the process of police surveillance. They demonstrate very clearly the way in which evidence was marshalled through press cuttings, soundings of opinion, records of

parliamentary debates etc., to give a particular context to the 'letter of the law' and its potential for execution between about 1900 and 1940. The other is a record of surveillance and arrests of homosexual(and Communist) sailors in Toulon and other major naval ports from 1927-32 approx, in the Archives Nationales under F/7/13960. For two different approaches to the problematic of this way of reading such material, that I have found a useful corrective to a more traditionally 'empiricist' practise of archival analysis, see Gyatry Chakravorty Spivak, 'The Rani of Sirmoor' in History and Theory, 3. 1985, and Arlette Farge, *Le goût de l'archive*, Paris, Seuil, 1989.

13  For the sentences from Adorno and Benjamin, see the translation of their correspondance over the Passages project in *Aesthetics and Politics*, London, Verso, 1979, pp. 110–141. Many of the sources I have used are ones picked up or only glimpsed 'en passant'. Record covers, booklets, novelettes and papers seen in the bouquinistes of Paris or in provincial bookshops, labelled but unauthored items from photographic archives, items in shop windows. For some, then, there are no references. Radiophonic scripts may be found in the Bibliothèque de l'Arsenal, Paris. *Louise, – roman musical en quatre actes et cinq tableaux*, text and music by Gustave Charpentier: first performed Opéra-Comique, Paris, 2 February 1900. For a general history of the opera, see in the Bibliothèque de l'Opéra, Paris, 'Dossier de l'Oeuvre, LOUISE' and the various collections of press cuttings in the Collection Rondel, Bibliothèque de l'Arsenal. For a fine general introduction, see Ginette Herry's article prepared for her 1983 production of *Louise* at the Théatre Royal de la Monnaie, Brussels, to be found in the libretto accompanying the recording of this performance, Erato, Num. 750843, 1984.

14  There are too many versions of this story to list here, but the most obvious and most discussed in the last decade is Marshall Berman, *All That is Solid Melts into Air*, London, Verso, 1985.

15  This could be traced almost entirely through city guides, or rather those specifically aimed at the male tourist or pleasure seeker, or those specialised sections aimed at him rather than his family. One trajectory might go from Alfred Delvau's classic, *Les Cythères parisiennes, histoire anecdotique des bals de Paris*, Paris, E. Dentu, 1865 to an English guide by John Chancellor, *How to be Happy in Paris, without being ruined!*, London, Arrowsmith, 1926. For a summary of the gender question here, see Janet Wolff, 'The Invisible *Flâneuse*: Women and the Literature of Modernity', in *The Problems of Modernity*, ed., Andrew Benjamin London, Routledge, 1989, pp. 141–56, and Griselda Pollock in her *Vision and Difference: Femininity, Feminism and the Histories of Art*, London, Routledge, 1988: the chapter on 'Modernity and the Spaces of Femininity', pp. 50–90.

16  One of the determinations on the unspoken relations between a writer like Bejamin and Mac Orlan is their common preoccupation with the radio and with the means available to them to work their cultural paradigms within its new possibilities. Benjamin, like his colleagues Brecht and Weill who very quickly turned their hand to a radiophonic cantata, the *Lindenburgflug* (1929), produced a string of programmes between 1929 and 1932; see *Lumières pour enfants* and *Trois pièces radiophoniques*, Paris, Bourgois, 1989 and 1987. For an overview of radio in the 1930s see Rudoph Arnheim, Radio, London, Faber, 1937 and later Alphons Silbermann, *La Musique, la radio et l'auditeur, étude sociologique*, Paris, PUF, 1954. Mac Orlan not only, as we will see, writes for the radio but fetishises the wireless itself as a romantic object alongside the gramophone. For him the sound of the 'poste de la TSF' is a new and sentimental relation of the individual to the world. For Benjamin on Mac Orlan, see his review of the latter's *Sous la lumière froide*, Paris, Émile-Paul Frères, 1927, in Walter Benjamin, *Schriften*, vol.iii, ed. Hella Tiedemann-Bartels, Frankfurt, Suhrkamp Verlag, 1972, pp. 174–6. I am indebted to Christopher Phillips for this important reference and for a summary translation of it.

17 I argue in chapter 3 that Colette occupies a kind of male space. For a list of her work and that of Victor Margueritte see Note on sources, and again, for Margueritte, chapter 3, pp .... For generalities on women after 1918, see Frances I. Clark, *The Position of Women in Contemporary France*, London, P. S. King and Son, 1937 and Dominique Desanti, *La Femme aux temps des années folles*, Paris, Stock, 1985. A fascinating but little-known feminist novel of 1930 which treats the conflict of public and domestic civil and legal rights is Magdeleine Chaumont, *Un mari moderne*, Paris, Albin Michel, 1930.

18 Paul Verlaine, *Femmes & Hombres*, various clandestine editions from 1892 in the *Enfer* of the Bibliothèque Nationale, Paris and more recently the collection edited by Jean-Paul Corsetti and Jean-Pierre Giusto, Paris, Terrain Vague, 1991. An appropriate parallel to what I am proposing here might be Kristin Ross's consideration of Rimbaud in her *The Emergence of Social Space – Rimbaud and the Paris Commune*, London, Macmillan, 1988, which radically widens the reading of textual politics.

19 When my work was largely completed Annie Stora-Lamare published a book on the legal, administrative and moral structures of censorship in the Third Republic, *L'Enfer de la III* république – censeurs et pornographes (1881–1914).*, Paris, Auzas/Imago, 1990. In my estimation this is an opportunity missed, and only marginally useful in the sense that it gives an adequate account of the development of the law, to which I will refer, and of the composition of the *Enfer* of its title, the closed pornography collection of the Bibliothèque Nationale. Stora-Lamare uses a rather different and earlier series of archives, with most of which I am not acquainted, but, alas, seems to be quite unaware that one can and must read between the lines of these, or any other, materials. She seems, for example, unable or unwilling to distinguish between moralising literature and gallant literature that knowingly plays with a moralising tone.

20 It was the Vichy government, for example, that specifically outlawed homosexuality, which had previously been affected only by laws governing public decency. This in effect turned out to be a perfect law for the moralisation of French society *after the war*, giving an emphasised respectability to the family and some kind of a legal status to the rash of homophobic moralising that partnered this attempted *revirilisation* of the Patrie. See Antony Copley, *Sexual Moralities in France – 1780–1980 – New Ideas on the Family, Divorce and Homosexuality. An Essay on Moral Change.*, London, Routledge, 1989, pp. 199ff. or Jacques Girard, *Le Mouvement homosexuel en France, 1945–1980*, Paris, Syros, 1981, pp. 7–29.

21 Clearly, the *trajet* is the pre-eminent record of the traces of the *flâneur's* passage through the city, and a highly finished genre amongst Parisian intellectuals, one might say a genre of genres, sometimes combining the *'récit'*, the memoir, the diary and different forms of fiction. For a critical perspective, see Augé's anthropological journey in the Parisian underground, *Un ethnologue dans le métro*. See also Michel du Certeau, 'Practices of Space', in *On Signs*, ed. Marshall Blonsky London, Polity, 1987, and Richard Fauque, 'Le Discours de la ville' in *A Semiotic Landscape*, ed. Thomas A. Sebeok and Julia Kristéva, Mouton, The Hague, 1967.

22 The dictionary is J. Laplanche and J. B. Pontalis, *Vocabulaire de la psychanalyse*, Paris, PUF., 1981. pp. 467–69.

23 On the historical and philosophical character of detective fiction as a form of knowledge, see Benjamin's great source, Régis Messac, *Le 'Detective Novel' et l'influence de la pensée scientifique*, Paris, Honoré Champion, 1929, which remains the most substantial work of its kind. Within a French context the works of Roger Caillois, *Le Roman policier*, Paris, Lettres Françaises, 1941, and his seminal 1937 essay in *La Nouvelle Revue Française*, 'Paris, mythe moderne', in which he emphasises the relation of Sir Williams, the master criminal of Ponson du Terrail's Rocambole series, to the modern city as the space of

crime. See Ponson du Terrail, *Le Club des valets de coeur*, 1865. Also Fereydoun Hoveyda, *Petite histoire du roman policier, préface de Jean Cocteau.*, Paris, Pavillon, 1956, and expanded as *Histoire du roman policier*, Paris, Pavillon, 1965. On more general questions of serial and popular literature, see Marc Angenot, *Le Roman populaire – recherches en paralittérature*, Presses Universitaires de Québec, 1975, and the essays collected as 'Poétique du polar', in *Roman*, 24, September 1988, including pieces by Gilles Deleuze and Daeninckx.

24  On the question of the series/totality relation in the everday, see Henri Lefèbvre, *Critique de la vie quotidienne II, fondements d'une sociologie de la quotidienneté*, Paris, L'Arche, 1961, pp. 183ff. See also Alice Kaplan and Kristin Ross, 'Introduction', to 'Everyday Life', *Yale French Studies*, 73, New Haven and London, Yale University Press, 1987. They treat the accretion of the everyday in the Annales school of history rather harshly, while I have found Fernand Braudel, *Écrits sur l'histoire*, Paris, Champs–Flammarion, 1969, very useful, especially Section Two, 'L'Histoire et les autres sciences de l'homme'. Although Lefèbvre has been one of the most systematic critics of structuralism, it is worth taking his notion of series and totality alongside that of Claude Lévi- Strauss in his 'Overture' to *The Raw and the Cooked*, London, Cape, 1970.

25  See Marc Augé, *op. cit.*, pp. 66ff. for an illuminating discussion of Lévi-Strauss's explication and extension of Mauss, which provides an excellent context for my point in terms of a discussion of Paris. For Chombart, see Paul Henri Chombart de Lauwe, 'L'Étude de l'Espace social' in *Paris, essais de sociologie 1952–64*, Paris, Éditions Sociales, 1964. pp. 22ff. The passage before my quotation reads: '[we speak of] not only a geographic space, but a social space; of a demographic space, a cultural space, a juridical space and a religious space ... the limits within which the life of a group of humans unfolds cannot be defined by a single criterion. It is the same for the divisions of space comprised within its limits. In reality, it is a question of a series of juxtaposed spaces whose structures sometimes cover each other and sometimes escape any superposition.'

For 'social facts', see Emile Durkheim, *Les Règles de la méthode sociologique*, Paris, Quadrige, 1981. As *Street Noises* is not intended to be a critical commentary on cultural philosophy, I have elided any detailed discussion on the problem of structuralist and post-structuralist difference/*différance* and their relation to Freud. This alone is worth a whole book, such as *Post-structuralism and the question of history*, ed. D. Attridge, G. Bennington and R. Young, Cambridge, CUP, 1987. However I have found J. Derrida's essay 'La Différance' in *Tel Quel – théorie d'ensemble*, Paris, Seuil, 1968, useful, especially pp. 57ff. – the discussion of the unconscious, the ontology of presence etc.

26  The work of Miller is too far from my preoccupations to have delayed me. However the work of Samuel M. Steward, *Parisian Lives*, New York, St Martin's Press, 1984, Elliot Paul, *A Narrow Street*, Harmondsworth, Penguin, 1942 and Ned Rorem, *The Paris and New York Diaries of Ned Rorem*, San Francisco, North Point Press, 1983, have all helped me to think through both gloomy and 'gai' Paris.

Although the film *Les Enfants du Paradis* was central from the very beginning of this work, I have often been guided in my choice of other filmic material by Ginette Vincendeau, and I am indebted to her astute advice.

27  After all, his initial concept of the everyday was thought through in conflict with that of the Surrealists – see *Critique of Everyday Life*, translated by John Moore with a Preface by Michel Trebitsch, London, Verso, 1991.

28  Jacques Rancière, 'Good Times, or Pleasure at the Barriers', in *Voices of the People – the Politics and Life of 'La Sociale' at the End of the Second Empire*, ed. by Adrian Rifkin and Roger Thomas, translated by John Moore. London, Routledge, 1987, pp. 45–94. Originally published in *Les Révoltes Logiques*, 7, 1978, the article typifies the innovatory work of that journal. The recent publication in English of Rancière's *La Nuit des prolétaires*, Paris, Fayard, 1981, as *The Nights of Labour – the Worker's Dream in Nineteenth-Century France*,

Philadelphia, Temple University Press, 1989, translated by John Drury with an introduction by Donald Reid, will doubtless raise a more thorough debate around the development of his thinking. Especially useful in its discussion of the relation of radical, bourgeois culture to 'proletarian' literature is 'Ronds de fumée, les poètes ouvriers dans la France de Louis-Philippe', *Revue des sciences humaines*, 190, 1983.

29   See Donald Reid's introduction to *Nights*, pp. viiff. for an excellent discussion of this matter, in particular of the controversy over Rancière's 1983 article 'The Myth of the Artisan', *International Labour and Working Class History*, 24, 1983. For a very different but appropriate discussion of class identity and history, see Peter Stallybrass and Allon White, *The Politics and Poetics of Transgression*, London, Methuen, 1986, p. 192: 'academic work clearly reveals its discursive mirroring of the subject-formation of the middle class'.

30   Denis Poulot, *Le Sublime, ou le travailleur comme il est en 1870, et ce qu'il peut être*, reprinted Paris, Maspéro, 1980, with an introduction by Alain Cottereau. This important essay on mythologies of popular identity is translated in Rifkin and Thomas, *Voices of the People*.. Georges Duveau, *La Vie ouvrière en France sous le Second Empire*, Paris, Gallimard, 1946. For a classic worker hagiography, see Maurice Dommanget, *Eugène Pottier, membre de la Commune et chantre de l'Internationale*, Paris, Études et Documentation Internationales, 1971.

31   Lucien Descaves, *Philémon, vieux de la vieille*, Paris, Ollendorf, 1913. In Commune historiography this work is generally taken as a source of documentary truth. Here it will be treated as part of the literary tradition of the Goncourt Academy, which is not to deny that its documentary status can, should one so wish, be confirmed, or not, against other types of historical sources.

32   For a good general survey of the role and status of workers and the working-class movement in France, see Gérard Noiriel, *Les Ouvriers dans la société française, XIXᵉ–XXᵉ siècle*, Paris, Seuil, 1986. In effect the wider context of a political and cultural struggle over Frenchness is that encompassed by Jaurès at one pole and Barrès at the other.

33   In 'Good Times' Rancière rightly distanced himself from Descaves–Philémon's pessimism, arguing that it cannot encompass any change or invention in social behaviour. Equally it cannot deal with long-term transformation of the popular and its new modes of affectivity. It is here, in imagining a new relation of people and technology that is both nostalgic and utopian, that Mac Orlan really is a crucial figure, linking a *fin-de-siècle* bohemianism to the inter-war years of the growth of mass media. Hence in his writings the multiplicity of the sites of this re-making, Java to Limehouse, North Africa to the French countryside, is of significance in projecting the imaginary space of those media back on to metropolitan culture. Here see Mac Orlan, *Dans le quartier réservé, grande nouvelle inédite*, Les Oeuvres Libres, Paris, Fayard, 1932.

34   Louis Chevalier, *Montmartre du plaisir et du crime*, Paris, Laffont, 1980. It is worth listing here some of the principal urban sociologists on whose work I have drawn. Of these Chombart de Lauwe can be seen as a middle term, paralleling Henri Lefèbvre in his cultural materialism, though from a less radical and innovative tradition of marxism. Louis Wirth, *On Cities and Social Life*, Chicago and London, Chicago University Press, 1964; Henri Lefèbvre, *La Production de l'espace*, Paris, Anthropos, 1974; Manuel Castells, *La Question urbaine*, Paris, Maspéro, 1972, tr. as *The Urban Question*, London, Edward Arnold, 1977; Pierre Sansot, *Poétique de la ville*, Paris, Klincksieck, 1984; David Harvey, *Consciousness and the Urban Experience*, Oxford, Blackwell, 1985. With Edward Soja, *Postmodern Geographies*, London, Verso, 1989, the idea of the city as a mode of representation becomes a paramount theme. Chevalier's reading of popular literature is extraordinary, and certainly distances him from the pitfalls of a sociology that might wish to quantify mentalities – it is interesting to compare this book with Castells's *Urban Ques-*

tion, written before Castells had begun to deal with issues of the urban symbolic. I know of no other work on Paris that establishes so many links between types of mass and popular cultures as does Chevalier's and on a number of occasions I have stumbled on obscure yet revealing anecdotes that I have then found already noted in it – see in my chapter 2, for example, the history of 'Casque d'Or'. Reading him is a stark contrast to Sansot, in whose *Poétique de la ville* it is quite hard to find any element of 'vulgar materiality' at all. Not only does Chevalier have no theory of representation, but his version of Paris, like that of Richard Cobb, is one that refuses any kind of politic(s) – except the unspoken one that controls their texts, the politic of the freedom of the *flâneur*, to master the appearances of things. See Richard Cobb's self-consciously plebeian *The Streets of Paris, with photographs by Nicholas Breach*, London, Duckworth, 1980. For an instructive comparison, of great interest in its method, see Anne Cauquelin's *La Ville la nuit*, which skilfully combines 'actuality', quantification and poetic speculation.

# 1

# The hold of Paris on history

They leaf through a marvellous 'Paris ancien', raise their eyes and, astonished, recognise it all around them. They make contact with a past which they renounced from ignorance, a capital where they were born but which they do not even look at; they are moved by the thought that it might have perished without their ever having truly loved it.   (Colette, writing of young Parisians in occupied Paris, in *Looking Backwards*, 1941/4, p. 111)

In my eyes Paris will remain the decor of a novel that no one will ever write. How many times have I returned from long wanderings through old streets, my heart heavy with all the inexpressible things that I had seen! Is all that a matter of illusion? I believe not.   (Julien Green, *Paris*, 1984, p. 12)

To continue I have chosen some fragments of entertainment and critical theory that brood over and reshuffle the archaeological layers of Parisianism. One set of images comes from a film, produced in the closing years of the Second World War, *Les Enfants du Paradis*. Another comes from the years just before the war, made up of scattered phrases from Benjamin's writings on the Second Empire. It is hardly surprising that the idea of Paris as a city of the people should have had a particular kind of resonance in 1938, but a very different one in 1943, however strong the continuity and integrity of its language. The time between the completion of Benjamin's *Paris of the Second Empire in Baudelaire* and the making of *Les Enfants du Paradis* was more of an epoch than half a decade, a chasm in time and politics between the end of the Popular Front and the latter days of the Occupation. So even if these two texts worked some of the same kind of materials, and both sought to embody a certain type of image of the city of eighty or a hundred years before them, in 1943 the grounds and implications of historical precision had changed – as much for the work of the historian and the cinematic script-writer as for the ensemble of their publics.[1]

The economic and military rigours of the Occupation, the Nazi programme for a new Europe, the fission of the social and political body, all reordered and disrupted the ideas of the nation and the popular that had contended in the 1930s. What images, of Paris especially, could nourish and represent the national and the popular? Those of glamour cut across the grain of hardship, they seemed egotistical, complaisant to the hardship of the times. And the all-Parisian habit of revolution could hardly fare better. Two such possibilities were equally blocked when either one or the other might register or excite discontent and resistance. A longing for a secure version of an authentic France was equally splintered. Which France, the capital headquarters of the occupier, its *beaux quartiers* the scene of Nazi pleasures? Its faubourgs and their poverty? The memories of one or the other in their intersection with the state of things could hardly sidestep a damaging equivocation and ambiguity. If the city before the war could be the unhealthy, filthy, despairing warren of a Céline or the elegiac poverty and popular spirit of a Dabit – without too much difference in its figuring as either one or the other – in 1943 the elegy or the despair could slip into more dangerous connotations, into collaboration or resistance. Likewise the countryside – how could the idea of 'deepest France' evade the 'volkish' myth? Maurice Chevalier's songs of these years – the 'Chant du maçon', or the 'Marche des semelles en bois' – were no more populist those he had sung in 1937, but they certainly sounded that way, and had a tone of possible collaboration. In a very short space of time words in popular cultures had changed their meaning. In 1937 a song about legionnaires evoked a polymorphous sense of colonial fantasy and sexual excitement. In 1944 the word Légion meant the LVF, the Légion Volontaire Française, the last word of collaboration as military heroics. The body of the colonial volunteer had been sexualised in a way that was inappropriate to the wartime soldier, unless at the expense of fascination with Nazi manhood.[2] The 'people' and the 'popular' had after all been at the heart of the confrontation of socialist and fascist ambitions, the contention of a communist Thorez and a populist–fascist Déat for a social base, for the loyalty of a class wooed by Blum's progressive legislation.

What could get by in 1943 was a vacant history, one that pictured the rich and the poor, the respectable and the criminal, the *menu peuple* and the Faubourg Saint-Germain, and the types of hero or heroine who came out of them, but which recognised them only through their nature as figures of convention: within a unifying emotion of the story rather than as a revelation of social structure and irreconcilable difference: or through difference as a game. Such a history existed in the currency of the means of representation. In 1943 *Les Enfants* managed to balance a striking reality of decor with a complete generalising of Parisian affectivities, creating a scenario in which a narcissistic gratification overwhelmed any uncomfortable presence. At the moment of its production, then, *Les Enfants* stood at a watershed in the imaging of Paris, satisfying a need to forget just some of the conflicts between its pasts and its presents. It was both a summation of the skills learned in the mass cultures of image, song or theatre, and, necessarily, a desertion of the terrain across which they had been articulated. The immediate modernity of context that marked Carné's 1930s films like the *Hôtel du Nord* or *Métropolitain*, and which drew on a well established tradition of the picturing of social difference, forcibly gives way to historical distance.

In fact many of these classics of realist cinema were under interdiction in occupied and Vichy France, and it is of interest to note that one of those passed by the French censors but banned by the German authorities, had been Abel Gance's 1938 version of Gustave Charpentier's opera *Louise*. This film was a model of traditional Montmartrois culture. It was a tribute to the opera that had first been performed in 1900, but only after a six-year delay of bitter disputes over what was seen to be its excessively direct representation of modern people. Once staged, it divided opinion. However, the critic André Corneau acclaimed it 'Dans *Louise*, le "plaisir parisien" joue le role du FATUM dans la tragédie antique'...[3] – a view that was to prevail, the opera yielding only to *Carmen* in its eventual success. *Louise* came to stand for the whole network of connections that could be made between the national and the popular through the streets of Paris, yielding up a succession of meanings for them in one and then another historical context. If the film version was seen as a high point of French lyric art, its temporary loss may be read as another effect of the imposition of a zone of silence around the troublesome particularities of Paris, the silence that *Les Enfants* tried to break.

Yet what significance was loss, when distance itself is a mark and the condition of the intellectual perception of the popular? As we saw in Campagne's lunchtime story, it was René Clair, not the firemen, who knew about the tenderness of Paris. In *Les Enfants* distance allows a projection of the means of representation back into their literary origins – which were generally understood to lie in the years between about 1825 and 1848 – that is to say, the first classic period of a literary bohemia as it was defined through the work of Balzac and Murger. A shift in time that permits a recuperation of meaning for the city in the twin shapes of pure history and of pure anecdote – spoken out of the present, but without apparant reference to its immediate origins and problems. In *Les Enfants* the exquisite, self-conscious, emotional dandyism of Jacques Prévert's scenario, the highly wrought informality of the performance and the poetic realism of the sets play off each other to allow a space in which the present is rescued from its grim equivocations, hidden in a historical romance whose every element is the substance of its mythemes. It was not so much a historical film as one that slipped behind the present and restituted its conventions of social distance.

Coming out finally only in 1945, a year after the liberation of Paris, the film nudged into the future an idea of the city, in an abstract and poetic form, that turned out to be if anything more appropriate to the post-war world than to the Vichy France for which it had been dreamed up. In their next film, *Les Portes de la nuit* (1946), Carné and Prévert used the lyrical realism of the 1930s to frame the horrors of the collaborationist mentality, surviving in the fabric of the city spaces. It met with refusal, by public and critics alike.[4] For one thing, unlike *Les Enfants*, this was an idea of the city both more compromised by wartime experience and more vividly outdated by economic and demographic change, by those transformations that not only destroy buildings and spaces but that in doing so suggest the urgent need for an archaeology of nostalgias to retrieve them and preserve them. *Les Enfants*, then, was able to escape not only reference to the moment of its production but also the as yet barely realised implications of the more dramatic changes of the 1920s and 1930s: changes that were entailed in new types of consumption, either of the means of production in the form of gigantic city plans or of luxuries and colonial pleasures in the exhibitions of decorative arts (1925) or colonial celebration (1931) and of ever more lavish and mechanised styles of entertainment.

Amongst such a complex of transformations, the competing plans for the rebuilding of Paris, from Corbusier's radial city downwards, sounded a deafening accompaniment. And no plan was more menacing to the meaning of Paris than the one actually to be put into effect. This was the demolition and redevelopment of Thiers's fortifications of the 1840s, together with the military 'Zone non aedificandi' – the 250 metres of officially bare land on either side of them. A grand plan for the rehabilitation of the entire Parisan periphery had been on the table since the 1880s. It was finally made viable by the defeat of 1914–15, which demonstrated beyond doubt that the fortifications had no military purpose. Their demolition was decreed in 1919 and a series of protocols for the distribution and use of the land elaborated in 1924. They proposed the construction of cheap housing, university lodgings, stadiums and gardens both on the site of the fortifications and in the Zone. A complex administrative and legal nightmare of public and private finance, expropriations, intermunicipal conflicts over the ownership of land and disputes between Paris and the national government was thus unleashed. And at stake were not only the future form of the city but the fates of the inhabitants and industries of the Zone. In 1930 there were some 125,000 people, in 15,000 'dwellings', 879 factories employing 50,000 workers with 180,000 dependants, and a source of some 10 million francs in taxes.[5] The plan supplanted a reality and a dream of the unhygienic, illegal and marginal life of the city edges with another, more organised one of the city worthy of the worthiness of labour, worthy of itself, and therefore in sections, the West especially, even more replete with bourgeois pleasures.

Yet if the plan took decades to bring to fruition – the ring road was completed only in the 1970s – the reaction of music-hall, night-club or cinematic song to its beginnings was rapid. Precisely because these margins were already the myth materials of a literary treatment of city spaces and social differences, and were already signifiers of nostalgia, the threat to their actual existence could only elevate their status in systems of representation. So, these fantasmagoric margins were consigned to the past and to loss if anything more rapidly in song and in cinema than in the execution of the city plan. The repertoire of the principal singers of the 1930s, amongst whom were Fréhel and Piaf, mourned their loss and celebrated the popular texture of their life, their marvellous sexuality, with songs like 'Où sont-ils donc', 'Entre Saint-Ouen et Clignancourt'

and ''Chand d'habits'. Their remains in the post-war world, the fleamarkets, were as open to firemen as to intellectuals, and sought by both for their recreation and amusement. The implementation of this project had indeed begun to bite deeply into the materials of fantasy, making their renewal all the more urgent. Van Parys and Clair were at the *puces* in 1951 because it was the idyllic survivor of these old margins.

The forgetfulness of *Les Enfants* after the war, then, may well have facilitated blindness to a present whose formation was a result of some unbearable complexities. For these changes in the urban fabric had been willed, albeit with different intentions, by a succession of inter-war governments of different political colours. More, they had in the end been partly consummated by the requirements of the occupier. Inevitably the German strategies for control of Paris readily embraced the politic of cleaning up the city, and large areas of the sheds (*barraques*) on the Zone were razed at their requirement in 1943–4. This coincidence is of an order that needs not to be noticed. Its repression could work all the more urgently through the fantasy of unitary origins in the city's myth, an escape from acknowledging those unintended complicities that are too revealing of the concrete forces of the power of capital, which that were neither purely French nor German. The purging and generalisation of sentiment is as beautifully adapted to the future as to the present. It exercised skills in representation to a point of virtuosity where they deny any world other than their own, and so helped to prepare Paris, and a generation of its entertainers, for consumption in a new stage of the development of the international culture industries after the war, as well as for a mode of adaptation to the futures of capital investment in its fabric.

The narrative of the popular in *Les Enfants* links real historical characters – Debureau (mime artist), Lemaître(actor), Lacenaire (criminal, dandy and homosexual)[6] across a framework of social and spatial geographies that are lovingly recreated in the details of the set. Yet despite this compelling reality of detail, or because of it, because each element signifies a recovered sentiment, the film evades any outcome that might open on to a perception of change and process, least of all any glimpse into the evolution and historical lifetimes of its own materials. The wholeness of *Les Enfants* denies that the film itself is only one possible outcome of their ordering. This is not just because of the reticence imposed by the moment. It is also predicated by the fear of the final disappearance of these materials, whether under the jackboot or under the developer's pickaxe. It preserves rather than resists, much more in tears than anger. Its crucial images are ones not of change but of exchange, of regression rather than progress, of circularity and loss.

This process is accomplished through a simple but rhythmically complex diegesis, that is to say, the 'straightforward' narrative of an impossible love that is lost in the crowds of *fête*-day, gets stilled in long and breathless digressions. The swift yet discursive opening sequences set up and define the character of the city and its protagonists, bringing them into relation with each other through a scale of open desires and smothered passions, only to dissolve into the first, tense dialogue of Baptiste and Nathalie. This unfolds at a snail's pace while all around the frenzied, comic crises of the Funambules surge ahead on stage and backstage. Specific time disappears, leaving only desire and its frustrations to take its place. However, structurally, the story's links are worked through a single figure, Jéricho, the *marchand d'habits* (ambulant clothes seller). It is he who passes goods and information from one character to another, securing their place in the narrative and their knowledge of it. It is he who shows that each interlocking part plays its role in a given space, and there alone. 'Here comes Jupiter, called Jéricho because of his trumpet,

called the Medusa because of the raft ... ' Thus Jéricho announces himself
with a listing of his names, of which each is also a name for some dream
state or mythic traces in the perception of city life. He sets values on
stolen goods and foretells the future. His tittle-tattle is truth or treachery
– even to the criminal:

> Lacenaire (*to Jéricho*) ... last night I dreamed of you, ... Yes, you went by in
> the street and shouted your cry: 'Old clothes, any old clothes to sell.'
> ('Marchand d'habits, avez vous des habits à vendre') (*High angle shot of
> Lacenaire*). And in my dream I heard something else: 'Old friends, any old
> friends to sell.' ('Marchand d'amis, avez-vous des amis à vendre') (Brooke,
> p. 78)

Jéricho orders a dreamworld of representations, of which reality is the
repressed, unconscious state, rediscovered only in the Vaudeville.

> The Director: [in] those noble theatres the public dies with boredom ... They
> doze off, their audience, with their museum pieces ... whereas here at the
> Funambules, it's alive, things jump, they move (*He almost dances*). Fairyland,
> what! ... Quoi? Things appear and disappear, just like life ... and then there's
> the tap dancing, and the fighting, just like life ... (Brooke, p. 46)

It is here that the film begins to share its images and spaces with
Benjamin's *Baudelaire* and *Passagen-Werk*. At the same time its feverish
representation of the urban mentality recalls one of Benjamin's inspira-
tions, Georg Simmel's essay *The Metropolis and Mental Life*.[7] The proximity with Benjamin is particularised in the figure of Jéricho, who resembles
a ragpicker, drunken and limping with his sack, and in whom Prévert's
poetry opens up flawed glimpses of the city, just as does Baudelaire's
'Rag-picker's Wine' to Benjamin. And it operates at a more general level
in the perception of history. With Benjamin the hard process of economic change is held in view through signs of loss that play on the edge
of the nostalgic: a new historical phenomenon can be the sign for the loss
of an older one. For example, the profoundly uninformed mass connoisseurship that frames the industrial consumption of the Expositions
Universelles is offered in opposition to that of the Passages (arcades). As
salestalk replaces the knowledge of the product in the intensified fetishism of the god-commodity, the Passages suffer a loss of meaning. And
that in the end is part of the process that will turn the *flâneur* of the mid-
century into the detached, fascist mentality of Benjamin's own time,
Henri Béraud as the *Flâneur salarié*.[8] But even as history is planted with
the seeds of a future dystopia, a space is implicitly opened up for a certain
atavism. Possibly, for Benjamin, one of a more truthful regime of signs,
rather than the yearning for the kitschy regime of the 'good old days'.

In the film, meanwhile, an important part of the fun and the horseplay
of the life of the stage depends upon the co-existance of different kinds of
theatre and of the ways that its regulation can give rise to comedy. This

emerges in the suspense and crisis that hangs over the mimes when a sudden and indecorous emotion breaks through their professional silence into a cry or a sound, and brings down a fine from the Director.[9] A fine, that is, to pay the authorities who at that time imposed them to maintain the distinction of mime and proper theatre. If, at that time, fines acted as a constraint on popular theatrical forms, in the film they are the source of a vanished possibility of expression, the invisible trace of a borderline between the illegal and legal that is transgressed as a site of amusement. The long-gone legal system, for all its absurd repression – even the pantomime lion may not roar – was something better than the modern commercial theatre and the imposed silences of the Occupation, whose breaking was more risky. Or whose keeping could only lead to the slightly absurd asceticism of Vercors's novel *Le Silence de la mer*, where the heroic price exacted for silence in the occupier's presence is the denial of love, the utter withering of affectivity.[10]

This is not to say that the critical history of Benjamin is a sentimental 'fiction' and the film a flawed 'historical' text, or that it doesn't matter which is which. Nor that our problem can be solved by recourse to a demonstration of their structural similarities. If they share the risk of atavism to illuminate the present, this is largely because, in the registers of change of the 1930s, both tracked across the same kinds of terrain to find their imagery – a terrain that was acceptable as the origins of modernity, whether by marxists or literary dandies, because it looked like a rediscovered master plan for the everyday that they knew. And both in their different ways had to represent the passage of time as a form of loss if they were sufficiently to underline or to realise the threats of the future or the present. They share, then, a tendency to substitute names for structures, to make names stand in for process and to act as feeling. The resulting equivocal relation of detail and narrative suggests that Adorno's insistence to Benjamin on clarifying the class structure, even if at the expense of detail, might just as well be applied to the film as to *Baudelaire*: 'I wonder whether such ideas need to be as immured behind impenetrable layers of material as your ascetic discipline demands.' But in that case they both might well be able to share Benjamin's defence of his philological method, his insistence to Adorno on the establishment of the entire series of nameable phenomena as a precondition of securing a meaning:

> Yet in each case it is this critique that provokes the philological effort itself. To use the language of *Elective Affinities*, it presses for the exhibition of the material content in which the truth content can be historically revealed.[11]

This shared risk may be developed by tracing in both the relation between the perceived shape of the city in the present and in the past. Benjamin, in sifting his sources from the time of Louis-Philippe and the Second Empire, worked through a knowledge that came both through his daily round and his discovery of the city, and through the literary and visual formulations of Louis Aragon, of the photographer Atget, of Surrealism. And Eugène Atget, whose work was so crucial to Benjamin's formulation of the modernity of photography, could himself only be read at that point within the double but related literary spaces of Surrealism and the 'social fantastic' of Pierre Mac Orlan, the 'domain of shadow'.[12] That is to say in a physical space and a literary world of which Prévert too was an adept, and whose nostalgias were a deposit of very complex sets of archaeologies of the popular. These spaces and forms of writing and diction were lived as everyday, and self-consciously composed and recomposed to investigate the past, to make a living out of writing, to entertain. As an identity, they condemned the author who could not sidestep them through either history or irony, to an endless repetition of his subjectivity, a repetition than took on the strength of an informal literary institution. They were thus parameters, which criticism might break, but not before it had passed through their nostalgia.

In this roundabout, *Les Enfants...* repeats, evades and hints at points and means of escape and distance. Garance, who is the only major character invented for the film, refuses to be the simulacrum of Beauty, and quits her job as a fairground attraction.[13] Baptiste mistakes her worldly gallantry for innocence. A single movement of the arms can both darken and lighten the screen, unsettling the cinematic image in itself. If the film moves through discourse, gesture, expression and the dislocating movements of its surfaces, as well as through anachronism and play in the unfolding of the narrative, it is not because of this that it enjoys less of an ironic tension with its atavism than does Benjamin through his montage. The problem for the survival of both is that, albeit in different degrees, their relation with the literal is too deeply embedded in the lived-out cultures of the moment of their production to make it clear that they have sidestepped their routines. As we shall see, the film could escape the Paris of Maurice Chevalier no more easily than Benjamin the romance of Paris formulated in Aragon's *Paysan de Paris*.[14]

In *Les Enfants...* Baptiste and Garance finally get together after the scene in the *bouge* (low dive), the Rouge-Gorge, at the Barrière de Ménilmontant, when Baptiste has fought Lacenaire's bully: a piling-up of readymades, of clichés, a Western-style punch-up in a suburban dance-hall out of a nineteenth-century Paris guide. The hooligan, Avril – who is actually a stock type of the *titi de Paris* – could be drawn from any number of *Détective Magazine*, *Voilà*, or contemporary guides to Parisian *populaire* dance-halls, such as this one of 1922:

> a young man has just come in, paleskinned with blue eyes so clear that they seem colourless, never looking directly, and avoiding any look. A supple way of holding himself, like the balancing of the shoulders, all comes together to give him a disquieting and threatening feel: he's dressed in black and his wide

open shirt displays his neck. We have already seen his like one morning at daybreak on the Boulevard Arago, when a man who was going to die came out of the van to the waiting guillotine. (André Warnod, *Bals de Paris*, 1922, p. 115)

Avril is a type who is as dangerous only as he is pitiable and lovable ('mon pauvre Avril' is how Lacenaire pets him), a regular denizen of the popular Paris of pimps and hooligans, *marlous* or *apaches*. As are the other stereotypes, of the master criminal, the 'blind' beggar, and Baptiste himself, as fit to defeat them all as Rodolphe, the hero of Eugène Sue's *Mysteries of Paris*, whom he resembles in much but his ultimate failure. However, in his fight Baptiste rescues not only Garance for his own love, but the narrative itself from complete dependence on its sources among the anecdotes of the criminal people. The fight is a ritual of separation that allows the story of their love to operate in seclusion, a dynamic from which it generates the light that it throws on its milieu as the decorative context of constraints that it will never transcend. This inverse relation of the love story to its circumstantial decor mirrors other changes in entertainment at the time. There was, for instance, a drastic swing in Edith Piaf's wartime repertoire when she declared, again in 1943, that she wanted to escape the realist song, with its 'dirty pavements seething with prostitutes' and to sing in their place 'simple loves, health and the joy of living, … the sunshine and Paris'. This coincidence is useful here, because it underlines the fact that the Vichy mentality had a productive effect in entertainment and in the career of an individual star. And it suggests that the role of the love story is not just a cultural 'universal' but a value at a specific conjuncture. Its resources as a sign are not limited or exhausted simply by reference to a set of sexual or literary conventions.

In *Les Enfants*, then, it is through the engrossing centrality of the love story that the historic image of Paris floats free from the distance of historical anecdote into a present of empathy and association. A contemporary identification can be made with its historical 'authenticity', for that love should be the narrative of the city is another comfortably acceptable and expected stereotype, one that makes possible the finding of sense rather than insisting on the effort of making it. That love should be fired through a glance at the fairground attraction (the naked Venus that was Garance when Baptiste sighted her), that it should be fleeting, that it should lose itself in the weft of social complexities and class difference, all these have the odour of normality in romantic narratives of the pre-war decades. The historical reconstruction both redeems the abstraction that is the love story, and in turn is given a purpose by it, a disguise for its metaphors of the present. The problem is that the film's very adeptness at irony is what turns it back in on itself as an exercise in virtuoso narcissism. The excess of naming disables the moment of critique, and irony itself ends up being only another name for Paris. In some respects too, we might argue, it is the beauty of the Passages in Benjamin that stops them from leading anywhere. To linger in them in the 1840s is to redeem the present, to re-live the pre-fascist *flâneur*.

Baptiste and Garance leave the *bouge* to walk together, and then she gestures across the gulf of night-time to her own origins as a woman of the people, to the clustered lights of Ménilmontant. Now we need be in little doubt that it is really the Ménilmontant of 1943, rather than that of 1830, the Ménilmontant of 1943 known throughout the world of cinema and gramophone as the 'Ménilmuche' of Maurice Chevalier. Louis Chevalier was later to put it definitively in his study *Les Parisiens*, though in terms that might remind us more of Prévert's poetic than of sociological enquiry. It is the people who define themselves:

> To know these quartiers, in the end, it's enough to ask the people who live there – as I did, with my students, in an attempt to delimit the uncertain but living frontier between Belleville and Ménilmontant. A cry of horror from the honest housewife who finds herself suspected of living in Belleville when all her dignity is bound up with her being an inhabitant of Ménilmontant. (*Les Parisiens*, p. 151)

And, writing of the distinction between the legal and the perceived or psychological existence of individual quartiers in the administrative maps of Paris and the minds of their inhabitants:

> Present is Belleville, but not Ménilmontant, of which everyone will avow, by the Grace of Maurice Chevalier, and to end of the world, that it exists and that it is not to be confused with its neighbour. (*ibid.*, p. 153)

In a way this is fair enough. At no point in the nine volumes of his autobiography does Maurice Chevalier allow for even the faintest of a blurring between 'Ménilmuche' and its neighbours, let alone the people of Ménilmontant and the French working classes as a whole. In the songs of the 1920s and 1930s it was they who were the *gratin du pavé* (the cream of the street) or the true *Paris parigot* (Paris speaking-Parisian). For Maurice the boys of Ménilmontant were always going up home, as he himself took care to do from time to time. And in wartime France his slightly tainted songs were not hopelessly sentimental, even coming from the mouth of this escapee from the working class. Underlining one's origins had its point, in contrast to Piaf's or Fréhel's pre-war songs where boys from eastern Paris were just as often going out, to fight for France in the colonies and conquer hearts. It is because Louis Chevalier's sociology is made within and out of this literature of the mutual and circular reinvention of character and place that his text so usefully underlines the inevitability of the reading imposed by Garance's gesture:

> Garance: Look at all those little points of light. The lights of Ménilmontant. (*Cut to a longshot of Ménilmontant by night, and several glimmering lights. She continues off.*) People sleep and wake up. Each one has a lamp that lights up

and is extinguished ... (*Cut back to her in close up, full face, he is backview, half out of shot.*) When I think (*very melancholy*) that I can't even recognise the room where I lived with my mother when I was little. (Brooke, p. 84)

If this inflexion was necessarily very precise, it was only the more so because of the sudden and uncharacteristic lapse into historical innacuracy in the set – 'flash sur un plan général de Ménilmontant'. For despite its obsessional demand for authenticity in each crease and fold of costume, the façades of the Boulevard du Crime or the distribution of theatre seats, the lights of Ménilmontant that Garance shows Baptiste could not have been seen in the 1820s. True enough the neighbouring village of Belleville had already grown to have a population of tens of thousands by this time, so that when it was annexed in the creation of Paris 'intra-muros' in 1859, it was already the thirteenth French town, overcrowded, swollen with immigration from central Paris and the provinces, with more than its fair share of property owners and rackrenting landlords living cheek by jowl with their tenants. But not Ménilmontant, and, as we have seen, the two are not to be confused. Maps of the 1820s to 1840s show how rustic this future refuge of the Saint-Simonians remained, in comparison to its neighbour, relatively sparse in its housing, certainly unable to project quite such a late-night cluster of glittering firesides and lamps.[15]

No, Garance gestures to a community that came to be identified as the bedrock of the working class, in their goodness or their horror, of the Third Republic in the last two decades of the nineteenth century. *Pace* the inhabitants, it bore the double name of Belleville-Ménilmontant, and was a community cut off from central Paris by its self-sufficiency in the circuits of work and pleasure and by the mythologies of its independence. A volume of 1943, *Paris 1943, arts et lettres*, issued by the Inspection Générale des Beaux Arts of the city of Paris, published a series of essays that lent an air of untramelled serenity to the wartime imaging of the city, a perfect continuity with the pre-war world. In the chapter on Belleville-Ménilmontant this independence is the key to associating the whole area with the social body of the entire city:

> Many quartiers live off Paris, feed themselves off her and profit from her generous life. On the contrary those that enable her to live, who nourish and support her, are but a few. Belleville is the foremost amongst them. Belleville is indispensable to life inside Paris, to her basic life, to her construction, to her strength.[16]

But for Garance, even in her gesture, she fails to recognise her childhood room. The time of growing up imposes invisibility. This is the more tragic because, in the circumstances of acute historical rupture that really lend the essays of *Paris 1943* an air of desperate insipidity, Garance's childhood is itself the childhood of the city. It can be conjured up but never retrieved through the insistent repetition of its tropes. Loss and identification are a palimpsest in which it is the both distance between and similarity of the overlapping texts that prevents their unscrambling. So too for Maurice Chevalier the life of work that is Ménilmontant can only be recognised through its refusal. Seized with the desire to sing from childhood, the virtues of work become a burden to him. To practise his childish repertory he has to hide in the lavatory at the drawing pin factory where he makes his pennies. And once, the rhythm of the song in his head and the dully repeated rhythm of beating out the pinheads clash: the hammer comes down on his thumb, crushing it.

Just as its values can only be discerned by breaking from them, by looking down or back: why else should the boys be forever going back, if they have not already left? In 1960 Maurice had himself photographed by Robert Doisneau in the street of his birth for his book *My Paris*. He stands at the summit of a street staircase, a rich, overdressed bourgeois. His famous smile substitutes itself for the scene, his history for its. The lens just catches the modern buildings at the foot of the hill, a sure sign that there is not much left to see, and that soon there will be less. This literal twisting of the viewpoint is symptomatic of the way in which the effects of change can only be handled or denied by the resort to metonym. Maurice is nearly all that is left, his smile wards off this uncomfortable knowledge.

In 1943, then, the ideal community of history and the fantasies of the entertainment industries, the masculine fetishes of wars and colonial glory, the glory of international stardom, all the elements of the idea of 'Ménilmuche' read an equivocal present back into an eclectic past. A casually inaccurate image of a history that provides a meaning for the present even while it censors itself, in a censorship made as easy by its complexities and by its complicities. The idea that Belleville-Ménilmontant might have no history could suggest another possible version, one offered by the same essay in *Paris 1943*, of a quartier – Belleville – that 'conjugates only with the future', whose moments of upheaval and revolution have 'never stopped the plane-trees budding, the old Faubourg from breathing ... this unforgettable odour of chips, cooked artichokes, boiled potatoes...':[17]

> The only quartier that has no ancestral regrets, no antiquated remorse. It is the one quartier that is always alive with the future, which it gets from a present without a past. The only one whose existence depends upon itself alone. There, everything conjugates with the future.

Though the idea of the present and the future is highly compromised in such a semi-official publication, it is in some ways unfair to make morally mechanical distinctions and comparisons between a text like this and *Les Enfants*. There were some strange unfoldings of these wartime complicities which turned out to reveal a harshly appropriate relation of Vichy morality to that of post-war reconstruction. Sometimes the traces refer to a future that they may not intend, and plenty of works that were formally collaborationist were little different from some that were not. *Les Enfants* had the good fortune to contain lines like that of Garance, 'me, I adore it, liberty'. The strategy of *Paris 1943* is easily enough recognised in this context: it is to get away with a history of one's choosing, and it tries to bargain away the image of red Belleville for an expansive dignity of labour, invested in this eastern working class, in this 'only living' quartier.

Benjamin and Prévert stumbled on strikingly similar formulations in their perception of urban humanity. Benjamin, in some of his notes on modern forms of lighting, used almost the same words as Garance when she looks at Ménilmontant. He wrote of a 'comparison of human beings with a control panel on which are thousands of electric light bulbs; first these die out, then others light themselves anew' (Buck-Morss, *Dialectic*, p. 309ff.). Neither he nor Prévert was far from Mac Orlan either in his early discussions of photography or in his attempt to make poetry out of the neon lights of Paris in 1937.[18] The difference between the three lies in their understanding of technology. If in Prévert the cinematic apparatus becomes the perfect vehicle of a pre-cinematic pleasure, and if Mac Orlan is fascinated by the failure of his own poetic of the gas-lamp in the confrontation with electricity, it is Benjamin who sees the development of lighting as a nightmare representation of the controlling power of bourgeois, fascist society.

More crucially, as I have already indicated, Benjamin's texts and *Les Enfants* overlap in the way in which they allow for an exchange of social relations and appearances through the two persons of the rag-picker and the ambulant clothes seller (*'chand d'habits*), those elemental figures of the nineteenth-century *bohème du travail*. These two Parisian forms of work had different activities and functions that coincided through the processing of waste. But in the long term, they lost this definition and had certainly became thoroughly confused in the 1930s cultures of poverty fetishism and bargain hunting. They had been allowed not only to overlap on to each other but to lose the previously well defined structures of their trade, through blurring the distinctions of employee and entrepreneur, wholesaler and retailer, buyer and seller, stallholder and ambulant seller. As with the shout in the theatre, their function as image transcends their legal status. In Benjamin and in Prévert the figures, or a composite, act as an arbitrator or as a handler of the truth, who both offers it in different forms to its participants and points to the processes of its production. The perception of social reality itself passes for a *déchet*:

The rag-picker is the most provocative figure of human poverty. Lumpenproletarian in a double sense, dressed in rags and having business them. (*Paris capital*, p. 364)

Above all let us keep this in mind: this man is no longer playing the game: he refuses to mask himself for the carnival, he has even left his doctor of sociology's hat at home, and with his elbows he makes his way across the crowd, here and there lifting off the most outrages masks ... (Wohlfarth, in *Passages*, p. 593)

In the first lines Benjamin echoes André Warnod in his 1927 essay *Les Fortifs*, though in comparison to Warnod his image of the demasking rag-picker is wildly optimistic. The difference is one of time – the historical time in question, the Second Empire and the 1920s. Of place – the nineteenth-century street as a *fête*, and the Zone after the First World War, with its elaborate social and economic structure. And, in Warnod, of a deep ambivalence in the face of the rag-pickers and their environment:

Here [Le Touzet, a sector of the Zone], garbage and filth overwhelm everything, here it's a heap of chicken carcasses, further on a pile of old Camembert boxes, elsewhere a little hillock made of rags: the same grime smears over the walls, the cobblestones of the street, and everything that lives in this empire. The humanity that swarms in this filth becomes a single body with it. (*Les Fortifs*, 1927)

The rag-picker and the *'chand d'habits* or *fripier* need to be elaborated more carefully as types in history and literature. In either case, he or she not only transfers commodities between social classes and strata, but, depending upon the nature and direction of the exchange, makes possible disguise and deception, appropriation and re-appropriation of wealth or pleasure, legal and illegal. And, at the same time, in certain forms of literature, the figure of the rag-picker or clothes-seller is also a disguise, the wearing of which became something of a cultural habit.

In thriller fiction from the Second Empire and before it is a degree zero of the passage through the city, unnoticed and omniscient, the clothing of crime or virtue, the form to be donned by the aristocrat–criminal or detective alike in their mutual pursuit – as, in its own way, *Les Enfants* is a disguise for the Paris of 1943, made out of historical relics. Both functions of the rag-picker, the *'chand d'habits* or *fripier* as provider and as disguise coalesce in the most popular detective of the late 1860s, the young Inspector Lecoq in Emile Gaboriau's *L'Enquête* (1867). It is Lecoq who initiates the systematic use of inductive reason to sift the mysteries and enigmas of city crime. In *L'Enquête* he loses his criminal, a duke in disguise, largely because he fails to consult the *fripiers*. If there is question of disguise, it is they alone who can trace it to its wearer. They are the starting point for the induction that alone is able to unpick appearances. As the Père Tabaret-Tirauclair, his master of inductive reasoning, explains to him:

Oh, my boy! what a way to carry on!. I, who am but a poor old fellow, I would have summoned before me the barons and the vassals of the Parisian *fripiers*, and, in the end, I would have winkled out one who would have blurted, 'These rags?... yes, it was me, I sold them to an individual who looked like this and like that, who bought them for one of his friends, whose measurements he brought with him'. (*L'Enquête*, p. 245)

In the sequel, *The Honour of the Name*, Lecoq finally traps his duke by the assumption of a successful disguise, one that ties a Gordian knot in the threads of the countless *faux-semblants* and false trails that make up his story. The creation of an image impenetrable to his adversary may put one in mind of Benjamin's 'dialectical images', those complexes of space, time and the materiality of daily life that serve as an access to the inter-weaving of ideology and production.

The rag-pickers or clothes-sellers are also figures that can be loaded with any form of social or political vice, depending on what you want to count as rubbish, and on how you value it. The *fripière* of the eighteenth and early nineteenth century stood on the borders of high life and the low, offering her services to the aristocracy from a position of privileged knowledge and amoral criminality that escaped the sordid dealings and ordinary dishonesties of the respectable *commerçant*. According to the *Grande Encyclopédie* it was she who could provide a countess with false jewels to cover the loss through a clandestine sale or illicit gift of the real ones. Or who could find the old, precious piece of Alençon embroidery lost during the Revolution. We already have a sense of a trade in history, the recovery of the fragments of social rupture, but one that evades the monetary values of bourgeois commerce to restitute a lost aristocratic ideal.[19] And if this mythology originated particularly in the eighteenth century, it was reformulated with immense popular attraction in Balzac's *Splendeurs et misères des courtisanes* (1838–47). In the figure of Asie, the *fripière* in all her museum-like magnificence, we find the material source of Vautrin's power over appearances. It is upon her resources that he relies to dress and redress himself and his human materials in the guises that allow them to circulate through all the strata of modern society.

'Rag-pickers provided the lowest proportion of Communards', says Descaves's critical old Philémon, speaking of the social composition of the Commune. And yet, as Descaves points out to him, this did not prevent the reactionary satirists from seeing the Commune or the Communard worker as a rag-picker, or rather as its lowest type, the *piqueur*, fishing the city gutters for the rubbish of red republicanisms. And even as he wrote that, Descaves was visiting the rag-pickers' cities of the Zone to write the most depressing newspaper articles on their wretched life. As Félix Pyat's famous play *Le Chiffonnier de Paris* (1846) had shown, the redemption of the repulsive rag-picker was arduous and difficult to accept at all. As a form of work rag-picking's connotations were systematically negative, subject to a rigorous system of regulation that forced it to the margins of time and space. Even as late as 1903 a report of the Parisian Labour Office picked over these connotations in assessing the state of rag-picking in the city. But it recorded that the rate of crime amongst rag-pickers was, in reality, very low, much lower than that amongst cart-drivers, and that their state of hygiene was better than might have been expected, given their environment of uncured rabbit skins and their hereditary vice of drink.[20] Sandwiched in statistics, opinion and moralities in this way, the integral role of the rag-picker in the economy of the city is readily disavowed as a normal or normative type of work. Equivocation of its image made the different elements of its very complete industrial structure available for different narratives. Hence the *piqueur* of the anti-Commune cartoons appears not as the true proletarian of the rag industry but as the lowest social type of all.

It is this denial or repression that opens up economic difference itself as a site of fantasy and pleasure. In this case difference is backlit against terrible signs of rags and rabbit skins, so that the particular trade disappears behind their abysmal stench and physical disorder. So, as they he or she processes the movement of commodities through the city, recycling them, the rag-pickers and *fripiers* seem to give rise to their own displacement and wandering life, which is actually controlled by law and the structure of their industry. If this is absent, then the search for their goods itself becomes identity, their resale another. From this abstraction of economic process as identity, the backing-up of the rag-picker and the *'chand d'habits* is only a small step, the observation of a homonym of displacement. And the build-up of their considerable population in the rag-pickers' cities, or on the borders of the city in *barraques* of the Zone and fleamarkets, condenses this identity of continuously displaced accumulations and sales into a more permament, or anyway a more evident, physical institution: a place where they are under the hand of the authorities, at the reach of the poor worker on the lookout for cheap clothing, or under the eye of the landlord, the social voyeur and the antique dealer. This concentration of a sub-class of rags also identifies the waste of commodities with the waste of people, offering the human jettison too for excessive consumption: in the form not of necessities by the poor, but of the superfluous consumption of poverties by the rich. Or their processing as anecdote and special knowleges of city life and its types by those only passing through them, the literary bohemia who name and list and moralise.

The very temptation to envisage the intellectual as rag-picker of history and daily life ineluctably proceeds from and consolidates a parasitism of identity. The illusory voluntary wanderings of the rag-pickers offer a mirror up to the intellectual's own freedom of choice. Benjamin noted this empathy, though not, it would seem, its implications for his own treatment:

A rag-picker cannot, of course, be part of the *bohème*. But from the *littérateur* to the professional conspirator, everyone who belonged to the *bohème* could recognise a bit of himself in the rag-picker. (*Baudelaire*, p. 20)

In some ways, in so far as it can be pretended that the process of rag-picking is itself unconstrained by rules or contracts, the indiscriminate element in it parallels the ideology of art for its own sake, as both yield up a vision of freedom and choice. But this misrecognition is also bound to lead to a scission of identity and work. In one direction it purges intellectual activity of the structure of work by denying that structure to rag-picking. And from another, the marginalising of everyone who deals with detritus suggests that critical intellectual work is, like rag-picking, necessary, but inherently marginal. It is among some of that increasingly great body of writers or artists who necessarily had to work outside the cultural institutions of the French state in the mid-century that we can find a social base for these kinds of belief. It is this misrecognition that wishes away the space between the problem of finding either work or a market, of suffering the constraints of a place of work, and the ideal of work as the *flânerie*. Seen without its own economic conditions, the *bohème du travail* is a source of subject matter, a means of identification with the city streets and a model of social freedom. In introducing the rag-picker through Baudelaire's poem, Benjamin both lighted on this and denied its deep effects. For one thing, it meant that the bourgeois perception of a popular culture, and the cultural ambitions of proletarians who refused this romantic sanctification of work, could never meet head on.[21] For another, that the mytheme of a special social unity that was implicit in the different meanings of *bohème* could only survive in the language of *déclassement*, where it did so for another century. It was only at a particular conjuncture that the different interests could overlap. The hugely popular song of the end of the Second Empire, 'La Canaille', was, at that moment, a successful attempt to unite the artist, the bohemian and the 'old, iron race' of Paris in the face of a common political enemy, 'c'est l'artiste, c'est le bohème'.

In his critique of the draft of *Baudelaire*, Adorno counselled Benjamin to look into the figure of the ragpicker in *Louise*, suggesting that he would find there a more completely socialised representation than that of Baudelaire's poem.

I am referring to the rag-picker. It seems to me that his destiny as the figure of the lower limits of poverty is certainly not brought out by the way the word rag-picker appears in your study. It contains none of the dog-like cringing, nothing of the sack on his back or the voice which, in Charpentier's *Louise* provides, as it were, the source of black light for an entire opera. (*Aesthetics and Politics*, p. 130)

And, one might add, an image more crucial to the 1920s and 1930s in so far as the opera must be seen as one of the most concentrated and complex depositories of Parisianism. Adorno's adjectives fit the *'chand d'habits* Jéricho quite perfectly, an uncanny prophesy of Prévert's invention. But Adorno is right about the rag-picker in *Louise*. There he is to be discovered at the heart of a to and fro of social relationships that unfold around pleasure and work, the power of representation and of its refusal. He appears in the long and complex first scene of Act II of the opera, which parades a range of Parisian types, – *métiers*, cries, cleaners and bohemians, through an equivalent layering of musical themes. Charpentier put together the artistic Parisian panoplies of a Raffaëlli or a Steinlen with the currency of the picture postcard. But rather than offering them simply as objects of a given cultural repertoire, *Louise* treats them as microcosms of the central, imbricated themes of the whole piece, the story of a working-class girl who breaks from the constraints of her parental home, to live with her poet–lover, Julien – and the display of the poet's life itself. These themes articulate a conflict of work and leisure, of artisanal work and artistic work, of generation and family, of recognition of a place in the scheme of the city and recognition of the scheme, of the power of sexuality in this difference. As the rag-picker appears on stage in Act II he is literally knocked over by the *noctambule*, the 'pleasure of Paris' as he calls himself, the seducer, the professional of self-amusement, who represents the egotistical glamour of the city, and who unifies it through his flirting:

> Le Chiffonnier (*aside*): Ah, I know the wretch, it's not the first time he's crossed my path … (*to the bricoleur*) … One evening a long time ago, it seems like yesterday, he appeared…alas that day he was not alone! … a young girl gave him her hand, smiling at his song! It was my daughter! I'd left her at work … he came, he whispered his wicked temptations in her ear, and she, the coquette, listened … flying with him she bumped me, and like today, I fell…
>
> Glaneuse: Poor man!
>
> Bricoleur: Bah, in all families it's the same thing, … Me, I had three daughters … I couldn't hold them … you can't blame them if they prefer the paradise that calls them down there to our life of hell …
>
> Girl Rag-picker (*aside*): Should not good beds and lovely dresses, like the sun, belong to everyone?

Here then the rag-picker stands in the same position as Louise's father, who is rather a workshop-based proletarian, but fired with a similar sense of self-pitying injustice, if without any idea of change. Yet for both the loss of family, its comfort and security, is played out around their contradiction with the Paris of pleasure. It makes them worthless in the eyes of their daughters. It destroys, not because, as they would like to believe, it is vicious in itself but because the utopian dream of equal distribution is itself vitiated by its exotic impossibility. In fact this fear of the corruption of the working-class female by parasitic, bourgeois sexual moralities is a current in nineteenth-century working-class discourses. The particularity of its emergence in *Louise* is that it has to appear as a flaw in the brilliance of the bohemian myth, represented by Julien, without calling into question the right to freedom, freedom to be and freedom to love, that this myth represents. It cannot but be complex and utopian as there is no way out of the grind of working life without it, no view of city life without it, but the conflict between honest hard work and freedom is irresolvable. The opera beats against the unspoken determinations of social structure, and, in doing so, restitutes rag-picking to work within the accepted depiction of the picturesque.

The most open conflict occurs when Julien's bohemian friends try to flirt with Louise's fellow working girls, who pay them scant attention. 'Their parents would like them to marry a middle-class man', says the philosopher. Jibing, they now turn their wit against the worker, because he wants to be a bourgeois: the bourgeois who wants to become a 'great lord': the 'great lord' who aspires to be an artist. But they sing glory to the artists, who alone can dream of being gods. In effect they repress another longing for social alterity that forms a sub-theme of the entire act. This is the reiterated desire of the poor and homeless child type-figures, the little girl-rag-picker, the cynical *gavroche*, to know, or even imagine, the life of the city of luxury; the life that they might see, only from far off, or trace in the piles of its waste. If Julien is the artists' archetype, then gods they really must be, for he alone can recognise the ensemble of city voices, overcome their discords, and turn them into a single affect:

> Julien: Ah! Song of Paris, where my soul vibrates and throbs! Naive and old refrains of the wakening faubourg, sonorous dawn that pleasures my ear! Cries of Paris ... voices of the street ... Are you the victory song of our triumphant love?

Nor does this resolve the access to representation. From beginning to end the opera forces on Paris irreconcilable but equal meanings, from Julien's cries of pleasure to Louise's father's final despairing shout of 'hatred and pain', O Paris!

Something of this emerges as a problem in *Les Enfants* when Baptiste's theatre company takes up the image of Jéricho as a character in a new mime, in which this composite of rag-picker/*'chand d'habits* sells his wares by night – another interesting solecism, given the strict regulation to day-time of ambulant sales in the Paris of the period, and the status of the *'chand d'habits* as a buyer and not as a seller of old clothes.[22] On stage Baptiste, as Pierrot, kills him to steal a costume that will enable him to get into an aristocratic ball in pursuit of his love. The 'real' Jéricho comes to confront old Debureau, to accuse him and Baptiste of the theft and then the murder of his image:

M/dH: Ah, there you are, plunderer, body snatcher!

DEB (*very dignified*): You're not going to start again, are you?

M/dH: You ought to be ashamed! To steal my outline, my identity!

DEB: You're raving! There's more than one 'marchand d'habits' in Paris. And then, after all, you yourself provided the costume!

M/dH: Ah, if I'd known what use you'd make of it!
When I think that every evening Baptiste murders a poor old man like me, … and just to amuse people too! Ah! What an example!

DEB: Be quiet my friend, you're drunk and you're peddling absurdities! You'd do best to go to bed!

M/dH (*to Nathalie*): Perhaps I am drunk, but that doesn't stop me having some morality, not me! (Brooke, pp 172–3)

This Jéricho is both the seedy precursor and descendant of Félix Pyat's penitent rag-picker, but perhaps also the Jewish *fripier* of the criminal class of receivers noted by Maxime Ducamp, or caricatured by Murger in his *Tales*;[23] he shares his wine with Benjamin's. The negative characteristics again link the different figures in a continuum. But he defends himself from expropriation that shatters his right of control over the exchange of truth. And he seems to inherit something from another *chiffonnier*, a real one, of 1924, who denounced the government's declaration of the Zone as a hygiene problem. Speaking to a reporter, he claimed that it was alcohol, not alcoholism, that was the birthright of the rag-picker. And to show the filth of the rich in contrast to his poverty, he emptied his *hotte* that he had filled from their dustbins the night before (*Le Temps*, 11 August 1924). If Benjamin as an historian adopted the gait of the rag-picker, he was all the more a product of the inherited mythologies of class redemption of the Paris of his time, even if he, as a good modernist, renounced the concealment of the modes of his control over the materials that he gathered for his works. In so doing he acknowledged the requirements of the poor, and exposed the rubbish of the manipulatory myth–history of capital:

> Method of this work: literary montage. I have nothing to say. Only to show. I will have nothing precious to conceal, nor will I appropriate any clever formula for myself … as for rags and waste I don't want to make an inventory of them, but to render them justice in the one way possible: by using them. (Wohlfarth, *op. cit*, p. 563)

However, it remains the case that, by the end of the 1930s, the transformation of the rag-picker's cities, the fleamarkets, into the cities of antique dealers was well under way. For Jéricho, who is curiously close to the object-haunted Benjamin of the *Moscow Diaries*, the misuse of the rubbish could constitute an affront – a fine ironising of a system of commodities, which sees the movement of its cycles as more important than their moments of arrest. Otherwise, to live out the jostling of the markets of the poor with with those for curiosities and antiquities required a faith in a social unity that itself could only be lived out through the idealised sharing of a culture. The democracy of access to rubbish, to find a necessity or a bargain, depending on your means, can only be valorised through the repression of difference in its causes, difference rooted in the nature of social production and consumption. Concomitant with this repression is an idealisation of one's self, of a social sharing that was realised in the literature of intimacy with the Zone or the radio-diffusions of popular song.

So, in looking into the past, the different ways of recognising or misrecognising the present, or rather the relation between them, is of elementary importance. Garance's gaze out over Ménilmontant was so deeply rooted in the culture of the 1930s that it is reasonable exactly because of its anachronism, an anachronism that is itself a condition of being able to see the city in this way at all. She and Baptiste look out from the Barrière de Ménilmontant. But the site that they see, or rather its troping, is quintessentially Montmartrois. It's a viewpoint on the city that later came to be possible from the summit of the touristic Butte of Sacré-Coeur and the literary optic of the Free Commune of Montmartre, beloved of atavistic bohemianism. A doubling of anachronism in the film, as the place from which these images-to-be of Paris came to be seen consolidated only in the Montmartrois cabaret cultures of the 1880s and 1890s. If they were already circulating in the politically wishful politics of Vermersch's writing in his journal *Père Duchêne* at the time of the Commune, then this underlines the fact that atavism too has an archaeology. An archaeology that is one of the institutions of literary bohemia, a register of its transformations of social composition and political complexion.

In *Louise* we find this archaeology on the borders of the self-conscious, both rejoicing in the sounds that Montmartre hears, and questioning the authenticity of the hearing, recognising the gulf between the power of representation and its objects. In *Paris 1943*, Malric puts it bluntly in the last lines of the paragraph I have already cited:

> Without Belleville Paris loses its strength and its prosperity. Belleville, an inexhaustible reservoir of energy, activity, abundance and vitality, which are the muscles, the nerves, the arms and the legs of Paris, as Montparnasse, Montmartre and the Latin Quarter are its brain, Passy, the Champs-Élysées and Auteuil the luxurious outfit. Belleville *makes* Paris.

To see those origins, that 'making', is a measure of a separation from them, for Garance as a sophisticated professional mistress. For Maurice Chevalier when he first senses his professionalism and ventures into the corrupt world of central Paris entertainment. For Yvette Guilbert when she re-imagines the people of Paris through Bruant's songs rather than through her own life, as we shall see in chapter 2. Or for Vermersch in finding the under-side of literature in the politics of the *menu peuple*.

Particular signs connect these images to another world, the funicular of the Rue de Belleville, for example, at the turn of the century: for Maurice Chevalier's generation, for Clément Lépidis in his recent memoirs, a means of 'going down into Paris'. For Jules Romains a passage of literary imagination that transports his universalising narrative in *Les Hommes de bonne volonté* up there, to the gestures and emotions of those people who are the alien, far-off bedrock of the city of the novel. His first description of the land beyond the funicular is like a visit to an anthropological field-site, a vision of strange comings and goings, of unknown codes.[24]

Now, to take them once again together, Belleville and Ménilmontant were the great centre of a revolutionary, popular republicanism at the end of the Second Empire. The Belleville Platform in 1869 pushed the bourgeois republicans like Gambetta further along the path of opposition than they would otherwise have chosen. And then, in May 1871, partly because of their geographical position, they were the last areas of Communard Paris to fall to the Versailles troops: and as 'last' itself is sufficiently strong a word on which to build mythologies, the population became the material of a conflict for the image both of Red Paris and of the good-worker-bedrock of a bourgeois republic. It is this that Malric tries to manipulate while incorporating the population into the definition of Paris. In their own way, but more systematically, it had been as important for the new social strata of the Third Republic to fulfil their conception of themselves and to consolidate their power through their place in the image of a people's Paris and their control over its representation – in a more strictly political sense of the word. The Red worker becomes the 'Belleville Battallion', the café-concert marching tune of an imaginary proletarian enthusiasm for post-war reconstruction.[25] Once it can be thought of as respectable, the quartier becomes inappropriate to the desires of the highly political artistic bohemia of the late 1860s, like Eugène Vermersch, when they had set out to 'other' themselves in the body, the language, the style of the people. Rough, libidinous and spontaneous. Belleville and Ménilmontant branded themselves on the Parisian social question, and, eventually, the Montmartrois tropings of the city were to become one of the means if not of healing the scars then at least of displaying them with pride. It was Montmartre's artistic cabarets that finally processed Vermersch's idyll of rough, spontaneous and libidinous working-class life into entertainment for the middle class. Nor was this literary language of amusement absent from the all-important contestation for the fidelity and support of Belleville-Ménilmontant by the communists in their political campaigns of the 1920s and 1930s.

Such an appropriation is episodically fissured by its implicit partner of hatred and refusal, the image of the self-same streets and places as harbouring the enemy of civilisation. This is a hatred that nourishes itself on the same tropes as pride, reworking roughness as horror, spontaneity as uncontrolled violence. The people of the Commune as Medusa, in an 1871 cartoon, burning the city while transfiguring the frightened bourgeois with its serpent gaze, is one such inversion. The companionable worker of *Père Duchêne*, who readily spills over into the embodiment of alcoholic vice in Maxime Ducamp's *Paris after the Prussians*, is another. And even later in Leon Daudet, writing of the Rue de la Roquette, there is a touching vision of the good people weeping at his father's funeral:

> The crowd was oppressed with a sense of personal loss, a wordless grief that made one realise the importance a novelist has in the social life of his time if he succeeds in translating into words that all can understand the pleasures, pains and joys of the common folk ...

A vision that rapidly gives way to something quite different as he reaches Père-Lachaise cemetery, and finds himself at the Communard monument, the Federals' Wall:

> Frequently here we have caught sight of slinking beasts of prey, young men and women whose nerves a concentrated hatred of the present social system have stretched to breaking point ... It is an ideal spot for meditation ...[26]

Even within a single text then, the author has to stretch the same people to figure both as 'absinthe addicts, nymphomaniacs, Juliet of the gutter accompanying Romeos of the slums', and as dreamers for a royalist France. In 1943 Malric simply slips the whole thing into the inconsequence of a few isolated memories, which don't 'stop the plane-trees budding'. As if there were any moment of history when the laws of nature went out on a political strike!

Further, alongside these diverse ideal images of the Parisian people, there is the choice of another 'people' altogether – of the country and the peasant farmer, and the politics of *France profonde* rather than of Paris. These were the people who were to find their way into the elaborate displays of the Musée des Arts et Traditions Populaires during and after the Second War. Clearly such differences articulate broad political and social distinctions of left and right, from socialist republicanism to monarchism. But the range of inflections that articulate the space between them is so complex, in their overlappings and slippages, that the anthropology of a van Gennep can just as well feed a left-wing historiography as a romance of the unchanging country – for example, the songs of the Breton royalist–traditionalist Théodore Botrel. In 1943 the great museologist Georges-Henri Rivière wrote some notes for the Musée des Arts et Traditions Populaires that do indeed read like a plan for the revenge of the rural folk on the capitalist city – an uneasy mix of populist–socialist and Vichy–national themes.[27]

Moreover, the sophisticated, professional urbanity of the Académie Goncourt can as well serve an industrialised culture of the gramophone as a Célinian pessimism of daily life. Its observations can spill over into the glitter of the music-hall or a new form of literary prose. The line between a virulent disdain for popular life and succumbing to the aura of its authenticity is thin indeed, and political identities are as jumbled on either side. Thus it may be that the introverted and self-congratulatory indulgence of authenticity that we find in both the book and the film of the *Hôtel du Nord*, can be read either as a phenomenon of the right or more liberal forms of populism. If there was a confusion in the political allegiance of the tropes of Paris, then this was productive for *Les Enfants* in its articulation of the moment between Vichy and liberated France.

Such conflicts should be seen laid over the other established archaeologies of popular entertainments. 'Going down from the Courtille'[28] – that ritual slumming of the 1840s, and picnics on the fortifications of the end of the century, that is to say, the story of movements to the barriers and margins in search of pleasure, is one. Its history is one of a quest for the popular areas as a site of spontaneous amusement, and of a desire by the people to find happiness in their turn on the grassy slopes of the fortifications. The juxtaposition of the search for the people as an idyll and of the people for an idyll endows the industrial strata of the eastern working class with the allure of a pastoral or urban–arcadian innocence that informs and perfects the idea of a popular city.

But these eastern people are in some ways quite different from 'the little people of the Butte (Montmartre)', for they do not share their precise status in the human bestiaries of Paris, and their being is rooted in the labour of their workshops. The distinction originates in the demography of literary production and of entertainment in the 1880s. The generation and projection of representations is the work of Montmartre, and the rest of the city the screen that it brings to light, and whose inhabitants are revealed fully clothed in the tropes of the popular, as in Garance's look, which follows the same sightline as Bruant's songs of the 1880s – 'À la Roquette', 'À Ménilmontant', and so on, the reiterated, distant vision of the city from high up in the cabarets of the Butte. It is to Bruant and Charpentier above all that succeeding generations will accord the golden laurels for picturing the city in the different spaces of entertainment, giving a social unity to the Opéra-Comique and the music-hall or night-club. Yet the self-same images could be found neatly packaged in a series of picture postcards, which pick up the physiognomies of the mid-century as a culture of souvenirs. Their currency, political as aesthetic, is inseperable from their banality.

A crucial effect of this division and specialisation is that city life is disclosed as a series of discrete and fragmented microcultures. Their separation from each other and the sharpness of their definition reproduces the habits, methods and individual experience of experts skilled in their observation, their picturing becomes their collective skill. And so their outlines as microcultures remain fixed for a long period of time within literary institutions. Their significance as origins derives from their role in the formation of this professional discourse. In Louis Chevalier's work since 1950 this reaches its sociological apogee in the minute differentiation between the essential nature of the same crimes committed on one street corner and on another not a quarter of a mile away. Or the 'authentic' representatives of Belleville and Ménilmontant, a Piaf or a Maurice Chevalier, learn to sing their authenticity through another register of this self-same repertoire. Their bodies, and through them the city, come to represent it – anyone speaking within the dominant literary culture will hear, utter, see, write and sing through its tropes as a matter of course. It is a type of urban nature, this language of the city. Entertainment is the privileged space of the forgetting this process. Its images, born from one kind of search for difference and origins, reinvent multiplicity in its modes of address and in its mass consumption.

The writings of Marx and Engels on Parisian revolutions too form one of the axes of this attachment. It was not only that the Revolution of 1789 produced the prototypes for many kinds of popular struggle, for their forms of conflict and their iconography, but that Paris brought the proletariat into Revolution. In *The Class Stuggles in France* (1871) they write:

> Thanks to the economic and political development of France since 1789, Paris has been placed for the past fifty years in such a position that no revolution could break out there without assuming a proletarian character, that is to say without the proletariat, which had bought victory with its blood, advancing its own demand after victory.

The clarity of these revolutions, already made text in the structural beauties of the *Eighteenth Brumaire,* contrasted so radically with the complicatedness of the situation in Britain, America or the semi-feudal relations of their colonies that they were instated at the heart of the theory of proletarian revolution as its clearest paradigm. In Lenin's *State and the Revolution* it is the Paris Commune that prefigures the proletarian government of the future. And, appropriately, ageing Parisian revolutionaries were regularly transported to Moscow to be fêted at the meetings of the International. Even as Marx and Engels were planning *The Class Struggles in France*, a young *littérateur* and satirist, Eugène Vermersch, was penning his revolutionary journal, *Père Duchêne*, which turned the speech and mores of this self-same proletariat of eastern Paris into the values and fantasies of the great bohemian myth of *déclassement*, of which they had been the sternest critics. It is with their review of Chenu and de la Hodde, a critique of conspiratorial bohemianism, that Benjamin opens his *Baudelaire*.[29] Yet it is difficult to pick and choose bits and pieces of a legend that is deeply inscribed in so many levels of a culture. Marxism contributed its heroic dimensions to the narcissism of Parisianism. It involuntarily helped to attribute to Paris a part of its charm, which can even be discerned in the review of Chenu if we care to read it for the way it gives a sense of the finely graduated sociability of overlapping political strata, and for its comprehensive view of the multiple relationships of intellectuals and people, their articulation through culture and mores, a gradation to which Marx and Engels belong, and which links them along with a whole scale of viewpoints and positions. An elite disdain for the urban mass, sometimes combined with a morbid curiosity. An anthropology of the street that often begins with a mediation like the image of the city in Balzac or Zola, and so gives new mediations a special authority that is as much guaranteed by a literary canon as by a fresh or telling observation. Or a form of slumming, political or social, slipping behind the back of the radical intellectuals to find an 'authentic' people who have not fallen for the radicals' image of them: and its corollary – going ahead of the detached *flâneur*, to find a politics more real than the politics of his pleasure. It seems reasonable that the Passage, with its function of linking of streets and often sharply contrasting social spaces, its reputation as a place of overlapping leisures, should have slipped into becoming a metaphor for passage, should have become so fascinating, whether as a way into the past or as a route between levels of experience.

So too the movement from the edges of Paris to the centre, and from the centre outwards, is a passage and sometimes a rite. When the young Maurice Chevalier had needed to buy music he had to 'go down into Paris'. The journey down the Rue de Ménilmontant took him to République and the fringes of the great, central area of the Passages, to Brady and Prado where the music publishers and agents had their shops and offices – 'a whole world of little tradesmen who had no other *raison d'être* but that provided by this multitude of the workers of song' (vol. 1, p. 74). There he saw the variety star Mayol, who lived nearby in the Rue Martel. And in one of those emblematic moments that mark the autobiographical accounts of so many stars' lives, the already great entertainer seemed to nod to him. To welcome him on his passage to the city centre, to look at him long enough to give him a permission to carry on. And to excite a frisson with a glance so lacking in innocence that Maurice himself began to lose the innocence of his origins, and to suffer the agony of separation that is the beginning of memory. A glance that was just one other exchange of the commodity system of this Passage – where began the commerce in entertainers and their songs, the great and not so great, the cohorts of second-liners, aspirants and failures. A glance that exercised the grip of the commercial city centre on the spontaneity and generative power of its peripheries, lured it with the temptations of its light and space.

So, the passages were a starting point for Chevalier's career as they were to be for Benjamin's historical work, and we will see that the singer's life is as much decked out in the promises of consumption as the windows of the shopping arcade. And that the social passage that links the imagery of success back to its humble origins is also an imaginary passage from the slums to the high life of literary bohemia, or from the high life of the music-hall to the real high life that was Hollywood. This is rather more than the fulfilment fantasy, of the type, let us say, of the working-class footballer. For it is deeply structured in the textures of Parisian life and the history of its representations. It is a visualisation of their grammars of difference, so that the shape of each singer's life gives a fresh order back to these textures.

It is the pervasive and endlessly modulated character of this popular that enables us to seek connections between a Benjamin, a Carné, a Prévert and Maurice Chevalier, and to see that something they do share through this figure of popular Paris is the status of the intellectual who is a part of the *bohème du travail*: a man who might not necessarily stand among the people, but who, in one way or another, within the contexts that we find him, stands in for them or for their interests. This can be seen as a distantly related homology of the role of the professional conspirator as a parasitic motivator of the proletariat as described in the opening pages of *Baudelaire*. The historian or the entertainer too come to depend on a movement in either the world of politics or the music markets, a shift in a social movement or a fashion, to give value to their work. It is the nature of mass markets, cultures and politics to set up and mediate this dependence. That an escape might be envisaged is as evident in Prévert's Lacenaire as in Benjamin's utopianism. He, Lacenaire, in his detached and intellectual indifference, his cruel pity for the human materials of his own crime-work, is an inverted version of the city addict. He reveals the underside of dependence, a strangely unbalanced need for a nourishment that he can hardly stomach. If he cannot spit it out, he might at least transcend his milieu. 'My poor Avril ...' For him the mastery of people is his escape from being one of them, and his only means will be the virtual suicide of waiting, stoically, to be arrested for his final crime. 'My poor Avril ... A person of my status cannot risk a provincial executioner.' In the prospect of his death he enjoys an anti-delectation of the city that only underlines the way in which individual identity is ensured through an insistance on its differences, the fascination of its overlapping and inseparable spaces.

The exercise of power over the imaging of the people and the city was polymorphous in its origins, its interests and its modes of access to its subject. It is criss-crossed by the formation and working lives of intellectuals, of poets, journalists, song-writers, or historians, cheap novelists and pornographers, who are occasionally the same individuals, as well as being sometimes trade unionists, communists, anarchists and fascists ... In fixing a memory or a personal history, or in finding a sense of themselves at all, they need to recruit the people. It is a knowledge of the people and their places, and the intimacy of their relation with this people that externalises the meaning of the self. In their different ways they need the anecdotal and the picturesque, in the full magnificence of hypertrophic fixity to underline the movement of their own trajectory, a trajectory in which the people are markers of change of which they themselves are not the subject. Nostalgia is at the heart of these histories, more a way of working than a mood or an attitude. In the late 1930s, whether for Benjamin or Song-writer X, or Mme la Grande Bourgeoise Y setting off for the flea market, rag-pickers and *fripiers* were in fashion, even when they had never set eyes on one, and probably could not distinguish between them. The terrain of entertainment is criss-crossed by these modes, and is so linked to their differing origins in an unconscious commonality or an involuntary sharing. Entertainment is necessarily a general category of all those sub-sets that flow together to give it sense.

History and poetry, cultural criticism and song-writing achieve, through works like those of Prévert or Benjamin, a solution to the problems of retrieving, remaking and living out conjugations of the imagery of the people. Prévert and Benjamin work from within a social formation of men who conjugate the city from a consciousness made possible by the complexity of the superposition of its spaces, of which they themselves are partly an effect. Prévert acts much as a mid-term between the Bibliothèque Nationale and the popular romance, evening out and re-working the differences between more savant and more scandalous or commercial rehearsals of the city. But again in his work, in Benjamin, or the Charpentier of *Louise* as well as in Louis Chevalier's sociology, the complexity and superposition in continuous change, and the further complexity of the technological development of the means of representation and the evolution of publics, present a formidable task. In an unselfconscious mode, a worked-up fragment or an individual state of mind can be adequate to a response. Or in a highly self-conscious mode, like that of Surrealism, the state of mind itself consumes and controls complexity by estranging it as the effect of thought. Otherwise the task is one that can only be broached with a self-defeating urgency to be comprehensive. If the nuances and chasms of change are to be registered, held in temporary stasis, and even understood, if montage, conjugation and narration are to exercise their power, the objects that are the materials of this power must always be held in sight, paraded in front of the eyes: an unending carnival procession, of which each attempted passage only adds to its length.

*Amours, Bals, Bars, Bordels, Bouges, Boutiques, Cabarets, Cafés, Dancings, Foires, Lieux, Marchés, Métiers, Rues, Types, Vieux Quartiers* ... Listing, cataloguing, mapping, the summing-up of repetitions and the conception of their topology, then provide the basis for the exercise of power on its proper materials. An 'almost incomprehensible number of writings [which procure a historical knowledge of] Paris by street, Paris by house ...' as Benjamin wrote of the previous century (in Wohlfarth, *op. cit.*) Ordering and re-ordering, and authoring each order as a position and as an individual relation to the lexicon become the means of forgetting the space between histories and other images, the differences between them. The image of the city is fixed, but it never comes fully to rest at a time or a place. It circulates like other commodities, no more so than the 'finds' of the fleamarkets. The virtue of the figure of the rag-picker is that it facilitates the relation of exchange and conjugation. It is doubled, or given a technological form, in the mechanisms and omnipresence of the snapshot camera, in the gramophone, in the stackability of photographs and discs, and the tuning dial on the radio.[30]

## Notes

1 For a brief but competent discussion of the issues at stake, which came to the fore very much during the period of the purging from 1944 onwards, see Pierre Assouline, *L'Épuration des intellectuels*, Brussels, Éditions Complexe, 1985. There are too many good works on the war period to list here, but see the classic Robert Paxton, *Vichy France:Old Guard and New Order*, New York, Knopf, 1972; Robert Aron, *Histoire de l'Épuration*, Paris, Fayard, 1975 and various works of Pascal Ory, e.g. *Les Collaborateurs 1940–1945*, Paris, Seuil, 1976. For cinema see René Prédal, *1914–1915 la société française à travers le cinéma*, Paris, Armand Colin, 1972, p. 285ff. (with a list of films banned under Vichy), and also J. P. Bertin Maghrit, *Le Cinéma français sous Vichy*, Paris, Cerf, 1984. My information on the suppression of *Louise* comes from an archival source, Archives Nationales, Paris: F/1/a 3742, in a dossier on cinema passed from a resistance agent called 'Nénuphar' to the French authorities in London. Too late for me to consider in depth is the excellent collection edited by Jean-Pierre Rioux, *La Vie culturelle sous Vichy*, Paris, Éditions Complexe, 1990, which contains an essay on Radio by Hélène Eck. Also see Laurence Bertrand-Dorléac, *L'Histoire de l'art – Paris – 1940–44*, Paris, Éditions de la Sorbonne, 1986 and *Collaboration in France – Politics and Culture during the Nazi Occupation 1940–1944*, ed. G. Hirschfeld and P. Marsh, Oxford, Berg, 1989.

2 The best general discussion of culture and politics in the 1930s is Alice Yaeger Kaplan, *Reproductions of Banality – Fascism Literature and French Intellectual Life*, Minneapolis, University of Minnesota Press, 1986. Along with the *légionnaire*, the *marin* and *matelot* too become figures of muscular and nationalist heroism in distinction to their everyday sexualising before the war. I found in the Archives Nationales, F/17/13369, a schoolboy novelette on the subject of the heroic sailor, forwarded to the wartime Education Ministry of Abel Bonnard by a proud mother. Jean Cocteau and Jean Genet were, of course, fascinated – Cocteau had been the lover of Hitler's favourite sculptor, Arno Breker, back in the latter's art-student days.

3 *La Revue Blanche*, Paris, 15 February 1900. My thanks to Jacques Rancière for drawing my attention to this source. Any discussion in this *Revue* is likely to mark a rite of passage into cultural value, and later I will quote from Félicien Fagus's article in the same number.

4 See Baron Turk, *Child of Paradise*, pp. 361ff. for a discussion of this film in Carné's postwar *oeuvre*.

5  From André Billy, *Adieu aux fortifications – eaux-fortes de Porcaboeuf*, Paris, Société de Saint Eloy, 1930. See also André Warnod, *Les 'Fortifs', promenades sur les anciennes fortifications et la zone – 40 lithographies de Serge-Henri Moreau*, Paris, Éditions de l'Epi, 1927. An extensive literature on the rebuilding of the Zone and Fortifications in the 1920s and 1930s can be found in the Archives de la Seine, Paris, under VM 17. This takes one into the fine details of types of building and ownership, planning permissions etc.

6  Cf. Baron Turk, who refers to debates around Lacenaire's sexuality. For a more complete discussion, see: Andrew Copley, *Sexual Moralities,* p. 104, and the whole section, pp. 99–107, on homosexuality and criminality in the nineteenth century. A 1936 number of the satirical magazine *Crapouillot* takes it for granted that Lacenaire was homosexual, suggesting that this was currency in the 1930s. I have not developed the point, as I do not believe that it has much bearing on my chapter 4. In 1990 a new, big budget film simply called *Lacenaire* went on show in Paris.

7  There is little need to underline the importance of Simmel's essays for Benjamin; see G. Simmel, 'The Metropolis and Mental Life' in *Classic Essays on the Culture of Cities*, ed. Richard Sennet, New Jersey, Englewood Cliffs, 1969.

8  At the time of publishing his *Flâneur salarié*, Paris (1927), with an introduction by Mac Orlan, essentially a journalist's travel diaries, Béraud had not graduated to the politics that were to lead him to collaboration and becoming, along with Robert Brasillach, one of the few intellectuals condemned to death by the *épuration*. See Assouline, *op. cit.* and Kaplan, *Reproductions*, for a wider discussion of the culture of collaboration. Béraud's sentence was commuted.

9  See Charles Constant, *Code de théâtre*, Paris, 1875.

10 Vercors was the resistance name of the *littérateur* and illustrator Jean Bruller. *Le Silence de la mer*, Paris, Albin Michel, 1951, was completed in 1941. It recounts the war of total silence waged by a man and his niece on whom an educated and francophilic young German officer has been billeted. The subtext is the simultaneous emergence and repression of love between the officer and the niece as her sacrifice of heroic resistance. The uncle loses nothing. See Michael Kelly for a contrary view of Vercors in his essay 'The Après Guerre' in Hirschfield and Marsh, *op. cit.*, p. 245.

11 *Aesthetics and Politics*, London, NLB, 1977, pp. 110–141 for the exchange between them, these from p. 127 & p. 137 respectively.

12 See Mac Orlan, 'Préface' to Atget, Photographe de Paris" in *Photography in the Modern Era, European Documents and Critical Writings, 1913-1940*, New York, MMA/Aperture, 1989, originally published in 1927. Although Mac Orlan developed the idea of the 'social fantastic' across the whole range of his writings, the resumé to be found in his *Lautrec le peintre*, Paris, Fleury, 1934, pp. 50ff. is particularly useful. Especially important on this question is Molly Nesbit's forthcoming volume *Atget's Six Albums*, and I am grateful to have been able to read the manuscript. However, see also, by the same author, 'Atget's Intérieurs Parisiens, the point of difference', in *Intérieurs parisiens*, Paris, Musée Carnavalet, 1982.

13 Ginette Vincendeau has pointed out to me the importance of the fact that the only major character not based on a historical model is Garance and suggests that this underlines my argument around her role in the articulation of memory and truth in *Les enfants*.

14 Louis Aragon, *Le Paysan de Paris*, Paris, 1926. For a convincing argument on Benjamin's relation to this text, see Jacques Leenhardt, 'Le Passage comme forme d'expérience: Benjamin face à Aragon' in *Passages*, ed. Wisman, pp. 163ff.

15 For a sentimental yet accurate history of Belleville, see Clément Lépidis, *Belleville au coeur*, Paris, Vermet, 1980. Also, Gérard Jacquemet, *Belleville au XIX^e siècle*, Paris, J.

Touzot, 1984, and various maps of the period from the Plan Verniquet of 1791 to the Plan Pierotte of 1874 in either the Bibliothèque Historique de la Ville de Paris or the Bibliothèque Nationale.

16  *Paris 1943, arts et lettres*, Paris, PUF, 1943, 'Belleville-Ménilmontant' by Henri Malric, illustrations by Marc de Béchillon, pp. 82–5. The chapter on painting, 'Salons et Tendances' is by J.-M. Campagne, pp. 92–3.

17  From Malric, *op. cit.*, here picking up the classic smells of popular food, the often idolised odour of cheap cooking becomes fabulous. This theme often turns up in books on the fleamarkets. See L. Aressy and A. Parménie, *La Cité des épaves*, Paris, 1943 (completed in 1939) for much on the bitter smell of frites. For a rather different view of the place of *Les Enfants* in this discussion, Garance as a figure of freedom, Jéricho as an informer and theatre as collective redemption, see Baron Turk, *op. cit.*, pp. 245ff. Also on the question of what is or is not a collaborationist song, see the important, but rather mechanistic, study of André Halimi, *Chantons sous l'occupation*, Paris, Olivier Orban, 1976.

18  See his essay 'La Publicité et le romantisme commercial et industriel' in the catalogue / memorial publication, *Gala du Commerce et de l'Industrie*, Théatre des Champs-Élysées, 9 Juin 1937, pp. 39–44.

19  *La Grande Encyclopédie, Inventaire raisonné des sciences, des lettres, et des arts, par une société des savants et des gens de lettres*, Paris, H. Lamirault, 1885–.

20  See Alain Faure, 'Classe malpropre, classe dangereuse? – Quelques remarques à propos des chiffonniers parisiens au XIX$^e$ siècle et de leurs cités', *Recherches*, 29, 1977. Of primary importance is the report of the Office du Travail, *L'Industrie du chiffon à Paris*, 1903. See also the *Monographies professionelles* of J. Barberet, or his *La Bohème du travail*, Paris, Hetzel, 1889, and the *Grande Encyclopédie*.

21  See Benjamin, *Paris Capitale*, p. 365, for his discussion of Baudelaire's self-recognition in the rag-picker.

22  I gathered the regulations from a single dossier in the Archives of the Parisian Prefecture of Police, DB / 194, which contains a series of laws and legal projects from the end of the Ancien Régime to the middle of the nineteenth century.

23  Maxime Ducamp, *Paris, ses organes, ses fonctions et sa vie dans la seconde moitié du XIX$^e$ siècle*, Paris, Hachette, 1869-75, sections on the rag trade. And Murger, *Scènes de la vie de bohème*, Paris, Hetzel, 1851, where, in one episode, it is the racially stereotyped Jewish dealer who 'helps' the bohemians by retailing paintings.

24  Jules Romains's epic masterpiece of modern life, the twenty-nine-volume *Les Hommes de bonne volonté*, Paris, Flammarion, 1929–, really gets to work by mapping out the different trajectories and spaces, work and leisure, of the Parisian social classes, their fractions, substrata and sexes.

25  Cf. Rancière, 'Good Times…', pp. 70ff.

26  L. Daudet, 'The Last Street of All' in Arthur K. Griggs, *My Paris, an anthology of modern Paris from the works of contemporary French Writers*, London, Methuen, 1926

27  See *La Muséologie selon Georges-Henri Rivière*, Paris, Dunod, 1989, for a fascinating and exhaustive account of his ideas. This does not cite the document from which I quote, found in the Archives Nationales, Paris, under F17 / 13369. Daniel Lindenberg, in his excellent *Les Années souterraines 1937–1947*, Paris, La Découverte, 1990, bears out my speculations on this matter in a detailed discussion of Rivière, van Gennep *et al.* in wartime France. See pp. 65ff. James Clifford has written well on these questions, but see especially his '1933, February – After two years of Ethnographic Research, the Mission Dakar-Djibouti Returns to Paris – Negrophilia' in *A New History of French Literature*, ed. Denis Hollier Cambridge, Mass., Harvard University Press, 1989, pp. 901ff.

28  For La Courtille and the romance of the dance-halls at the *barrières* in pre-1859 Paris, see Rancière, 'Good Times', and for a detailed statistical and chronological study, see François Gasnault, *Guinguettes et lorettes, bals publics à Paris au XIX<sup>e</sup> siècle*, Paris, Aubier, 1986, pp. 116ff. Also Nicholas Green, *The Spectacle of Nature, Landscape and bourgeois culture in nineteenth-century France*, Manchester, MUP, 1990, pp. 76–7, for this and generally for an innovative discussion of nature and the city.

29  See Marx/Engels, *Collected Works*, vol. 10, London, Lawrence and Wishart, 1978, p. 311. Cf. Benjamin's review of Mac Orlan, cited above p.XX. Benjamin sees Mac Orlan as one of the 'most important' writers engaged in the 'hopeless dream' of finding a space 'to stand outside both the bourgeoisie and the working class'. Mac Orlan is the Sterne of this tendency, he suggests, while Carco is its Richardson. Here we may discern a very close link between Benjamin and the classic class analyses of Marx and Engels in the *Manifesto of the Communist Party*, their reveiw of Chenu and elsewhere.

30  For a recent summary of Adorno's ideas on these matters, see Tom Levin in *October*, 57, 1991.

# O Yvette, O Maurice,

... les gens de la haute
ne sav'nt pas faire l'amour ...    ('Entre Saint-Ouen et Clignancourt')

Julien: you regret nothing?
Louise: no, I regret nothing,
what could I regret?...    (*Louise*)

My love,
My slumbers were broken with little 'erlebnisse' all impassioned for you –
with the result that I slept really badly. I had a charming dream about
Maurice Chevalier who was at the same time Colette, and who was really
astonished: 'But is it not a woman?', he was saying.
   (Simone de Beauvoir, *Lettres à Sartre*, early 1937)

That night I dreamed of angels with faces of the faubourgs ...
   (Maurice Chevalier, *Ma route*, vol. 3, May Day 1945)

How to put a life together? The question is rich in the banality of its
answers, but we must be careful not to resolve it with too easy a resort to
a critical theory of narrative. In the end, for example, Louise's life has no
end, though by the end of the opera she has acquired something to
regret. This something is not that she went to live with Julien but that
she then returned to her parents, to re-learn their unhappiness and their
miseries of blind self-hatred. As the opera draws to a close she quits home
for the second time, once and for all. This costs her a nightmare of
affective torment, a yet more tortured passage from domestic enclosure
to the open perspectives of the city. But what will happen? To which
place can she go that is not already imagined in the music? The question
stays hanging in thin air, although it is the only crucial one. How will she
put together the rest of her life?[1] It is left only to our good sense and our
feeling for romance to assume that Paris remains the sign of her life's
contentment.
   But of Paris we know something else: Louise might just as well end up

on the prostitutional scrap-heap of the Rue Pigalle as a poet's companion. And next, cocaine-wrecked, or run down by her pimp in his motor car, she would finish in the municipal cemetery at Pantin. A good ending for a popular song about the dregs of prostitution, like Les 'Mômes de la cloche' – 'the day death cuts us down, it's our finest day' – or for a bittersweet romantic novel like Maurice Dekobra's *Grain d'Cachou*, 'The great cemetery is empty. Perched on a branch above Grain-d'Cachou's grave, a sparrow screeches desperately.' Or, more optimistically, she might have got a job as a salesgirl, and eventually become a head of section, in ladies' lace, perhaps at the Galeries Lafayette, with aching feet and bulging varicose veins.

Even as Julien's lover, what would she have done for the rest of her life? His socks? A little sewing? Prepare *fêtes* for him and his friends? Happiness was her only vocation. Not much to survive on in a world where neither a humble craft nor a million francs would be certain to purchase it and where misery was at a premium. However you look at things, she can't have turned out as well as her fellow seamstress and more or less exact contemporary, Yvette Guilbert, who became a rather distinguished and celebrated woman. And even if she had turned out as badly as Edith Piaf, who was both a celebrity and a wreck, we know that, in the very end, she could still have been allowed nothing to regret, at least no regrets to aknowledge in public. For the 'nothing to regret' is the city itself, the careful *bricolage* of types and lives in the elaborate sound-plan of the score, an image and a space that predicates its own perception as a poetic abstraction, its experience as epiphany rather than damnation, as the freedom of subjectivity rather than as subjection. So sings the Street Sweeper in *Louise*:

> [The Street Sweeper]: Me, twenty years ago, I had horses and carriages...
> ... (*triumphant*) I was the queen of Paris! (*comically*) What a downfall! eh? but I regret nothing!... I had such a good time. (*sentimental*) Ah! the good life! the joyous, the tender, the unforgettable paradise!

None but the most severe moralist could have wished either the Sweeper or Louise to regret the story of her life and to undergo the exemplary opprobrium due to one who willfully leaves home and abandons herself to pleasure. Yet, as we shall see in the next chapter, such folk, the organised keepers of public morality, did set themselves against the rounds of Parisian pleasure. Like Louise's mother they mistook pleasure for debauch, and so condemned it to debauch, just as she did in refusing Julien's offer of marriage to her daughter.

Guilbert makes a perfect counterpoint to either Louise or to Piaf because she was a woman who managed to equip herself with choices and made her career deliberately, out of her own intentions. At the same time, her life was no less like fiction than theirs. Her autobiography, *The*

*Song of my Life*, opens with a cool, almost sociological account of herself as a type of young woman coming from a petit-bourgeois social stratum that is prey to an economic instability and misfortune in which the role of Paris is contingent rather than sufficient – a decor rather than a cause. As a child in the 1870s Yvette helped her mother to make hats. She worked as a seamstress and learned about the cruel indifference of her clients, their failure to pay their bills, their uncaring snobbishness towards her class. She became a shop-assistant and stood for such long hours that she became ill. She loved entertainment, going to concerts and perform-ances, and longed to make entertainment in her turn. To feed herself and her mother she learns to live off her wits, to practise some clever, city ruses that are close enough to theft. Later, she comes to think of her work as a singer as something that draws on the experience of this class of young working women and that her career is a means of redeeming them. In this she fulfils the purpose of the opera *Louise* rather than the longings of its heroine. For Charpentier intended that his work should give the working girls, at last, the chance to see themselves as subjects of the city. Anyway, Guilbert's experience as one of them taught her to know how virtue is a matter of the hairline indifference between choice and necessity. Not easily to be subjected to a moral discourse, however well meaning:

> I have always kept a special fondness for all those who sew. I love them. It is to the Parisian working girl that I owe the root of my talent, for it is from her that I learned life, the lot of poor girls who have no one to protect them, nothing but their common sense, their modesty, their religion …
>
> By the time I was eighteen I had learned of every masculine trick, of every trap laid by men. If my body remained pure I felt my soul in danger and my mind soiled.
>
> Living among such miserably poor and terribly young sinners made of me a girl strangely womanly and sad and serious and bitter – ah, how bitter! It is certainly from that atmosphere that my art as a singer drew its deepest, most human, most sincere tones, for I have really known all the griefs of life. …
>
> Ah, how I promised myself that I should be good if only some day I were rich! (pp. 21-2)

With all its quirky cynicism, this is an important and radical refusal of the contemporary clichés of easy virtue. For one thing, the easiness is seen as the difficulty of being a young woman rather than as the amuse-ment of the male *flâneur*, needed by him for his pleasure. It's clearly demarcated from the viewpoint of a chronicler and literary journalist like Gérard Bauër, whose *Recensement de l'amour à Paris* (1922) typifies the *flâneur*'s narrative of the city as a mnemonic classification of women and sites, of places where the women are for the taking, just as, for another, it stands off from the demands of moral puritanism for easiness to convert itself back into virtue. She and Louise in some ways overlap with the dressmakers, typists or shop-assistants condemned by the moralist Paul Bureau for the imputed opportunism of taking advantage of their modest independence 'to set up housekeeping with a young man': a group of young women of whom the feminist Madeleine Lepelletier noted that, unable to circulate alone in the male world of streets and cafés, they had to take a lover 'in order to be able to go out'.[2]

Guilbert does not offer herself for moral reproval, or enclose herself in the image of the 'congenitally' degenerate strata of the urban poor. Nor does her life conform to the happy, image of the little *midinette* (dressmaker) as an archetypal Parisienne, mouselike but brave, even if *midinette* in part is what she was. The ambition and the decision to cross the borderline between the spectator and the performer, between the represented and their representative, immunises her from the unselfconscious animality of being a type, unlike Piaf, who never had to cross this line of her own volition. For being a street singer Piaf was already a type, a type of cultural value, a figure of Paris and, as such, a performer of Parisian rites. The boundary that she crossed from street to night-club was one inscribed in the markets for a 'natural talent', for images of a vice as easy as any virtue. With Guilbert, then, the experience of the friction between ethics and necessity is such that she does not make the error of confusing happiness with 'being good'. As with Louise, her life shows that their conventions neither can nor should be identified with each other. In living this out she demonstrates a viable means for the difficult conjugation of women / pleasure. But one that is none the less consigned to the imaginary of fiction or the *faits divers* by the exclusive privilege and exemplary luck of her success. And this success permitted her a second more respectable, gracious repertory, in which she turned her back on the popular and became a leading researcher into and exponent of Old French Song.

However, as a woman who did make choices, Guilbert, unlike Louise, didn't need to live with a poet to identify herself. When she married it was to a fully prosaic bourgeois, a doctor. But she did need several poets to locate herself and to supply her with the verses through which she constructed a particular and highly specialised persona in the Parisian cabarets They were or became famous poets at that – Xanrof, Jean Lorrain, Aristide Bruant, and a host of others. Many of them Montmartrois poets who would have fitted the mother's description of Julien in *Louise*: 'This scoundrel, this debauchee, this bohemian, this barprop, whose existence is the scandal of the quartier'. Yet the threads connecting her and their identities were woven with greater complexity and subtlety than those that link Louise and Julien. In her extensive correspondence with the great men and women of her day, or portrait pen-sketches of them, Yvette assumes a place of her own amongst these professionals and geniuses. From Freud to Loti or Duse she treats them as fellows and as equals, with a grandiloquence that reduces Colette's espistolary tone to mere coquettishness.[3] For the poets she is someone as necessary to them as they to her, for she is the one who endows them with a voice and who creates a public for them across Europe and America. It is she who makes the culture of the Montmartrois cabarets part of America's view of Paris – Ezra Pound translated one of her song books in 1911.

But this relationship is also articulated by the assumption of their viewpoints and modes of perception. She herself becomes a palimpsest in which the original, naive picture of herself is later overlaid with the urban *imaginaire* that is fabricated in their works, and through this she also becomes a part of the Paris of worldly guidebooks. So, in her autobiography, Yvette performs two quite distinct processes of self-realisation. One is the naturalistic, narrative account of her childhood and her emergence on the stages of the music-hall – as I have just summarised it. The other is a re-appropriation of the people through the Montmartrois perspective, the truth according to Aristide Bruant. When, as a newly successful *diseuse*, she sets out to rediscover the meaning of popular Paris she goes back not to her own chidhood, the workshops or her old music-hall haunts, but to the worst *bouge* in the Rue Galande, a species of place sung as hell by Bruant. She speaks with the most decrepit, downfallen of the women, 'a woman disfigured by a red stain that seems to cut her face in two', once the mistress of the criminal Gamahut. She reconstructs her Paris in the contrast between the scandal and misery of the ruined courtesan, who speaks of her lost love, and the space of entertainment:

> Yes, that's me, Lie-de-Vin, who loved him ... but the brutes cut him off. But I'm told he's to be at the Musée Grévin There'll be a fine bust of him and an inscription giving the story of his crime. I shall go there and kiss him, and I'll kill any blasted bourgeois that tries to stop me ... (*Song of my Life*, p. 122.)

In this account of Guilbert's the confrontations between her own former self as *midinette* and her new self as an artistic *chanteuse*, and between her own ascent and the fallen whore, together dramatise the precarious making and unmaking of a life as a narrative of Paris. This making is like the reading by the *midinette* of the sentimental novel or the *faits divers* as belonging to each other in their elision of the spaces between violence and romance: a disjunction at the heart of the autobiographical text, in the slippage from life to literature, as radical as it is natural. From now on Guilbert understands Bruant and his song 'Saint-Ouen', its whole gamut of wretchedness ... with its one consolation':

> Dans la plaine
> Ma mère m'fait – dans un coin –
>   À Saint-Ouen!...
> L'cimetière qu'est pas ben loin ...
>   À Saint-Ouen.

# Comment elles lisent...

## DÉTECTIVE

### Les midinettes
*Heureuse diversion aux sou-cis du travail... Comme leur*

Importantly, then, this palimpsest itself overlaps with the narrative conventions of romantic stories, the young woman rescued by her handsome knight, or plunged to her ruin by his sham. Here the dream of escape, and its sexual fantasy, can share their images in the ways in which it becomes possible that a young woman, someone shut in, might furnish her imagination at the point at which the *faits divers* of the newspapers, song, entertainment or romance bleed off into each other. Thus the enquiries of *Détective Magazine* into the criminal elements of the industry of prostitution, the gallant, illustrated romance of *Pages Folles*, the elegant novels of Maurice Dekobra and night-club songs track the same ground. The ground at the limits of entertainment and the social spaces of the city streets, of aspirations to freedom and the heart rolling in the gutter. In *Pages Folles* a man writes to his lost love, lost to the 'street corner', the young, provincial girl brought up to Paris by her lover, trying to earn enough for them to marry until, one day, he quits her:

> You were too proud to agree to see once again our village amongst the roses. And first you faced up to life. And life conquered you. That rascal life, it was she!
>
> You found men as you went on your way, who were good liars, and who knew to pay when hunger pushed you reeling into their arms. You lunched on a milky coffee, and had champagne for supper. It always starts like that … and then … (*Pages Folles*, Nov./Dec. 1934)

This resigned story of masculine reproach is less bitter an image than the one in a song recorded by Piaf in 1937, 'Mon coeur est au coin d'une rue', harsh and spiky:

> Mon coeur est au coin d'une rue
> Et roule souvent à l'égout
> Pour le broyer les chiens se ruent
> Les chiens sont des hommes, des loups.

And less plaintive than another much favoured song of the the late 1930s, 'Comme un Moineau'('Like a Sparrow'), in which the gutter-born singer (Fréhel or Piaf) has only to stagger from one depth to a lower one. Corrupted in body, yet pure in her soul, she walks the pavement from first love to prostitution, on sale for her cynical boyfriend's profit. Crushed by the shortening syllables of the verses, the 'pavé brutal' limited by the astutely measured crudeness of their rhyme, 'mon seul bien / ce pauvre corps je le sens bien / déjà se lasse', her life's melody quietly, inwardly turns a social condition into something to be hummed.

In all of these, the liminal is on the edge of the amusing, yet intensely sad. A step aside from daily life, an image that can be represented as can the truths of a theology or a religious catechism. Here the catechistic element is the broken body of the city woman of the streets, whose shattering and death are clues to the passage of the pleasures that are her fate. Thus the eponymous heroine of *Grain d'Cachou*, a schoolgirl angry with her teacher, steps out of her training college into a life that will lead her to a prostitute's grave at Pantin, through a string of clients rich and poor, a poet-lover and a surfeit of wartime (1914–18) starvation and cocaine. A girl of strange beauty, born to the 'most virtuous and least amusing of marriages', she is condemned:

> Through subtle irony had fate marked her with the indelible ectype of the sensual delights that kill? Why had this hot-house flower, this troubling orchid, been germinated in the sad vegetable garden of a bourgeois couple? (*Grain d'Cachou*, p. 9)

# TON CŒUR AU COIN D'UNE RUE...

par Max-André DAZERGUES

Cette lettre te surprendra, évidemment, Georgette ! Que veux-tu ! je n'ai pu résister au désir de t'écrire... Ça n'est point pour te faire de la peine ; j'en ai trop moi-même. Mais il faut bien que je te dise...

« A quoi bon ! Oui, sans doute. Tout de même. Écoute :

« Lorsque je t'ai aperçue, il y a deux heures, marchant à petits pas sur le trottoir humide et toujours revenant à ton point de départ, la façade grise, sinistre, de cet hôtel borgne, mon sang, comme l'on dit, n'a fait qu'un tour. Je t'ai reconnue tout de suite : depuis tant d'années que je t'avais perdue. Mon Dieu, Georgette, c'est donc toi !

« j'étais sur la plate-forme d'un autobus jaunas de sauter en marche bien tôt trouvé

ET PUIS VOICI DES FLEURS...

In *L'Ingénue libertine* (1904 and 1925) Colette had already proposed something like this set of narratives as the elaboration of a feeling of oneself for a very young woman when still confined within domestic or private spaces.[4] As an adolescent, the heroine, Minne, reads the newspaper rubric 'PARIS LA NUIT' under the cover of her homework. The stories of gangland conflict on the fortifications, of the Frisé and his formidable moll 'dite Casque de Cuivre' (Copper-Head) on account of her superb hair, suggest a powerful, indeed overwhelming sense of the possiblity of being other. Clearly based on reportages and dramas in the press of 1900 about some battles and killings between the Belleville gang and their rivals, over the sexual favours of one Casque d'Or, the novel imagines these intriguing, violent items at the moment of their being read.[5] They become a way of imagining the sexual when it is a subject clouded in a terrible ignorance. For Minne almost any passing, youthful figure, any pale *voyou*, could be the Grand Frisé, waiting now to take her as his mate. And these stories give access to the city space that is the Zone, only across the *boulevard extérieur* from Minne's house, yet as inaccessible as it is mythic in its dangers, its mystery and its un-form of liberty. The interweaving of violence and pleasure and the audacious freedom of the Zonard women – 'she boxes, wrestles and, when it's called for, uses a revolver' – to dominate the male society in which they reign, these are the themes that lead Minne towards an idea of pleasure that she will pursue through the rest of her childhood and her youthful marriage to an adoring cousin. A search that will slide from fantasy to real physical danger as the girl goes wandering on the night-time Boulevard Mortier in search of her Frisé. It is a boulevard also celebrated in about 1900 in a series of illustrated postcards of Bruant's poems, a tacky, cheap, blue–grey drama of a rainy Boulevard Mortier that seduces Minne, rather than the more finished and literary perspectives of a Zola. And for the young married woman, her quest for knowledge and sexual pleasure is a wandering out from middle-class matrimony into the streets and strange men's apartments. It will not so much culminate as expend itself through her curious but innocent adultery with a string of men – the adultery signified by the 'Libertine' of the novel's title.

The starting point for her search pinpoints a reading of the newspaper as fantasy, invention, mystery, mingled uneasily with the expression of a conventional and official morality of disapproval. A morality that is itself furnished with the same imagery as the artistic cabaret, peopled with the same figures, no doubt, as are the police files, and the autobiographical *récits* and *flâneries* of the Montmartre poets. As Mac Orlan put it in his *Rue Saint-Vincent*:

> you had to have a sister in St-Lazare [the prostitutes' prison], a mother doing housework at La Villette, and a 'dab' buried at Pantin, in the corner that the justice reserves for those whose existence it has abridged.
> I had none of these qualifications. (p. 58)

Colette does not need to spell all this out, only to take a thin, translucent slice of the sense-making of the time, but tied into the asking of a question that was unaskable out loud. What is pleasure for women as a subject in the city, and why is it not the same as man's? Why is one's libertine and the other's 'normal'? Why should it not be a mutual and considered choice for both, in reality? It is of the possiblity of this, the order of the real, that Julien tries to convince Louise, even as she lives it:

Julien: Your dear body desires me?

Louise: I want pleasure! Ah!

Julien: Take me.

Louise: Formerly you took the loving virgin, all naive in her springtime; but today the woman-lover wants in turn to take her lover. Come! oh my poet! Handsome knight, be my conquest! Ah! come to die beneath my kisses!

Julien: Oh my love, carry off your conquest! make me die beneath your kisses!

Louise: This is paradise!

Julien: No, it is life!

Louise: It's a fairy story!

Julien: No! It's life! everlasting, all-powerful life!

And here the public spectacle, in one of its most respectable forms, the Opéra-Comique, hovers on the edges of pornography in its admission of such an ecstatic pleasure. 'Louise is the poem of desire', commented Félicien Fagus in 1900:

> but the desire that is particular to the beings of this time, the desperate struggle of the individual against an anonymous collectivity that gobbles up and suffocates ... 'Every being has the right to be free, every heart the right to love' cry Julien and Louise ... (*Revue Blanche*, 15 Feb.1900)

Yet where was freedom to be found, in what image of life? If an urban culture is such that it links the idea of pleasure to its margins or its underside, how can a life that is not a sacrifice find pleasure? From *Louise* to Piaf this question turns around the image in the song and the image of the singer, the *faits divers* and the fictions of pleasure that narrate it as danger as well as the idle *flânerie*.

More important than the answering of these questions is to see how they direct us to a configuration of something that we can call the everyday: an overlapping, or a presence of complex processes of representation in the most banal of gestures and social routines. Adorno noted this collage at the heart of another opera, Georges Bizet's *Carmen*, a work that Charpentier saw as the premonition of his own, a first stage in the demythifying of ordinary human passion. Locked at its heart is the trio of the Card Scene, when Carmen's companions use the cards to tell themselves romantic life stories of rich lovers and passionate horsemen, while she reads only her death: the infinite possibilities of the cards on the one hand, and of the organisation of melody and harmony on the other, produce the metaphor for the irreconcilable trajectories of life as endless, repetitive narrativity and as fatality. 'In myth', Adorno writes, 'death is inscribed in the order of the living, without our making a distinction between the one or the other'.[6] Press cuttings, romance and *faits divers* between them provide one of the possible ways of constructing a life. As Susan Buck-Morss notes of the press in the middle of the nineteenth century:

> One has only to regard the format of a nineteenth century newspaper, in which the feuilleton occupied the bottom quarter of the front page, to see, literally, how thin was the line between political fact and literary fiction. News stories were literary constructions: feuilleton novelists used news stories as content. (*Dialectic*, p. 140)

In the Rondel Collection at the Bibliothèque de l'Arsenal there is stored a great depository of volumes of press cuttings that follow the careers of hundreds of every kind of theatrical star. Under the rubric 'Music-Hall' we find eleven volumes for Chevalier, four for Piaf, only a few leaflets for a lesser singer and but a single volume for another who might have been important in her time like Lucienne Boyer. And so on.

Often these cuttings add up to resemble the story of a life as it was told by the stars themselves either in an autobiography or as journalists mediated it for them in interviews for the tittle-tattle of theatre columns. As she or he becomes known and their performances get reviewed, a singer's life takes form. Little by little we can see anecdotes congeal into memory and historical record. Types of anecdote that have come to delineate a category of singer are refined and focused for an individual, fitted to a character or a particular type of life. The anecdotes of origins, perhaps classed under 'from rags to riches' or 'from bourgeois career to the music-hall' are examples of this medium of exchange that is the typological archive of entertainment. And the minor variations in stories, often so hotly disputed, serve only to indicate a baseline of veracity, a core of desirable reality in the narratives of myth.

Experience is fixed in reportage, and reportage corrected or refined through the memory that comes to serve it. Separate lives are sometimes unexpectedly or randomly connected in the *fait divers*. In one number of *Détective* Piaf's emergence from the *pègre* (underworld) is sensationally presented, while tucked away at the bottom of another page the well established family favourite, Marie Dubas, loses her diamonds to a petty crook. In a few months the two women will dispute the famous 'Légionnaire' in their competing recordings of Asso's poem, and the chance encounter of *Détective* incidentally becomes the substance of their right of access to the possession of this beautiful but questionable body.

The striking resemblance between the press cuttings and the volume of a star's autobiography, the book reviews that then compound it by knowing repetition of the already anecdotal, is no innocent matter of fact. It is an imprint of the matrices of amusement in everyday life, a deposit of the workings of the industries of pleasure on their markets.[7]

And how could this be otherwise? We know pretty well that the lives of international performers, whether film stars, entertainers or opera singers, are one of the spectacles of our time. Their turning into spectacle long predates the development of the electric and electronic mass media and in Paris it emerged out of the complex of the popular theatre and the music-hall, around the middle of the nineteenth century. The figure of the specialised star or music-hall turn was in part a sign of the growing division of labour and the separation of work and leisure that characterised the development both of industrial production and of commercial entertainment at a time of diverse and deep going transformations in the industry and social relations of the modern metropolis.[8] The types of entertainment and their sites, as we have already seen in chapter 1, both represent the social geography of the city, the pathways and transitions through it, and are traces of a archaeology. So, in the Paris of the 1920s and 1930s the overdetermination of conjuncture is absurdly rich.

Given the peculiar nature of entertainment as a business and as a source of pleasure, it is neither surprising that the forms of investment in it, whether economic or psychological, should be so lavish: nor that, as a new social fabric takes shape, so many of its significant representations should be precipitated around entertainment. The institutions and images of entertainment are open to many kinds and levels of investment. For one, a very high level of capital investment and a massive flow of revenue are required to create the economic conditions for the modern star to flourish and to play her or his part in this social imaginary – upon the success of which the rate of return on capital depends. A process obviously accelerated by the whole gamut of technological developments of the 1930s and the relations that develop between them. And at the same time, the star comes to occupy the different if interdependent attentions of the broad groupings and social strata of the public, including journalists, social commentators or moral reformers. Today, or rather since the rise of professional cultural and media studies, the star is as much a preoccupation of the interested academic as of the original reader of *Picturegoer*. As the former watches the latter watching and decodes, quite different institutions and ideologies of pleasure or scholarship are brought into a relationship with each other.

Perhaps the possibility of such a diversified sharing lies in the way in which stars' lives weave together an existence as commodified as that of wage labour with the apparently unfettered action of free will and choice. In Maurice Chevalier alienated labour-power is recognised with the same prestige as capital. As spectacle, it is massively rewarded and assuaged for its inauthenticity by becoming the repository for memories of an idyll of the people. Philosophically complex, stars' lives are as open to the projection of utopian possibilities and dreams as to the analysis of the vagaries of the labour process, or the ironising of any kind of industrial or professional work.

Maurice Chevalier has already appeared as a significant figure in the imaging of Paris and of Ménilmontant in particular. I have suggested that his person and his career can be thought of as a kind of map of the city, a formal abstraction of some of its knowledge and characteristics combined in the specific configuration that bears his name. In one reading, his map coincides with that of a Guilbert or a Piaf, or several other Parisian woman singers: it includes many of the same points of pleasure and geography, the sites, streets and types that give visibility to the idea of the people. Guilbert and Chevalier, for example, share the impossibility of reconciling the topographies or the rhythms of work and pleasure, the *atelier* and the concert. As we have seen, Chevalier tells us of his hammer hitting his thumb to the rhythm of the song in his head, or hiding in the workshop lavatory to practise his infantile *Tour de chant*. Guilbert recounts step by step quitting her life as a seamstress. This is something that neither of them has in common with the wandering and rootless life of Piaf, a life outside of work, of singing outside, on the street. Yet all three of them are shared by the industry in their overlapping and in their difference. All three emerged to their stardom in the face of a fierce and relentlessly competitive market ordered by hazards, the capital flows and technologies of a system of entertainment that could never have enough mappings of the city at its disposal, in its archive of nostalgias.

Whatever their common elements might be, the map changes radically beneath the woman and the male singer. Their set of representations is determined by the wider network of conventional codings of male and female and of their reproduction as specialised codes through types and traditions of song.[9] Within these traditions there are roles for men and women, some of which are more or less exclusive and others less so. The laughing, stand-up, patter comic, with his raucous horseplay, for example, is an almost entirely male type in the period from 1900, quite distinct from the female *fantaisiste*, while after the First World War the realist song of the tragedy of urban life is a largely female attribute. The environment of the brutal pavement, the street corner, the grim dawn outside a prison, the street without a name, circumscribes the horizons of its inhabitants, and by the extension of a pathetic fallacy, of its singers too. With the exception of Joséphine Baker, who was a black American, women singers never make love to the city in a song. Baker's famous theme song, 'I have two loves, my country and Paris', was the proclamation of her adoptive Frenchness, a move so crucial to her image that it gave her the man's rights to address the city as a lover. But for the ensemble of women singers, they never, so to speak, embrace it as a whole. If Chevalier has the right to sing Paris as if it were a woman, the woman singers are never more than one of its types of woman, even if, like Mistinguett, they might masquerade the whole gamut in a single show, and even though, once famous, they might get to choose their leading men as colleagues or as lovers.

Apart from their conventionality, the category of these differences is not so much Frenchness in general as Parisianism in particular, as the supreme category of the national. This metropolitanism is distinctly underlined in Maurice's memoirs in his friendship with the Marseillais male *fantaisiste* Vaquier, a few years his senior and enormously successful in his own province. While Maurice stands in awe of Vaquier's experience, he comes to realise that in fact it is the other who defers to him:

> Every little repartee that I made found him ready to burst into laughter. I soon realised that, face to face with me, who was so in awe of him, he had a sort of inferiority complex. The cause of this complex? But, Paris!... He was a fellow who saw Paris and the Parisians as certain foreigners imagine them. (*Ma route*, vol. 2, p. 59)

As Jules Bertaut wrote, 'it's something from our country, and better than that, from Paris'. It's important to hold in mind this ability of Paris to swallow up and represent, because it is a process that does not go uncontested, even if it cannot but impose itself. I have already indicated that a kind of regionalism and a sense of moral purity can coincide in the face of city culture. But, in the end, the tropings of entertainment as a whole must submit to Parisian histories, be mapped on to Paris, which also forms their markets. In an age of industrialised pleasure Paris was on the route wherever one might be coming from and it was the best of origins to claim for oneself.

Even so, none of these relations is entirely mechanical and it has to said that while Parisian traditions form the matrix for any development and change, they do evolve. They lend their tropes to a social world in transformation, in which the slippage of meaning in presents and in memories is continuous and sometimes definitive. Especially after the First World War, the further glamorising of the grand spectacle music-hall and the emergence of sound cinema have to meet a new demographic configuration in France, together with the twin siblings of tourism and the international amusement market. From the 1920s jazz sweeps on to the homeground of French music, while in the 1930s, just as increasing numbers of American films rate high in Parisian critical estimation, so American acclaim of French stars becomes important for their glory.[10] More than ever, their image has to make sense to an international public. Maurice Chevalier records his success at his first New York recital, but only after he has framed each song with an explanation:

> I bring to the USA songs that they don't know and a way of singing that they have never suspected. Novelty! With Al Jolson, Harry Ridman, George Jessel, they have very good popular singers, with superb voices and extraordinary dynamism. But what they don't have, it's my little manner all of my own, naive and natural. That evening I hit the Number One. I'm in the money. (*Ma route*, vol. 2, p. 137)

Also, the assumptions of gendered and class viewpoints are complicated by their intersection with different and changing moralities. These unfold and take hold within the space of a star's lifetime, affecting the ways in which they can recall a memory and so depict it for the present.

An entertainer's autobiography, then – which may or may not be ghosted – is liable to be a representation of many representations. Amongst the earliest of the 'autobiographies' of modern, French popular stars, those of the 1860s café-concert entertainers Rigolboche and Thérésa were written by men who were both professional journalists and vaudevillists of the Second Empire.[11] They may be seen as a means of cashing in on a fashion and as a particular genre of social and literary polemic. To begin with, they make elbow room for a type of radical, freelance, professional writing in the competitive market-place of the daily press as entertainment. To this end they exploit the figure of the star to invest its potential explosiveness with social and political scatologies and immoralities that have in common a special allure, that is to say the timeless allure that roots them in a conception of popular life as an elysium of freedom, insouciance and self-motion in the face of dominant normalities and restrictions.

In best-seller 'autobiographical' treatments of them, Rigolboche and Thérésa share their origins with the 'virtuoso of the sidewalk' of the popular sociologies of prostitution, whom we find in the writings of Alfred Delvau and Charles Virmaître, as well as with heroines of the closely related romantic narratives of the serial novel and detective story.[12] This can be sited too in a much wider framing of experience across the forms of entertainment. For example one of the most popular songs and the most read detective story of the late 1860s share a phrase. The great communal refrain of 'La Canaille' ('The Rabble'), 'And me, I'm one of them', which Rosalie Bordas's audience would sing back to her, can be found again in Gaboriau's best-selling 'feuilleton', *M. Lecocq,* as the whispered password for the mutual identification of the plain-clothes police, 'j'en suis'.

Like young prostitutes Thérésa and Rigolboche are set on their path as singers by the unavoidable hazards of provincial womanhood on the one hand – a sexual encounter that frees them from the constraint of respectability, a grasping mother who puts them out to 'work' – and, on the other, by their instinctive love of song and dance, the uncontrollable energy that was associated with the prostitutional character. Usually it is a man who sets these young women in motion, who releases them from moral constraint, or nods them beyond innocence, into another world that licenses their nature. With Guilbert it was the great impresario Zidler who noticed her at the theatre, spoke to her and pushed her on her way without her choosing. Grain d'Cachou is set on her career by the worldly and literary *maître d'hôtel,* M. Edmond, who recognises her potential for vice, and installs her in his restaurant as a facility for his clients. Piaf was chosen from the street by the wealthy night-club owner Louis Leplée when he heard her as he queued up for the cinema. This progress, then, follows on from an exercise of power by the man which is both sexual and economic, which holds up an escape from the confines of an everyday morality, whichever one it is that traps you, and a means of making good. Even for Maurice, Mayol's almost imperceptible nod sizes him up, sexually, in a way that lets him know that he must lose his working-class innocence if he is to become a professional performer.

The rise of that first generation of women, in the Second Empire, was accompanied by a frenzied, mass popular following – a phenomenom that caused some bewilderment at the time. How should it be read? As yet a further demonstration of the drunken degeneracy of working-class morals? – a right-wing, Catholic interpretation. Or the symptom of the loss by working men of their traditional, revolutionary dignity? – that is how Philémon would have understood it, and many revolutionaries of the 1860s did. Or perhaps as a harmless letting off of steam, the beginnings of a mass industry of remissive leisure, useful, profitable, to be encouraged.[13] This last clearly had political economy on its side, but it must be said that all these viewpoints, and others, between them elaborated the meaning of the site of entertainment. The more it was susceptible of a multiplicity of readings and projections, the more crucial it became that the stars should be seen as the freely willed expression of all its viewpoints. So it is to satisfy these publics that they exercise the freedom to trade themselves and their talent – a pure, disinterested investment in the using-up of themselves. In the memoirs it is often this freedom that is exalted at the expense of recognising the impossibility of doing otherwise, of having any other choice. It is a trade of which the chosen inevitability allows both talent and self an innocent disengagement from the vagaries of life, while allowing them to emerge across its buffeting and to be seen as a register of its shocks. A life whose unashamed pragmatism is itself a critique of bourgeois hypocrisies and whose reward, like those of hypocrisy, may be wealth and fame. Clearly such a life-cycle is one that might just have suggested a tempting homonym for that of the hack journalist who ghosts the memoirs, and who also aspires to stir the masses.

For the journalist ghosters of the Second Empire the figures of their stars are both a model and a *travesti*, a projection of their own desire for fame and scandal and a site to live it out. And this investment in the figure of the woman singer becomes a trope of long-lasting significance, one that outlives the political and social complex of its origins. It is especially important in the transference of the people/bohème atributes on to each others' terrain. As late as 1965 the elder surviving master of bohemian Parisianism, Mac Orlan, was insistent that the status of woman in his work could achieve a substantial value only in so far as she could voice his feelings. Of all his modes of writing, and of all the types of women, the song and the singer alone were able to complete this transference, this realisation of self in sexual and social alterity. For Mac Orlan, Germaine Montéro, who performed and recorded his work in the 1950s, was not so much an independent presence as a projection of his consciousness. As we will see, Piaf herself was to emerge as a condensation of the homoerotic subcultures of 1930s Paris. And, at the same time, she, like Fréhel, was a convincing representation of a deep sense of social dispossession. The mass demonstrations at her wedding and funeral in 1962 and 1963, the memories of city space that congealed around her songs in a changing Paris, underline this association.

Where an autobiography really is written by its subject, we find that this argument about its relation to a field of social meaning is confirmed. For if, like Maurice, you do write your own, the means that you find to represent yourself are, by and large, already made in the existing mythologies and annals of music-hall, in the press dossiers that comment on your career, in the prosody of entertainment. We have seen with Guilbert how she adopts two viewpoints, and how these represent an ambivalence in the overlapping relation of the singer and her public and of the singer and her own origins. Her life, as written by herself, is no less composed of her *faits divers* than Piaf's was to be when she spoke it to her writer in 1958, but in the voice and tittle-tattle of the journalists who first wrote about her in 1935–6 in *Voilà* or *Détective*. Given that this short-circuit is inherent to the genre, the autobiographies may as well anyway be understood as *travesti*, and with Guilbert or Chevalier a *travesti* show that is both long-running and well staged.

When Piaf made her first appearance at Le Gerny's nightclub, one of the most expensive spots off the Champs-Élysées, in 1935, it was if a figure like Casque d'Or – whose myth was still alive in Colette and *Détective Magazine* – had crossed over from the Zone to the world of *Paris mondain*. She was perceived within a network of images, filtered down through the archaeologies of their origins and worked through the fetishes of marginality current towards the end of the 1930s. She sang 'Les Mômes de la Cloche', the story of the brief life and death of the *purée* of prostitution, as if it were her own life, although the theme was an especially popular one. This version had been penned by one of the most successful writers of the time, Vincent Scotto – composer of at least four thousand songs over his working life.[14] No doubt when Louis Leplée, her first patron, named her, he had but little need for reflection, for naming was a privilege of his class of men:

> – You're a real Paris sparrow, and the name that would suit you would be Sparrow. Unhappily, the *môme* [kid] Moineau is already taken ... In slang a sparrow (*moineau*) is a 'piaf'. Why should you not be the *môme* Piaf? (*Au bâl de la chance*, p. 20)

Nor indeed were the very first witnesses of her night-club rehearsals at a loss in responding to her genre of *chanteuse réaliste*, knowing how to vary or to garnish it according to the fashion of the moment. Yvonne Vallée, already an established star, gives her a 'magnificent scarf of white silk':

> – I want to make this little one her first gift as an artist. Realist singers all think that they can't do without a red scarf. It's an absurd fashion. I'm against it. The *môme* Piaf will not have a red scarf ... (*ibid*, p. 21)

'It's strong, it's truthful. Piaf is a pure product of our tormented age.' So Maurice commented on a 1946 concert with the Compagnons de la Chanson

# la môme piaf

Effondrée, la môme Piaf assise aux côtés de Laure Jarny, aux obsèques de Louis Leplée, son bienfaiteur.

Marcel MONTARRON.

in an interview with *Paris Matin*. It was one of the many such judgements he was called to pass upon new generations of singers, and fairly typical of the early reception of Piaf whose very first recitals he had witnessed at Le Gerny's. If, with him and Yvette Guilbert, it seemed that certain themes of innocence and experience had a special significance in their presentation of their history, another related question is implicit in Maurice's language here, one of the perception of experience as if innocence. This is the innocence, so perfectly envisioned in Piaf, of 'Comme un moineau', that is the essential innocence of the criminal childhood of Paris. We could trace it in many forms, perhaps in the sentimental image of popular childhood in Poulbot's drawings of big-eyed deviant urchins, or Doisneau's 1940s photographs of kids playing in the street or on the Zone. It is a state of being that is, above all, innocent of the processes of its own fabrication, self-absorbed even when conscious that it is under observation. Its presence in a new figure refreshes the spontaneity of the popular as a renewal of its tropes. There is, in the very earliest reportages on Piaf, an uneasy mix of sexual and social instabilities that fit neatly with the context in which they were undertaken. This was the murder of Louis Leplée, probably for money, and possibly through a homosexual underworld of pick-ups and rent boys. Her hanging out with the *titi* who might be just her boyfriend, but also her patron's murderer or his lover, her living in cheap hotels, the possbility that she has been forced to sell herself to eat, all of this is crucial in establishing her as a natural member of the seething marginalities that made up the urban fauna. Though her biographers argue that Leplée's murder was a terrible setback for her – it left her without a patron, liable to the accusation of complicity, the subject of scandal and gossip – in the end her association with the dark side of the cityscape only added to her fascination.

In Marcel Montarron's report for *Voilà*, the trip up to Montmartre to find her is a ritual passage to a land of margins. In the page-layout, her image is surrounded by sparrows, accordions and the profiles of Sacré-Coeur and the Butte Montmartre. She belongs to the class of *légionnaires*, cheap gunmen, sailors and *voyous* of popular literature. Access to her is found by the Montmartrois *littérateurs* in the pages of *Détective* and *Voilà*, who shower her with the images of the eternal little people, their suffering, their anonymity, their accordions, their knowledge of the street, instinctive, sexual and material. This allows her songs and performances their significant ambivalence and ambiguity, for they conjugate with what is known and expected of the city. Then, little by little, as her career advances on radio and gramophone, the marginality that she lives cedes to one that merely provides her with a context, the substantive becomes a decor. As her repertoire expands, the men, the women in the songs come to be thought of as the projection of her own experience, and they become her life, woven into press reports and critical reviews. She acquires a biography that places the rudiments of her 'lived' life in the everyday life of the city-tropes.

Thus when the next stage of her career unfolds in 1936–9, carefully plotted by the writer–musician team of Raymond Asso and Marguerite Monnot, with Jacques Canetti as fixer, their inventions are passed over entirely into her personality. The man-object of 'Mon légionnaire', or the fleeing, night-time criminal of 'Paris-Méditerranée', are read and valued as anecdotes from her life, written into the short notices and reviews of her appearances and discs. In the process Piaf's performance first adjusts from that of the street singer to the taut and refined address of the small, expensive night-club, with its solo piano or small group accompaniment. It is here that songs are launched and tested, sifted for the radio and a wider public.[15] With success, and especially the accolade of a national status as a singer for the troops in 1939, the next stage is that of the big music-hall, the orchestra and the backing choirs. And this overwhelming context in turn reworks her 'littleness', her pathos and her being-a-victim, so that she appears almost crushed in the context of the industry that has in turn taken on her attributes as its own. The sparrow motif, song or singer coincide and intermingle in their passages and between them circulate an identification and a recognition in their different appropriate forms between their different publics.[16]

Later, in the biographies of the 1960s and 1970s, for example, this evolves into a retroactive proof of Piaf's status as a norm of French womanhood, both loving and suffering. Through the accumulation of tiny points of evidence, detailed yet circumstantial, Monique Lange, for one, has her inspired, emotionally or musically, by a series of lovers. She more or less forces Piaf into bed with Asso, marshalling the witness of her girlfriend's account of how often she had to quit their shared hotel room at night to leave the couple alone. The stake in these accounts is not exactly what took place, whether or not Piaf really did have sex with Asso, and then X and Y and Paul Meurisse, but what must have happened to give substance to one of the types of popular French femininity that came to dominate the international market after 1945, and that Piaf was to represent in its seamless integrity.[17] The uneven time scales of the stories of sexual and social marginality recompose themselves in step with one another in the figure of Piaf. The long-gone prostitute of the fortifications is reborn from the petty criminality of a changing city in the culture of luxurious night-life, to find its way back to a public who can realise it as subjective memory over the radio-waves and on the gramophone. And little by little, as her fame develops, Piaf herself becomes the name for those collections of images and histories that first named her. In 1939 she has shed these details and what is left of them she dominates: her empty, tragic gaze cuts over ours, but directs it back to Paris, back to the weeping walls, the cobblestones, the wretched old lady, for whom

VOILA

L'HEBDOMADAIRE DU REPORTAGE

9ᵐᵉ Année - N° 449
CHAQUE VENDREDI

L'élite de nos artistes et de nos chanteuses part au front divertir nos soldats. VOILA a recueilli leurs confidences de là-bas

Étoiles au Front

EDITH PIAF

she can sing her wretchedness. Yet this startling cover is still only a fragment of the people's image, and is perhaps not so poignant an access to its meanings as that other voice, the voice of 'our great Maurice, national and international'.

Maurice Chevalier – for we must now return to him – was born in 1888 and died in 1972, and was for over fifty years one of the most successful music-hall and cinema stars in the entire international industry. He partnered Mistinguett at the age of twenty-two, and playing in London in the late 1920s he was already billed as the 'highest paid performer in the world'. When he went to Hollywood at the beginning of the sound cinema, it was his style that helped to define French male charm for generations of Americans. Although he toured the world throughout his career, his image was, in the final event, probably fixed in Minelli's film of Colette's *Gigi* – a look of a stupidly stereotyped, classy French elegance that is more often than not taken for bourgeois. This belies the symbolic value of the straw boater by mistaking it for chic, when the hat was the emblem of Maurice's origins in popular music-hall, one that he saw himself as wearing through his life on behalf of the 'little people' of Paris. Not because it was a working-class hat, but because in wearing it for his performances after the First World War, he had felt that he was holding out a vision of a new life, one of the reasonable aspirations to ease and pleasure, a popular access to a more sunny world of middle-class leisure.

At the same time the image in *Gigi*, with its theme song 'I remember it well' ironically makes nonsense of the possibility that such a figure could produce a long and interesting autobiography, *Ma route et mes chansons*, which runs to nine volumes of over two thousand pages. Over the years he was writing the style develops and varies, feeding off a gamut of literary conventions from the formal diary to a stream of consciousness. Consistently the volumes are as full of wild bouts of self-congratulation and bragging at each success and triumph as they are shot through with a studiously exaggerated modesty, punctuated by terrible crises of confidence. The conflict between these extremes is in itself an important thematic of the text, structuring the space of private and public, inner doubts and outer confidence, past and present. The whole story makes for a complex and intelligent account of the evolution of the world of modern entertainment, and one reading of it may suggest ways of outlining a topography and a politics of the 'popular' across the output of the 'factories of pleasure', to use the phrase of Maurice Verne's.

Both the bragging and the self-negation suggest the ways in which Maurice, as a son of the Parisian working class, has been able to make a space not only for himself but for it, too, in the firmament of which Marlene Dietrich, Al Jolson, Charles Chaplin, the Duke of Windsor and a host of kings and princesses, René Clair, von Stroheim or Louis Aragon are only a sample. In his passage through life Maurice's humility flatters his working-class origins, which he trails behind him as the titles of his authenticity. The generosity, the simplicity, the artless criminality of the people, are recorded and the record repeated. In the second volume he tells of how, as a child performer, a pimp from the passages stops him in the street and offers to help him with money. And this from nothing more than a disinterested generosity, a love of the boy's singing that he has heard in a local *boui-boui*. Of course he bluffs and refuses, yet 'I felt he was my friend. I didn't know his name' (*Ma route*, vol. 2, p. 65). And then, years later and a successful star, when he is taken to witness an execution in the Boulevard Arago, it is only to find his old friend on the scaffold. The man dies with dignity, 'calm, strong, dominanting the tragic situation', refusing a priest with a look that says 'You don't imagine that I can shed my pride?' Maurice's heart beats with joy, 'I was proud, as if a friend had just acquitted himself well'(*ibid.*).

Here too the passing interest of the *faits divers* turns tragedy into charm, the criminal into anecdote and the people into honour, all within the timescales of the singer's memory. And through his memory those two largely discrepant categories of the working classes and the popular classes meet up and are reconciled.

Maurice's mission is bathos as well, pricking the pretentions to the greatness which· he admires, but which take him from his people. He remembers his first meeting with the Duke of Windsor, recalling it as he sees him again on the golf-course at Nice in 1939. 'He pleases me, that prince.... I was introduced to him once in London, and that evening he reigned over Ménilmontant' (*Ma route*, vol. 3, chapters. 6 and 7). Maurice meets *many* princes. He salutes the Duke, who appears not to see him, while his caddy, with all the nagging insistence of a music-hall monologue, pleads to be taken to 'Ollivode' with him on a future visit. However in the next sequence Maurice is sitting down to lunch with the Duke, and, in all probability, so does Ménilmontant. But that, no doubt, is one of the reasons why the Duke invites him. During lunch, the radio announces to them the declaration of war. Emergency! Maurice and the Duke never find the time for their intended round of golf. At one meal, the extraordinary is banalised and the banal elevated, walking once again that borderline of news and fiction.

After the war, Maurice is accused of collaboration, of singing for the enemy, of being, along with other artistes, part of a group of *mauvais français* (*ibid.*, pp. 82ff.). His only possible misdemeanour, according to his version of the story, was to have sung in one German prison camp, Alten-Grabow – the one in which he himself had been incarcerated in the First World War and only on condition that the German authorities released ten boys from Belleville and Ménilmontant.[18] The accusations were not to stick, and he was eventually cleared by the *Épuration*, but the game was far from clear and the situation sufficiently tense to throw him into a period of acute anxiety – somewhat relieved by a visit from Marlene Dietrich to assure him of his reputation in Hollywood and New York. (Her wartime record was beyond reproach.) The mud did stick for a few years, and people still refer to 'Chevalier the collaborator', though this is probably a disguised aesthetic judgement.

It looks as if a young and militant section of the communist partisans were out to get him, to win a manoeuvre in an internal struggle with their leaders, and what was at stake, very precisely, was the loyalty of the people. On the parade that year to the Federals' Wall at Père-Lachaise it was, rather, the literary pin-ups of the Party, Aragon and Elsa Triolet, who persuaded him to march with them in the intellectuals section, and so to show himself to the people. The pages that follow are an idyll. They, the crowds on the street, welcome him into their arms:

> Ah, look there, Maurice! – Right, get a look at Chevalier! – O.K. then, he's not dead! Eh, Maurice, good-day to you! it's good to see you again! ...
>
> All the same, these are nothing but cries of affection, of love, you could well say. Bravo Maurice! – It's cool of you to be here with us! – I knew well enough that he's on the people's side, Maurice! He's a worker's son! – Long live Maurice! – Long live Ménilmontant....
>
> Aragon and his wife smile at me, stirred! – It's a true plebiscite, Maurice. You can be happy! The people adore you...
>
> The proof had been made. In the street, there is no reproach against me. (*ibid.*, pp. 105ff.).

It is tonight that he sleeps smiling, to 'Angels with faces of the faubourgs'.

In looking at Maurice, then, any of his fans who feel themselves to be a member of his class become their own voyeur, taking a representation of the people from *la haute*, the part of it that is tied up with Maurice. This social switchback connects an unstable relation of narcissism and metonymy, which is a deeply ambivalent exchange in class relations. Exquisite too, because for that other audience from *la haute*, Maurice is a means of looking at the popular class, finally conquered as the legitimate and handsomely rewarded object of amusement. Maybe, as I have hinted, Maurice's virtue was to make so convincing a reality of the oh-so-classic dream of bourgeois economics that the virtues of capital and labour can be equally rewarded, even though this means that the ultimate commodification of labour power is voluntary – like that self-use of Piaf or of Fréhel through the hard work of amusing others, through the alcohol and drugs that turn their lives into the metaphor of amusement. 'Je n'attends plus rien / rien désormais ne m'appartient ...', nothing is left but old stories at the bottom of her memory in one of Fréhel's hits. And Maurice's own smooth-running public figure is nicely set off by his crises of confidence, breakdowns and attempted suicide at the age of seventy-five. The pathologies of their class claim these singers as a condition of their being seen and heard and the fixing of social relations is reproduced in an image made irreproachable by their success.

This ideal role is an obsessional object of attention, and when the heroine of Faubourg Montmartre says to her sister, 'We, we are poor, no one looks at us', she is suggesting the fiction of the invisibility of poverty that makes its baroque and distant representation through Piaf or Chevalier all the more alluring. In one of Berthe Sylva's songs, the beautiful, diamond-glittering women with haughty airs may well look down on 'us':

mais demain, peut-être ce soir
Dans nos musettes [elles] viendront nous voir
Et nous lirons dans leurs yeux chavirés
Le voeu qu'elles n'osent murmurer...

C'est un mauvais garçon
Il a des façons
Pas très catholique ... ('Mauvais garçon')

This is why, for Maurice, looking back is so important. His remembering sutures a decomposing, poor artisanal working class of the late nineteenth-century economic crisis with the modern, industrial population of the Popular Front and the labour unions: and binds this complex, often violent political and social evolution to a relatively stable, if also polymorphous, archaeology of the people as a national value. In *Maurice Chevalier's Paris*, the CBS television programme outlined in my Introduction, we can see him sliding fatally into metonymy, picking up the inscrutable fragments of a hoped-for history. Through his work he makes possible a looking that, with the autobiography, he enables himself to share.

In volume 5 of *Ma route, Y'a tant d'amour*, there is an extraordinary passage that reveals something of this complexity of a journey across social frontiers, as well as through time, the subjective time of the memoirs, and the time of their writing. Here Maurice, who keeps abreast of literary developments, annotates a reading of André Gide. It should be noted that by now, 1952, the seventh year of the project, his own writing is loosening up, becoming more experimental. Maurice is assuming his part as a member of the national cultural elite. (Elsewhere, he recounts a conversation with the aged Colette about how he wrote of her in volume 1, his lascivious comments on her body as a young artiste. She is flattered rather than irritated.) He is aiming for an easy mixture of long narrative passages with with quick asides, confessions, and pages of free-versified patter. The whole is geared to the expression of the anguish of an ageing male sexuality, for he is involved with a much younger woman, and feels he can only be bad for her or to her. Suddenly Gide appears as a model, not only of great man of letters but of a sexual ideal as well. A strange choice for the singer of Paris the pretty blonde:

In the most recent volume of his journals André Gide confides in us that, in the month of June 1942 – at the age of 72 – he knew ectasy for two nights long, which came from paradise or hell, call it what you will.

The miracle took place in Tunis and had the features and body of a ravishing fifteen-year-old boy.

André Gide informs us about the the quality and the variety of the pleasures procured with the adorable cupid …

Excuse me, but this reading troubles me and leaves me dreamy …

What an ace! (*Ma route*, vol. 5. p. 100)

If, then, he dreams of finding the same pleasure, except that 'you won't mind if I prefer a girl', the dream integrates him into a worldly circle of famous men as one who has nothing to lose or to risk other than that he might not be seen as one of them. The phrase 'What an ace' both bonds with Gide and makes light of him. However, the contrast with his memories of adolescence in volume 1 could not be more stark. In this episode he is flattered to take a drive home from a performance with the friend of a new and famous colleague. He is excited to be in a proper, horse-drawn cab. But then:

With a pull of his arm, suddenly, he brought my face up to his proffered mouth, and holding me squeezed against him as in a vice, frenziedly tried to press his lips against mine. Horror struck, I protected myself like the devil. This repulsive battle lasted a few minutes … Going back up the stairs [to his family flat], I felt that something so serious had happened that I couldn't tell Paul and La Louque. I feared that they might drag me from a world and a milieu where such extraordinary things could happen so easily …

(*Ma route*, vol. 1, p. 91)

The shock is mixed, mitigated even, by this sudden accession to social grace. To arrive home in a *fiacre* was as much a pull from his origins as the unexpected sexual encounter, and the coincidence of the two events mingle pleasure and self-satisfaction with a horror and fear of separation. What Maurice will do in order to resolve this conflict is to take his origins, his class, and in particular, his mother – 'La Louque' – with him throughout his life. As he becomes rich and famous, he will publicly perform acts of piety to the people of Ménilmontant and of filial piety to La Louque, their daughter.

This will also help to recuperate an image of the people and of Frenchness in a longer-term redemption from the pessimistic populism of the right, so completely compromised by the wartime experience. It will facilitate its dynamic insertion into a post-war world economy, for which Maurice's enthused acclamation of the United States will now work so well: 'Formidable, really, indubitably formidable this *Broadway at night*. Orgy of lights, of signs, of titles, of slogans' (*Ma route*, vol. 2, p. 132).

Maurice's love of America and Americans, which he proclaims through Hollywood, the wild success of his New York performances, his friendship with the roster of great stars, and his insistent opening-up of a space amidst it all for Ménilmontant, makes for dramatic contrast with L.-F. Céline, for example. In his *Voyage au bout de la nuit* Céline tracks some of the same ground and circuits as does Maurice's life, through an iteration of the popular that now compounds it into the purely negative. The details of daily suffering in Céline block even an imaginary escape from exploitation – trapping it in a dead end that is confirmed by the experience of America as both even more categorically negative and, at the same time, un-French. With Céline, the anti-Semite and ardent collaborator, populism as cultural form and the conservative reaction to international capital are identified with each other.[19] Maurice comes closer to the enthusiasm of Elisabeth de Gramont, an idealised, pro-Americanism that goes back to a de Tocqueville or a Champfleury in the middle of the nineteenth century. Writing in 1937 she painted this idyll of New York:

> As for the circulation of traffic, facilitated by the grid plan of the streets, it is so well organised that anyone could cross New York on foot, reading the bible, without having to look up.[20]

The absurdity of accusing Chevalier of collaboration ironically lies in this element of un-Frenchness, in his other, long-established and willing, collaboration with the increasingly internationalised cultures of the allied bloc. If there were an element of active collaboration with Vichy morality in his songs, then this was already long since inscribed in the mythemes and the pathos of the popular, in its historical ambivalence that we explored in chapter 1. Anyway, as Maurice astutely perceived, he was saved from radiophonic collaboration by his truly terrible speaking voice.[21]

After the war he began the autobiography at the suggestion of the publisher Bernard Grasset, and also to understand the crisis that had been precipitated by process of accusation and *épuration*. The accumulation of narratives, each represented both in its original state and through the interplay of different, successive moralities, map on to each other the cultures of working-class innocence, of the sophisticated and 'naughty' world of music-hall and literary worldliness. If anything this means that, in the post-war years, Maurice could be seen in contrast to the grimly moralistic reconstruction of French civil society, with its legalised insistence on the Vichy values of family and work, its atmosphere of homophobia and homebuilding. It was the government of liberation that confirmed the Vichy laws against homosexuality – the first of their kind in modern French history, and, as we have seen with Maurice's praise of Gide, he comes to embody a tolerance and openness that could no longer be heard on gramophone or radio. At the same time, his own individuality of the ageing *coureur de femmes* is hardly redeemed by his sedulous attention to La Louque and his morale becomes increasingly unstable. If the image of the working people in Maurice and Yvette is rooted in the social forms of the 1870s and worked through the gallant' languages of pre-war entertainment, then, by 1945, their sublimation of the conflict between 'people' and 'working class' must be consigned to fantasy and concealment, or taken as an abstract ideal. Like *Les Enfants du Paradis*, they confer a future on lost meanings, make memories of what is becoming unknown. In a post-war, working-class Paris, described with brutal simplicity by the Swedish journalist Stig Dagerman, where could we find this amusing, troubled Maurice?[22] Dagerman travelled there and wrote about the life of a 'typical' working family from the Place Stalingrad. Through them he saw Paris as a city without comfort or choice, trapped in 'material and moral ruin', in the decay of its fabric as of its history. The version according to Maurice pales, his comment on popular song sounds pathetic:

> I'm still waiting for the little fellow who will come up from cobblestones ... who on his own will embody the people of Paris ... Trenet, Montand, it's sturdy stuff, but it doesn't seem enough like the faubourgs, do you understand ... (11 December 1946, in *Paris Matin*)

A little like the bird in Baudelaire's 'Le Cygne', Maurice, gorgeous in his plumage, treads clumsily between two worlds, this 'wretched being, strange and fatal myth'.

### Notes

1  As with Nora's departure at the very end of Ibsen's *Dolls' House*: see Lu Hsun, 'What happens when Nora leaves home?' in his *Collected Essays*, Peking, Foreign Languages Press, 1969.

2  See one of the classics of the French moralist movement, Paul Bureau, *Towards Moral Bankruptcy*, introduction by Mary Scharlieb MD, MS, London, Constable, 1925, pp. 94ff. Originally, *L'Indiscipline des moeurs*, Paris, Bloud et Gay, 1920.

3  See, for example, Colette, *Lettres à ses pairs*, texte établi et annoté par Claude Pichois et Roberte Forbin, Paris, Flammarion,1973. For the following point concerning the relation between Guilbert and her writers see the Recueil Factice on Xanrof, Bibliothèque de l'Arsenal. In an interview Xanrof in later life admitted that he ended up in quite serious conflict with Yvette who refused to announce his name during her performances, and he resorted, unsuccessfully, to singing his songs *chez* Bruant. Unsuccessfully because Bruant too could admit no competition and made his own deafening noise while Xanrof sung.

4  For comparable questions of the female spectator and German popular literature, see Patrice Petro, *Soulless Streets, Women and Melodramatic Representation in Weimar Germany*, Princeton, Princeton University Press, 1988. I have not here taken up the important question of mass culture as 'female', originated by Siegfried Kracauer, and discussed by Andreas Huyssen in his 'Mass Culture as Woman – Modernism's Other' in *Studies in Entertainment, Critical Approaches to Mass Culture*, ed. T. Modleski, Bloomington, Indiana University Press, 1986. Petro, *op. cit.*, pp. 8-9, comments acutely on a problem that I have let fall in so far as I feel that the routing of cultural identity through 'women' is quite a distinct issue from that of the 'mass' as other to a masculine modernism. In the next

chapter I continue to develop my theme in a manner that diverges further from this debate while converging with Petro's position in her chapters 2 and 3. For a study of the young woman reader in Colette, see 'La Révolution Claudinienne' in *Autour de Colette à St-Tropez*, France, Cogolin, 1987. There is an extensive recent literature on Colette, with some 121 items in the current MLA listings, and for a collection of essays see *Colette: Nouvelles approches critiques*, ed. Bernard Bray, Paris, Nizet, 1986.

5 See Louis Chevalier, *Montmartre* p. 282, where he gives an excellent account of this affair, the survival of its notoriety up to being filmed in 1952 by Jacques Becker. That it remained of interest is evident in the first annual of *Détective*, in 1930, where the story is recapitulated with a photograph of Casque d'Or. A new, popular paperback came out only recently – Pierre Drachline and Claude Petit-Castelli, *Casque d'Or et les apaches*, Paris, Renaudot, 1990. This has a useful chapter on the *apache*, his characterisation and topography. See pp. 169ff.

6 Theodor Adorno, 'Fantasia sopra Carmen' in *Quasi una fantasia*, Gallimard, Paris, 1982, p. 68, and my own 'Carmenology', *New Formations*, 5, 1988, pp. 91–107.

7 For an account of some of the myths of singers' origins see the discussion of Damia and Fréhel in my 'Musical Moments', *Yale French Studies*, 73, 1987, pp. 121–55, and Ginette Vincendeau, 'The Mise-en-scène of Suffering – French Chanteuses Réalistes' *New Formations*, 4, 1987, p. 107–28. From the extensive discussions of the 'star system' see Edgar Morin, Les Stars (third edition), Paris, Seuil, 1972.

8 This question has been much debated in recent years: see Rancière, 'Good Times'; T. J. Clark, *The Painting of Modern Life: Paris in the Art of Manet and his Followers*, London, Thames and Hudson, 1985, especially the essay on the *Bar at the Folies Bergère*.; François Gasnault, *Guinguettes et lorettes – bals publics à Paris au XIX^e siècle*, Paris, Aubier, 1986; Philippe Gumplowicz, *Les Travaux d'Orphée – 150 ans de vie musicale amateur en France, harmonies, chorales, fanfares*, Paris, Aubier, 1987; A. D. Rifkin, 'Cultural Movement and the Paris Commune', *Art History*, 2, no. 2, June 1979. Much of this discussion was originated by Siegfried Kracauer in a book that is the contemporary of Benjamin's *Passages*, his remarkable *Orpheus in Paris – Offenbach and the Paris of his Time* (1937) translated from the German by Gwenda David and Eric Mosbacher, New York, Knopf, 1938.

9 See Ginette Vincendeau, 'The Mise-en-scène of Suffering'; Rifkin, 'Musical Moments'; Anouk Adelman, *Chansons à vendre*, Paris, Cujas, 1968, puts it well: 'Even the realist song never makes a description of the real, but a description of the fashionable image of reality', pp. 128ff.

10 Even a rough count of articles and reviews in late 1930s French cinema magazines underlines both aspects of this point. Opinion on jazz was divided, and traditionalists expected and hoped that it would die. See Collection Rondel, Recueil Factice on Maryse Damia for her views and James Clifford, *Negrophilia*.

11 E. Blum and L. Huart, *Mémoires de Rigolboche*, Paris, Dentu, 1860; H. Rochefort, E. Blum and A. Wolf, *Mémoires de Thérésa*, Paris, Palais Royal, 1865. These ran to at least six or seven editions. Blum, who published his own *Mémoires d'un vieux beau*, Paris, Ollendorf, in 1896, has six pages of vaudevilles to his credit in the catalogue of the Bibliothèque Nationale. For a discussion of this see Gasnault, *Guinguettes*; A. D. Potts, 'Dance, Politics and Sculpture', *Art History*, 10, no. 1, March 1987, which is a review of Anne Middleton Wagner, *Jean Baptiste Carpeaux, Sculptor of the Second Empire*, New Haven and London, Yale University Press, 1986, who also discusses Rigolboche as an image of popular freedom.

12 Generally this literature is well treated in the classic work on prostitution in France, Alain Corbin, *Les Filles de noce – misère sexuelle et prostitution aux 19^e et 20^e siècles*, Paris,

Aubier, 1978. Charles Virmaître, *Paris impur*, Paris, Dalou, 1889.

13  See Honoré Bondilh, *L'Art pour le peuple: Les cafés-concerts et les cafés-théatres*, Marseille, A. Arnaud, 1867 for an early expression of this view.

14  For information on 'music-hallistes', see C. Brunschwig, L.-J. Calvet and J.-C. Klein, *Cent ans de chanson française*, Paris, Seuil/Points Actuels, 1981, an excellent scholarly and critical dictionary.

15  See Jacques Canetti's memoirs, *On cherche jeune homme aimant la musique*, Paris, 1978, for an account of this and his talent spotting activities first for Polydor and then Philips. Though far from critical, Canetti's account of his work points to the network of influences and decisions that lay behind the selection and promotion of individual talents.

16  A useful critical framework for listening to these forms of song could be found in Barthes's theory of bourgeois vocal art – his comparative analysis of Fischer-Dieskau, Gérard Souzay and Charles Panzéra in the essays on music collected in Roland Barthes, *L'Obvie et l'obtus*, Paris, Seuil, 1982, pp. 236–59. Similar distinctions to those he makes between the maudlin Fischer-Dieskau and the bodily Panzéra might be made between Piaf, late and early, or Piaf and Fréhel, usefully indicating a shift in public and with it, in modes and qualities of attention. Asso was not alone in feeling that Piaf's decline as a singer began with her rise to mass popularity in the years from 1939–1943, and that purity of diction and expression were sacrificed to emotional effects.

17  Monique Lange, *Histoire de Piaf*, Paris, Ramsay, 1979. Simone Bertéaut, *Piaf*, Paris, Robert Laffont, 1969, is especially important as Bertéaut was her street-friend at the start of her career.

18  See the press cuttings in the dossier Maurice Chevalier, Bibliothèque de l'Arsenal, Rondel Collection for an extensive coverage of his period of 'difficulty'.

19  Alice Yaeger Kaplan, *Repetitions*, provides a subtle analysis, pp. 107–21, of Céline's fascism within a contradictory framework of 'modern/international' and 'French/national'.

20  Elisabeth de Gramont, 'L'Attirance de New York – conférence faite à l'Assemblée Générale de la Section Française des Amitiés Internationales, 13 Décembre 1937', Paris, Denoel, 1937.

21  Kaplan, *op. cit.*, again, for the fascist uses of the radio and the importance of the radio-voice in pre-war and wartime politics, p. 133ff.

22  Stig Dagerman, *Printemps français*, traduit du suédois par Philippe Bouquet, Paris, Ludd, 1988. See also the Swiss author C. F. Ramuz in his *Paris*, Paris, Gallimard, 1939, who also emphasised modesty and neediness. In the 1988 edition of *Printemps* one of the surviving children of the Régnault family, who were the subject of Dagerman's attention, takes issue with his pessimism and suggests that he was something of the dupe of his own intervention. André Regnault was kept by the Dagerman family in Sweden during the war. Dagerman himself committed suicide shortly afterwards.

# 3

# Some snapshots

Monsieur Guillaume Balthasar, I welcome you amongst us. By the way, M. Ahmed, have you received my record: N.B. 6722: *Cries of the Police in a northern night?* (from Pierre Mac Orlan, *Dans le quartier réservé*)

My eyes seemed to play the part of a photographic lens, and the scene of the murder fixed itself on my mind as on a prepared sheet of glass, with such precision, accuracy and effect, that even today I could draw from memory the bedroom occupied by the Little Old Man of Batignolles, without forgetting any single object it contained...
(Emile Gaboriau, *The Little Old Man of Batignolles*, 1888)

This chapter is about the sight-plans and sound-plans of the city, perspectives that are seen or heard from a diversity of positions, filtered through interests and desires. It develops the idea that these are articulated both through informal, professional structures such as the Académie Goncourt and through specific institutions of the state, the culture industries or the press. It takes the snapshot as a paradigm for the illusion of disinterest that is a prevailing condition of urban subjectivity, of seeing and hearing each event and sound as a confirmation of your relation to the city.

Sound, like vision, is configured in moments and in spaces. To hear, at the point it becomes to listen, is to constitute random combinations of noise or music as meaning, as a point of access to the inductive unpiecing of Paris. In the paragraph from Mac Orlan's *Dans le quartier réservé* the police chief welcomes the Parisian record seller to North Africa, at the same time turning to the outgoing shopkeeper to confirm an order. A brief and enigmatic passage, but one that points in miniature to the inseparability of Paris, crime, the exotic, to the catching of their combination in sound and vision, to their enjoyment in the banal technologies of entertainment.

In the closing moments of the film *Faubourg Montmartre*, the heroine, played by Gaby Morlay, an innocent saved from the Parisian rounds of

7ᵉ Année - Nᵒ 271      1 FR. 50 - TOUS LES JEUDIS - 16 PAGES      4 Janvier 1934

# DÉTECTIVE

# 1934

ouvre ses yeux inquiets,
affolés, sur l'avenir
lourd de haines, de drames
et de catastrophes

drugs and prostitution, has found love and safety in a sunny provincial village. Newly rescued from the cruel if picturesque realities of the faubourg she wants only to hear it once again, to listen to its sound-collage of motor-horns, voices, engines. Fear and terror are transmuted into nostalgia and affection. She phones her old aunt, the manageress of a respectable *chocolatier* of the faubourg and has her hold the receiver up to the open door of the shop. The film, which began with a dramatic, high-level, compacted vision of the street ends with the electric reproduction of its sound.

Gaboriau's narrator in *The Little Old Man of Batignolles* is recounting how he became a detective. Arriving by chance at the scene of a crime, he discovers that he has a gift of vision, of the ability to imprint an event on his mind in a plenitude of detail that provides the conditions for induction. This gift prescribes his future. His description precedes the development of police photography by more than a decade. Recomposing such a vision will become the habit of the entertainment industries.

Seeing is in one sense the most voluntary of activities, like talking. It seems voluntary because of its intense individuality in the zoological identities of the city crowds, and because you can close your eyes and choose to see nothing at all. Baudelaire's conception of modernity, for example, was conjured out of a very particular exercise of vision. He constructed a field of view that wove together the trope of the city crowds from Poe with the *concerts populaires* of Paris and the drawings of Guys. He microscoped the poetic exposure of an exotically alienated but private sexuality with its representation in the most public of spaces, the discovery of its *semblable* amongst Delacroix's ceiling decorations in the Louvre or the Palais Bourbon. In the subsequent development of cultural history this astonishing skill in the combination of the disparate elements of urban subjectivity has been taken as the epigone of modernity. Roger Caillois's influential essay *Paris, mythe moderne* (1937), for example, both interrogates the Baudelairean moment of modernity and congeals it around the figure of the poet. The city in Baudelaire becomes the decor for something that can never be fully understood other than through the unfolding tradition of its realisation in literature.[1] Yet it would be useful to account for the survival of such a compelling vision elsewhere than in a literary heritage, to see it, rather, as an epiphenomenom of an altogether other modern.

One way of broaching this is to take up Benjamin's argument, in *The Work of Art in the Age of Mechanical Reproduction*, that the articulation of the new often has to find its means of expression within technical limitations already prescribed and formulated, a relationship typified by that between Futurism and painting. A view of the world takes shape before it finds a technology that can be made to mirror it, like the photographic seeing of Gaboriau's detective. As Benjamin was to put it:

The history of every art form shows critical epochs in which a certain art form aspires to effects which should be fully obtained only with a changed technical standard, that is to say, in a new art form. (*Illuminations*, p. 239)

If, then, this nineteenth-century conception of modernity, as the shifting imbrication of the complexities of city life, not only survived into the 1920s and 1930s, but flourished, we need to look for a means of survival, a source of strength that carries it beyond its literary formulation and finds it a place in a series of presents. To acomplish this we might well turn to the technologies of the culture industries, the gramophone, the cinema and, above all, radiophony. That is to the emergence of a technology capable of representing the urban sound-plan, the mimesis of its noises in their superposition, of defining a space for their control and subjection to the tropings of the urban poetic, and so of working for their consumption.

As a technology radio emerged and began to mature along with the secure establishment of a turn-of-the-century literary bohemia who worked across and through a wide range of the products and media of mass culture. Their matrix of production really became industrial in comparison to that of Baudelaire, in its morality, in its techniques and in the forms of attention that it pays to the city scene. For one thing its practitioners, who number writers as disparate as Colette and Mac Orlan, are no longer tormented, as Baudelaire had been, by a conflict of commercial and artistic interests and intentions. On the contrary, they live out and think through this new world. They are comfortable at whatever level of commercial culture they are able to insert themselves. They readily shift from the luxury edition of erotica to the pornographic magazine, from the music-hall performance to the radio, the novel of modern life, the reportage of the illustrated magazine, or the beauty shop. But often, through an atavistic reference to the earlier models, which extend from Villon to Baudelaire, they collapse this living of the modern world into nostalgia. Radio manifests its techniques as a new privilege of the *flâneur's* movement through the city. Mac Orlan uses it to imagine the accordion refrains of Parisian dance tunes on the shores of Tampico. It was the very availability of a public for such a new mode of address that also led Benjamin to make radio programmes, as did Weill and Brecht. The choice imposed itself.

This spread of intervention across a disparate, technologically and socially complex field underlines the significance of difference in the paying of attention. In the previous model listening is privileged over hearing. Significant sounds are discerned despite unimportant noise – Baudelaire catches a Wagner overture at an outdoor concert 'symphonic extracts from Wagner echoed every evening in the casinos open to a crowd in love with trivial pleasures'[2] – while in the scripting of radiophony overhearing becomes an authored activity in its own right.

Mac Orlan and Béraud find a poetic in the sound of motor horns. For the modern *flâneur* (his) hearing imposes itself as the listening of the audience, unless they, like him, escape through the inattention permitted by the radio – and the author dies even as the listener tunes. In fact such a relation of attention and inattention will become more important as we proceed, as a marker in the handling of irresolvable confrontations of meaning and intention in the field of entertainment. The crucial transformation for hearing is that, in becoming authored, it also becomes voluntary, and so achieves equality with seeing. For, after all, it is easier to close your eyes than your ears, a discrepancy that was to be worn down by the gramophone and finally resolved by the radio. The modern world, as in Baudelaire, could still appear to be both a stage of civilisation and an act of volition. The instatement of peripheral noise at the heart of modern mass cultures became a fulfilment and a pleasure, if not, in this case, before a technical means of figuration and narrative had evolved to represent it amongst them.

Like talking, seeing and hearing are dialogic. They occur within socially coded – if highly differentiated – conditions that are fissured by the multiplicity of levels of attention. In music, this is a discovery that emerges in the collage-work of Gustav Mahler long before the radio could mime the textures of the social. Ironically it was, in the symphony, a discovery that drew on commercial and mass cultures before it was used by them, figuring them as the nature of peripheral noise. In photography, where the photomontages of the war and the Commune of 1870–1 spring to mind, the snapshot had to be invented before it became technically possible, in order to produce the fetishes and talismans of social and political neurosis. In these images of massacres and orgies, the 'natural' or the 'caught in the act' exist because they are a representation of ideologies. Before the invention of the snapshot camera people knew how to look, as much for the unknown, the unexpected and the instantaneous as for the known and the fixed.[3] The unexpected itself is always one of the codes of difference. This means that the nature of surprise in the learned world is both highly controlled and also equivocal. The unexpected, which is a source of surprise, is a part of the learned world, and the surprise of the unexpected is as much the demonstration of the codings of the normal as is an improving sermon. For it too derives its frisson from and points to the fund of moral imperatives that are the dialogue and condition of perception, and it underlines their coherence and confirms their normative value. So there is nothing necessarily shocking or disjunctive about the unexpected, even though it might well get registered through reactions of approval, disapproval, disgust or sudden pleasure. Contrary to Simmel's belief in the mechanical artificiality of the urban mentality, its pace is no less natural than that of any other form of mental life.

Glancing around, behind curtains, into or out of the glare of a spot-light or flashgun, over a shoulder or even through key-holes – in short the ensemble of glances, looks or peerings that make up seeing – is important for the look of things. Each sightline has its legitimations and its improprieties. These readily reverse the relation of expected and unexpected, depending on the interests, the pleasures, the legalities that they articulate or that set them in action. For example, let's take a very common, everyday transaction: the search for a gallant postcard on a news-stand. The hopeful and skilled rummaging of the collector who knows where to look, or knows that the vendor has a 'special' box: the expected but unpredictable sighting of the same card by a moral guardian – unpredictable, as it must appear to him as a symptom of the state of things, and not as the product of his search: the investigatory peering of the police, or the disabused appraisal of the high-up legal official: these all produce the postcard as an object within a set of social spaces, more or less in the foreground, more on one or another side of the boundaries of infraction, in one way or another fulfilling or failing their expectations. Their sightlines mark out social space and difference in the ways in which they seize on the phenomenom and fashion it, in their interaction with each other.

An exception to this, a self-made exception, is a way of making the unexpected take on the look of the uncharted, by playing around with it and giving it the allure of an achieved experience. This is the self-conscious infraction of the mundane that became a social skill or habit for some groups of Parisian intellectuals of the 1920s in the shape of the Surrealist bluff of inaccessible knowledge. This pre-emptive appropriation of the 'unknown' offers a mirror image of the naiveté of those who are genuinely affronted by the unexpected. Here we find the mixing of innocence with myopia in an undifferentiated world, the projection of the restricted codes of a social position. In Clément Vautel's novel *L'Amour à la parisienne*, the eminent banker is deeply shocked that one of his middle-aged clerks writes *chansons idiotes* under his blotter, and that the clerk's daughter dreams of being a music-hall star. When in the film *Métropolitain* an honest worker goes to a music-hall, not for amusement but to unravel a crime he thinks he has witnessed from the overground Métro, he is lured on a journey of misadventure by a ravishing magician's assistant. She takes him to a high art-deco upper-class night-club, replete with every stereotype of decadent bourgeois pleasures, loose women, svelte men, drugs, sex, alcohol, where his innocence is reduced to dumb-struck astonishment. Seeing really is disbelieving, the starting point for repression. These two examples from popular cultures do suggest how the perception of the unexpected is closely interwoven with the veils of social distance and difference. But at the same time they unveil the absurdity of such innocence as a trope of social comedy. After all it is precisely one of the functions of popular, mass culture to interweave these images, to make them known to each other. But innocence is necessary to accord status to expertise.

For there are professionals of seeing, for whom social difference is no barrier, or who are trained to be unaware of its existence. Amongst them we can number the likes of art historians, collectors of human types, connoisseurs or policemen. For such experts seeing is learned. And, especially, they learn how to see phenomena in isolation from each other, but strictly related to a unifying code, be it an economic or an aesthetic definition of authorship, a set of moral commandments or a legal system. It is the repression of this ordering element that offers such professionals the semblance of neutrality, that lends their skill the look of a disinterested passion. For this they often become moral exemplars in modern, petty bourgeois societies. (Today they appear on quizzes, antique guessing games on television or radio shows, which admit the wide public to their skills.) They exercise with a deliberate eye all those observations and judgements that other folk either don't make at all or do make, but only by chance. A cheap-looking table, at a glance, turns out to be real *Louis-Quinze*. An innocent waif who is not really pathetic but playing innocence for the sex-market. The crucial clue in the *Détective* story.

Where the police detectives and the connoisseurs differ is in the emphasis of values in the unveiling of a fake and the discovery of the true, in the narrative that follows the observation and in its outcome. The police that is, are taught always to see innocence as a ruse, and to expect infraction. Therefore they are the masters of the inverse relation of normality and the unexpected. For them as for connoisseurs, beauty is suspect, but so too is the ordinary or dross. The plenitude of their work is the evocation not of authenticity but of its absence or its *faux-semblant* in the routines of infraction. Jean Genet glosses the implications of this in *Querelle de Brest*:

> For society, the police are what the dream is for everyday activity: what it forbids for itself, polite society, just as soon as it can, it authorises the police to evoke. It is perhaps from this that there comes the mixture of sympathy and disgust that we feel for them. Given the task of drawing off dreams, the police hold them in their filters. (p. 262)

For the connoisseurs, on the contrary, whether of things or of people, the recognition of the authentic is the bottom line of their virtuosity.

However even this distinction can break down where groups of civilians assume police duties in the regulation of daily life, or where connoisseurship itself specialises in the illicit, and either hides or emerges as a social avant garde. Genet himself is an example of the latter, while the moral purity movements of the early 1900s can be taken to exemplify the former. The last decade of the nineteenth century saw the growth of such movements, though of differing political complexions and social objectives.[4] The leading group, the Ligue pour le Relèvement de la Moralité Publique, held its first Congress against Pornography in Bordeaux in 1905. Its proceedings suggest that it was both Catholic and republican. It saw its combat both as the pursuit of the principles of the 'Déclaration des Droits de l'Homme' – a freedom from sexual subjection – and as a return to the habits of their Gallic grandfathers, who dedicated their mistletoe to 'strength, beauty and light'.[5]

While initially a provincial movement against the decadent power of Paris, these groups proliferated everywhere, and had the support and leadership of leading politicians, the Senator Henri Bérenger above all. Inevitably they threw up experts in the discernment of the obscene, the illicit or the abnormal: experts who share a field of interests with a writer like Jean Genet, and, indeed, help to invent it for him. In the first forty years of the century groupings like those against La Licence de la Rue, or of Pères de Famille, threw themselves upon the news-stands and book-shops from the provincial towns deep down in the south-west to the boulevards of Paris. They rummaged them for postcards, for dubious drawings in weekly magazines, for pamphlets on sexual education or contraceptive advice, and invitations to outrage in the personal columns of the papers. (The *petites annonces* were legally categorised as subject to discipline in 1898.)

In the *Proceedings* of 1905 a speaker read out sixteen examples of these *annonces* to shock his audience, and twenty years later they were still a major preoccupation with moralists and police alike. They sifted through the reproductions of salon paintings and volumes of artistic instruction. They reported lurid posters advertising music-hall performances, and the performances themselves, especially where these offered a hint or more than a hint of nudity. They established systems of classification and did research into the market – for example they knew which magazines sold best in which areas. Almost none that were gallant were for sale in Belleville, Ménilmontant and other working-class areas. Expensive art magazines like *Le Nu Artistique* were to be found in Passy, *Frou-Frou* and *La Culotte Rouge* at Batignolles. They passed all this information on to the police, and they demanded suppression under the law.

Their moralism, like that of the lowest grade of police officer, thrives on ignorance, if of a different quality.[6] For reasons either of professional rigour or moral conviction, neither can afford and must, indeed, refuse to accept that the glance is an integrative activity in handling the differentials of city life: a means of registering difference within irreconcilable subjectivities and moral positions, without either the binding commitment or the analysis of the studied look.[7] Like the collage, this refusal gives away the codings of the glance, the fact that its masquerade of informality is the masque of its overdetermination. The moralists, then,

# "VOULEZ-VOUS JOUER AU DÉTECTIVE"

# L'ASSASSINAT
## DU
# TAILLEUR

**1.** *[texte illisible]* ...leur, Fluet ouvrier... tailleur dans un tout... ...travaillant de la... ...situation de leur pa... tron G. Needles lequel... ...vient de vendre sa... propriété de Vernon.

**2.** G. Needles a re- çu une partie de la vente de sa propriété. Il reçoit la visite d'un voisin, de réputation douteuse, qui vient d'y venait commander un complet.

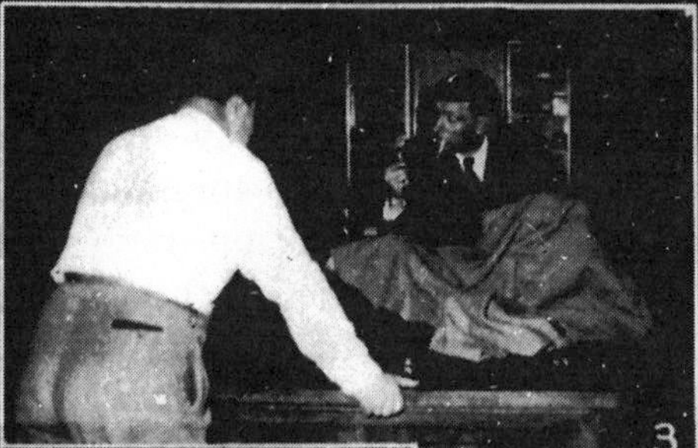

*[texte illisible colonne gauche]*

**3.** *[légende illisible]*

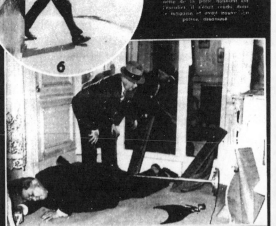

**5.** — Le tailleur est découvert, étendu dans le salon d'essayage, étranglé, au milieu d'un grand désordre : pièces d'étoffes dérangées, fauteuil renversé, l'un crier tombé de la cheminée.

**6.** *[légende illisible]*

**6.** Henri Fluet se rend au commissariat où il déclare que quelques minutes après la fermeture de l'essayage du client dont il avait situé le départ par le son nette de la porte donnant sur l'escalier, il s'était rendu dans le magasin et avait trouvé son patron assassiné.

**7.** — L'inspecteur Piget, après avoir fait préciser par Henri Fluet que le cadavre avait bien été trouvé par lui dans cette position et que personne n'était entré entre dans cette pièce examine scrupuleusement les lieux, ce qui lui permet de désigner le coupable.

## CONCLUSION

Il a suffi de l'examen des lieux, des objets conte- nus dans la pièce et des circonstances du drame pour que l'inspecteur Piget se fasse une conviction.

Vous possédez autant d'éléments que lui pour asseoir la vôtre. Examinez avec soin les photos et lisez avec attention les textes, et vous pourrez dési- gner le coupable.

are unable to see a joke or an ambiguity, and come to relish the whole lexicon of signs as if they have no grammar other than the master-code of their own circle. In whatever place, order or relation to each other they appear, the signs' single meaning can only be the one that is produced through this code's flattening effects. Unlike the moralists, the amateur detective readers of crime fiction or the picture puzzles of *Détective Magazine* live in a far more abstract and sophisticated culture. They at least are freed from the letter of the code by those literary laws that enable entertainment through the ways in which they govern the mystery of the 'locked room', and unlock the content of a clue. If their world is essentially one of grammars, that of the Pères de Famille and the police is made up of signals, each of which unleashes a moral or a legal crisis.

In effect the moralising societies, along with the police, come to make up a significant element of the public for pornography or gallant literature. They must be counted amongst its connoisseurs – even though it obviously penetrates the ranks of middle-class men by other channels than their own surveillance of it, and even though 'hard' pornography is strikingly absent from their discourse. For it is they who find a *louche* magazine placed too high on the news-stand for a child to reach, take it down and announce that it can corrupt the children. They interpose themselves between youth and its corruption, between their woman and the women of the news-stands and the city streets, to save her, so they say, from the burden of recognising her own degradation in the others' image. They outstrip the circuits of the vice squads and, taking the letter of the law for its meaning, subvert the unconscious quality of the day-to-day.

The Pères de Famille, then, are not unlike the vice police, such as the special squads organised by the Prefect of the Var in the years 1927–32 to clear up a long-running sexual scandal in the navy.[8] They both break open the boundaries of the private and the public with shocking and lubricious narratives, infringing the privileged knowledge of the male *flâneur*: 'at 21h.10 the officers themselves penetrated into the men's lavatory (*édicule*) and found the two men in question there together, but in a correct attitude' (F/7/13960).

It would probably have been much easier for these *flics*, out in pursuit of homosexual sailors and their friends, to have glanced what they were looking for over a shoulder than to march straight into the pissoir only to miss the act.

One advantage of the unexpected sighting is that it at least offers the certainty of a 'catching in the act'. Like the photographer in search of the spontaneous, everyday details of human life, the glance dissembles that you know what you're looking for, and for some lightens the burden of your expertise in the deviant or the unexpected. A glanced sighting is just another good job, simply configured by the hazards of social relations, out of their unseemly complexities. The images already held in the mind's eye, too consciously projected on to the scene of desired or supposed guilt, reflect back an excess of knowledge and a complicity. Or if they are not found, their lack becomes a moment of frustration or disappointment. The unexpected, as in turning the pages of a porno-graphic magazine (hastily, on the news-stand), allows the disavowal of the precision of the quest, but allows the bravura of its accomplishment. The snapshot is the paradigm of this dissembling. And, in the end, these flics, like the Pères de Famille, in taking the unexpected as normal, have to identify the moment that they elicit it with the moment of its repress-ion, the elimination of pleasure.

In this the police and the moralists are once again different from the city poet or the connoisseur, whose training leads them as often as not to the same point, but as the point of pleasure. And the poet, in constructing images out of the materials of the glance, gives them permanence and monumentality – qualities that alone can guarantee him possession of himself: a self-possession that achieves itself through the perfect recogni-tion and fixing of the ephemeral. The hidden codings of the glance, then, pull the ephemeral or fleeting into an open and permanent relation with normality, so lending its routines some of the charm of the unexpected. The observations of the city poet produce a *récit*, the account of a life, or of an urban *trajet*, which drafts the outlines of an identity. And this too differs from the accounts of the police, which can only achieve the status of poetry when they transmigrate into crime fiction and fantasy. The police, even if they are the audience of their victim's *récit*, are unlikely to get the same gratification as the public of a *tour de chant*.

More often than not they have to establish guilt through a confession that is an account of something that they haven't seen, recount a tale of which they are not the author. In distinction to the song, the police report is not the event. And to catch a crime 'in flagrante' may result in the task of writing up a report that, however complete its narrative, may be neither an author's *récit* nor an emotional response. When, as happens from time to time, the police are sent into a music-hall on the look-out for obscenity, they are diverted from any pleasure in the spectacle. For them, identity and identification don't overlap as they must for the poet or for the amusement-seeking public. The cocaine- or alcohol-soaked body of a song like this, for example, offers a logistical problem rather than an affective drama. And certainly not the casual melodrama whose repetitive transience is scored in the studied and off-hand modernity of the piano part in Piaf's recording:

le bonheur quotidien
vraiment ne me dit rien
la vertu n'est que faiblesse
je préfère la promesse

des paradis artificiels …
je sais à la porte d'un bar
où j'aurais bu jusqu'à l'extrême,
on aurait porté quelque part
mon corps brulé sur un brancquart
je bois, quand-même.[9]

Yet still in their different ways the evasive and fixing glances of the police and the poet are the armatures for modelling the fetish types of the conjugation of the city and a structure for experience. All the while knowing what lies there, and how to see it, they root behind appearances as the surface of a mystery. Their knowledge intercedes between their audience and the inaccessible, which is seen over their protecting and preventive shoulder.

> For me, this streetlamp marked the entrance to a country subjected to laws of whose code I knew nothing. And to feel myself thus defenceless at the gateway of an astonishing world left me feebly undecided between the certainty that I could, one night, penetrate this mystery of the depths and the fear of some deep and ferocious danger. (Mac Orlan, *Rue Saint-Vincent*, p. 57)

These phrases, with their hint of a half-formed, sexual excitement, echo the impatient and thwarted wait of the Toulon flics, but they are, in contrast, both coy and disingenuous. Of course the poet does march into this other world, and sees just what he wants. Poetic licence guarantees it. In this single daring action he subjugates both his materials and his readers. Without him we would know no more of the city than we would of a remote Amazon tribe without an anthropologist, for in effect it is we who are ignorant of the code. Clearly this is one form of the commonplace, literary authority of the narrator – its presence and narrativity itself are inseparable. So here its significance must lie in its specificity as a deposit of the social formations that it articulates and represents, with the way it makes possible a vicarious slumming.

Mac Orlan evolved a particular form of instantaneous narrative from his *Inflation sentimentale* to his *Poésies documentaires* to give a image to the 'social fantastic' which nods to Baudelaire's *Spleen*, but really resembles the effects of flashlight photography. His writing on photography suggests how vision and revelation are closely identified in the discovery of the urban decor as the assemblage of fragments of material that predicates a meaning for the life that inhabits it. It is a way of seeing, then, that also resembles the metonymising viewpoint of the detective, from the startling intiatives of Poe and Gaboriau to the popular currency of Mac Orlan's own time – the atmosphere-swilling figure of Inspector Maigret, for whom the scene of the crime is in itself a clue to the decisive, all revealing empathy with the criminal.

In the *Poésies documentaires* each brief, fragmentary passage takes the informal, momentary punctum of the snapshot as its intended purpose rather than as its chance effect. This has the strange yet artlessly masked result of ruining the document in honour of the act of its creation. In consequence, the inherited tropes of Zola's Paris, the glistening pavements in the fine rain, the peeling surfaces, the dark light of the gaslamp, or the feeble glare of a ray of sunlight, which in his writing are the signs of economic and social difference and the symptoms of a moral state, are turned into a repetitively fetishised decor. For if in Zola, and the Goncourt brothers, these iterations of the minute details of the material fabric of the city are means of signalling the nature of the social, in Mac Orlan, Carco and very often in the entourage of the Goncourt Academy, their fragmentary perception becomes the means of signalling the unity of the observing subject himself – an essential subject who survives their complexity of appearance and and of meaning. Zola's ethnocentric viewpoint is naturalised into the linguistic apparatus of a literary formation. Metonym slides into the metaphor of the poet's seeing.

It is in large part through this repetitive literary work that the archives for the turn-of-the-century amusement industries are assembled, from the cabaret or music-hall song to the picture postcard and the weekly press. Mac Orlan became a focus for the inter-war art of book illustration, working with a group of draughtsmen and photographers who re-appropriated his methods as a mode of artistic *flânerie* – one that, ironically, now seemed to escape the the photograph in favour of a sentimental, hand-made ontological imagery.

He and Carco formulated the poetic, literary song that Prévert was to elevate to the international hit with 'Feuilles mortes'. This first appeared on the soundtrack of *Les portes de la nuit*, in 1946. Along with a second lyric song, 'Les Enfants qui s'aiment', it is put into the mouths of the film's protagonists, of its street singers and characters, and into the background noise of Paris and the radio-waves. They are heard as phenomena made out of the nature of the city and the minds of its inhabitants. The authors of *Les Portes* slip their own product in among the tropes of city life, the means of whose reproduction they have inherited and developed. *Les Portes* is as near as possible a perfect summation and resurrection of their pre-war narcissism in its mapping of their identity against post-war Paris.

The mirror for this narcissism, its site, is crucially quite specific. 'Les Enfants qui s'aiment' is first heard in the opening sequence under the ironwork stairs of the overground Métro between Stalingrad and Barbès. A crowd of the people listen, entranced by the music, which is sung as a ancient dirge by a street singer, a poor but youngish man. This place is mythic and of the nature of the city, for the stations at La Chapelle and Barbès were where the young *littérateurs* disembarked when they came to find Montmartre for the first time. In the opening radio programme of

# Toujours Vingt ans!
## Francis Carco

*" Mais tu es morte*
*Et ton ombre depuis est toujours à ta porte "*

*" J'attends l'heure où la plus belle*
*Viendra m'ouvrir sa porte et tout bas, tendrement..."*

A UX Noctambules, Francis Carco chante. Le jour qu'il débuta, le « fin diseur » qui lire dans *l'Intransigeant* : « On parle de Francis Carco pour remplacer Léon Hennique à l'Académie Goncourt. »

Le lendemain, *le Figaro* publiait le *Petit Caboulot* (avec la musique) et insinuait que Carco pouvait prendre la place de Bourget chez les quarante... Je gage que M. Varna doit s'en mordre les doigts ! D'ailleurs, le soir de la générale, c'était bien un tour de chant académique.

Sur un strapontin, M. Mario Roustan s'agitait, riait, s'attendrissait, lissait deux mèches folles, applaudissait et serrait les mains de ses voisins. Dans une loge, M. Marcel Prévost essuyait son monocle ; la comtesse de Chambrun — qui fut princesse Murat — tapait sur l'épaule de Pierre Benoit de l'Académie Française, cependant que Roland Dorgelès de l'Académie Goncourt prenait les mesures de son candidat.

Et Carco riait, avec ses petits yeux effilés dans l'expression blême de sa joie.

Il lisait :

*Villon qu'on chercherait céans*
*N'est plus là, ni Verlaine...*

Il ne voyait pas ce qu'il lisait parce qu'on l'avait noyé d'ombre rouge, comme Damia dans la Berceuse Cruelle. Il demanda des lustres ! Et la lumière fut ! Alors, il chanta. Il chante « ses gestes », il lance une main grasse par-dessus l'épaule et qui se jette en avant, avec l'air de dire :

— Ça va, Toto !...

S'il parle d'amour, sa main vient sur son cœur automatiquement. Sous les applaudissements, il fait une révérence de cœur... des miracles. On dirait un Georgel qui s'en fiche, qui n'y croit pas.

Dans un coin, Jef Kessel sourit.

Entre deux chansons, Carco s'adresse aux copains, ceux des Académies :

— Tu te souviens, Roland et toi Pierre, c'est la chanson de Mac-Orlan.

Puis à la dernière strophe, il s'arrête :

— Dernier couplet, annonce-t-il : A la Kipling, comme disait Mac-Orlan.

— C'est très beau, dis-je à Carco, lorsqu'il eut satisfait aux exigences des photographes, mais parlez-moi des dames du temps jadis...

— A Montmartre ?

— Mais non, ici dans le secteur...

— Mais je l'ai récité. En ce temps-là, il y avait le caveau de la rue Saint-André-des-Arts, où j'ai connu Villon ?

— Non.

— Si, c'était un grand type maigre, avec un manteau à martingale de velours qui croyait fermement qu'il était Villon. Personne n'a jamais su son autre nom. Il servait d'entremetteur, de procureur comme on disait au Grand Siècle. Il adorait les poètes !

— Et vous aimez la poésie ?

— Tu parles ! quand j'étais au service, j'étais caporal vaguemestre.

— Ah ! oui.

*« Caporal Carco vous n'êtes*
*Pas un gradé sévère. »*

— Non, je faisais des poèmes sur les plis du colonel en revenant de la poste, puis comme j'avais peur de me faire enguester, je fichais les plis dans ma poche.

Il y a pas mal de messages confidentiels qui ne sont jamais arrivés, pour cause de poésie.

— Mais revenons au quartier !

— Eh bien ! tenez, là où il y a le Gernuy, rue Cujas, il y avait jadis les *Muses*. C'est là que j'ai connu Mecislas Goldberg — le père de Charrier, l'assassin du rapide de Marseille. Le pauvre gosse — oui, monsieur, l'assassin était un pauvre gosse, son Mecislas de père n'avait pas un rotin, il l'élevait dans le tiroir d'une commode... Les *Muses* était un ramassis de gouapes, de fauchés, de crève-la-faim, de receleurs... Dans des boîtes comme ça on lisait mieux son humanité que ses humanités.

Carco roule son manuscrit.

— Ça, dit-il, c'est la *Rose ou Balcon*, vingt pages de poésie pour les amis. Parce qu'il ne faut pas foutre du lyrisme à n'importe qui. Il y a des gens que ça détraque ou sur qui ça n'opère pas.

Un admirateur éperdu qui avait lu la *Bohème et mon Cœur*, vint faire signer son programme.

Et puis, c'est pas tout. Je file. Je travaille à un film et je vais écrire un Bourget intime qu'on n'a pas connu.

Il se lève et me dit en confidence :

— Mon vieux, j'ai vu Bourget pleurer en lisant du Baudelaire, du Laforgue ! Hein, ça vous la coupe !

Poésie ! poésie ! poésie !

**Pierre HUMBOURG.**

*Reportage photographique*
*VOILA-BRODSKY.*

*" Villon qu'on chercherait céans*
*N'est plus là, ni Verlaine..."*

*" J'ai changé ma manière pour elle..."*

*" Et c'est pour ça qu'on t'aime !..."*

a 1948 series entitled *Comme aux bons temps* and advertised as a reflection on the *poètes maudits*, Carco put together much the same sound-plan of Barbès as do Carné and Prévert. The programmes take the form of a sung and spoken dialogue between the author and the actress Jaqueline Morane, who recite his and others' poems, prose works and songs, as they journey around Paris, overhearing its sounds and listening to its noises.

Their purpose is the working of the present as the shadow of Carco's memories, and its value as the present is wholly entailed in its susceptibility to represent his loss.[10] The sound effects are precisely indicated to frame the long *trajet*, yet they could also have been found over twenty years before in a written text, Henri Béraud's *Plan sentimental de Paris* (1927). Here, writing from the fastness of his study, Béraud hears the city and imagines the klaxons of the cars to be horn calls from *Louise* – 'Paris – Paris' – Or these sounds can also be found in the final phone-call of *Faubourg Montmartre*. The script for the programmes begins like this:

> Noise of the crowd coming down the stairs at Barbès. Cries and rolling sounds of taxis – vaguely in the distance, the snuffling of an accordion.
> Morane (*reading*): The Boulevard de Clichy flattened its rows of trees against the low October sky with its crushing clouds ...

The crowd, the metal staircase – the ever-present Métro, the motor vehicles, the half-human, half-mechanical sound of the nasal accordion, the boulevard that flattens its trees against the sky – their ensemble marks the ground that poets patrol, defines an entry to seeing and hearing, a coding of decors as the subject of the discourse. A single space wraps round itself in the radio and the cinema. And out of this variation in repetition, the material of the mass culture industries is reproduced by feeding off these highly authored novelties of the already known.

One way in which this framing is geared to different types of consumption and to multiple subjectivities can be seen in the editioning of ephemera undertaken by Mac Orlan in his book *Images secrètes de Paris* (1922). Here he makes a series of verbal snapshots of twenty typical Parisian brothels or types of prostitution, one for each of the arrondissements. In it the bravura of the connoisseur at the height of his powers of recognition orders the reading of each ensemble and of its details. There exist a simple, textual version of *Images secrètes* and a luxury edition in which each chapter is accompanied by an etching in three states. And through the technology of the print each state decomes a separate moment of the glance. Each different detailing in its difference from the others offers a frustration or a completion, a more or less seeing of a little less or more of the minutiae of flesh, gesture or expression, of what the writer's glance has known. The refusal of precision realises the power of his discriminations. In the snapshot stillness of the figures the fixing of the glanced moment becomes the means of holding or controlling them in a state of accessibility to fantasy, to a fantasy that passes through the abstract connoisseurship of the print as the measure of the author's gift. The overlapping of the visions of the connoisseur and the voyeur in the hunt for significant or illicit details normalises the one into the other their power of purchase over art or bodies.

Such bravura, exercised outside its specific domain of the market for art or *objets de vertu*, takes on a particular power of denotation, a manipulation and purchase of a human other. It gives its type-figures the status of purely formal objects in its discourse, which in turn is structured by connotation, itself extracted by the snapshot-glance from the grammatical structures of the social. And, quite casually, the writer renounces any engagement in this decor that might go beyond moment of his piercing insight. 'A public woman is only worth the decor that surrounds her. In a choice landscape, a public girl may display a literary value ...', but none, for certain, in the 'mediocrity of her bed' (*Images secrètes*, p. 22).

The worldly recognition of the utterly known valorises recognition over its objects. So, in many guidebooks, *récits* on nightlife and mores, such as those of Francis de Miomandre or Gérard Bauër, it is the act of revelation that entrances as much as the scenes of gigolos, lesbian dance-halls or shop-girls in glamorous jewellery shops. The raising of the peep-hole cover is an act of knowing, of bravado, of power, exercised by the seeing, bourgeois man.[11] The readers can make their own snaps over the explorer's shoulder, within the codes he offers, in what amounts to an experiential or affective proxy. Here the narrative convention of the vicarious exceeds its conventionality in the polysemie of its different spaces, be they those of the guidebook or the spotlights of the music-hall. The field of meaning of the music-hall sketch or a weekly magazine are disclosed as elements of this social lexicon, a mode of access to it.

Texts such as Mac Orlan's poetic documentaries and city *trajets* and are best situated in the institutions and careers of the early twentieth century publishing industries, in the overlapping language of guidebooks and in urban tourism. For while they can also be understood as the descendants of the earlier nineteenth-century taxonomic tradition of Parisian *Physiognomies* or *Typologies*, those had more than a passing relation with the contemporary arts of social statistics. Mac Orlan or Carco do not allow themselves either to feed from or to bleed off into quantitative description, in which connoisseurship plays only an undeclared or secondary role. And while even in the 1930s statistics may need to borrow a turn of phrase from city-poetics, their representation of common sites is profoundly incompatible. And where a sociology like that of Louis Chevalier is rooted in the city-poetic, numbers loose all significance.[12]

Yet this writing's investment of the transitory in the subject of the writer himself also strays from the modern beauty of Baudelaire and Guys – that is, from the search for the eternal element in the ephemeral.

Their fixing derives not from the discovery of some essence or eternal character of the modern but from character of their author's materials as his used-up experience. As Mac Orlan put it in *Rue Saint-Vincent*, 'There's not much left of those lights, or those washed out girls, too stupid for a retrospective pity to intervene on their behalf', nor is there any reason to regret the 'stupid little people made up of tarts and young men whose only interest was to go and bawl revolutionary songs or student ditties in the brothels of Paris' (pp. 73–5). Or, in the same mode, insisting on the decor:

> The girls of La Villette, the ones with a black velvet bow around their neck and their hair got up in a beehive, who used to pace the Boulevard, are no longer there to give a special meaning to the shadows of the street ... (*Images secrètes*, p. 7)

Apart from his experience of them these materials have no motion. Locked in the memorial of the author's texts, they do not even have the voice to utter their own transience. Glancing or snapping is a gaze that sees through the gauzes of appearance to discover the omniscience of the identity that is the author's subject. And the distance between its presence and the absence of its figures itself becomes an overarching moral and social judgement, the shape of social space that hides in the techniques of representation:

> Here [in Montparnasse] there was certainly a change from Montmartre, where our girlfriends were sitters and models rather than humble girls devoid of intelligence or imagination ... (Francis Carco, *De Montmartre au quartier latin*, p. 127)

With writers like Mac Orlan, Carco or Warnod, Descaves or Billy, the seizing of ephemera often takes on the character of a compulsion or of a hysteria, which is masked by the apparently normal process of connoisseurship and listing as the natural outcome of the well schooled glance. Judgement hides not only in the distance but in the slippage between the name and the metaphor, a cultivation of descriptive skill in which human material is worth little more than a shop-front or a popular song. The wretched immigrant population of Grenelle, the working-class Kabyles, Mac Orlan places deftly in a social and ethical limbo, in the language of his own fascination with sexual violence:

> In general they love women in a jealous, powerful fashion, made bloodthirsty by a drop too much of spirits ...
> They prowl round the white, soft flesh of the girls of prostitution like wolves that are sick with hunger ...
> Every Saturday Grenelle blossoms in a magnificent, puerile joy, with an Orient of the lower class ... (*Images secrètes*, p. 70)

So there is little presence in these lists of adjectives, this exercise of discrimination but the reflection of the poet's own wandering, his realisation of difference through his movements and his quest for novelty. His insatiable hunger is shifted on to the Tunisian workers. That this movement and choice are underpinned by the most banal of social relations, and that the poet's freedom and man's are each other's paradigm, is recalled at the end of Bauër's *Recensement de l'amour à Paris*, where the old gallant sums up his city tour to his young acolyte:

> I've broached each one of those sectors of Paris where love appears to dwell ... Believe me, you have to be philosophical and take women as they go by, for, whether they might be lustful or cold, tender or dissolute, the principle is to take them. (p. 190)

The activity of the city–author then is dependent upon the contradictory process of fixing the ephemeral with a charm that denies the existence of any such contradiction. The draining of motion out of the materials of ephemerality into the activity of the author can be seen as a transference of their energy through which his subject is substituted for the world or through which the author invents a world of what still seems like a document of reality, or substitutes it for himself, as we have seen with *Les Portes de la nuit*. Indeed the movement from glancing to fixing is implicated in the renewal of the avant garde, which itself shares a form with the market for commodities, with their renewal and redesign. Or, as Benjamin once noted of the development of new skills of consumers' expertise that grew in proportion to their ignorance of the process of production, the transference of change to the subject masks the impulses and forces producing change in the system of commodities and in the forms of city life. At the same time, the redesign, the fresh individualities of the author–subject, now appear to be self-willed.

So the discovery and listing of people and places and the mapping of a topology, and the means of registering their spaces, is itself a register of social difference and movement, of technologies of pleasure and the industries of entertainment, of the modes of intellectual life that evolve around them. Consider too that the condition of being the material of representation is to live out one's life through those restricted codes of which only the subject–author can master the context and turn the key that unlocks the full articulation of the lexicon of memories and feelings. Like this brief glimpse of the life that cannot represent itself:

> les filles qui la nuit s'offrent aux coin des rues
> connaissent de belles histoires,
> qu'elles disent parfois, mêlant aux phrases crues
> les chers souvenirs que gardent leurs mémoires ... (Jean Boyer, 'Les Filles qui la nuit...', 1936)

In its loosely institutional shape the name for this handling of life is *Académie Goncourt*.[13] Loosely, as the Academy neither includes police and music-hall directors, who are, in their own fashion, as responsible for the coding of the city as are its members, nor do the Ten make up more than a handful of the writers of their kind. At the same time the Goncourt type of voice is made up of many conflicting voices. Institutional, because the members of the Académie individually and collectively produce the kinds of work that are the summation of the experience of troping city life, award prizes to such works, review them in the press and elect themselves from like-minded authors. They eat together in the chaste and abstract surroundings of the Restaurant Drouant, while the city jingles in their ears. And they return to their country houses, to the *bouges* or the brothels, to shape their magic of social reality, to write the songs which underpin the music-hall with literary quality, and which laminate their own possession of the varieties of social space with a knowledge of the vulgar.

At a certain stage of their career some may write for a magazine like the weekly *Paris Sex-Appeal*, amongst the most tacky of all its genre – before he became Mac Orlan, Mac Orlan was Sadie Blackeyes, specialist in a literature of lesbian flagellation.[14] Later it will be for Gaston Gallimard that they write, and many – Carco, Mac Orlan, Warnod, Dorgelès did worldly chat-shows and music programmes for the radio both before and after 1945. Through the film scenario, or adaptations of their work – *Quai des Brumes, Hôtel du Nord, Faubourg Montmartre* – they are present in the cinema, amongst the classics of the 1930s and 1940s. Individual careers may last for decades – Carco and Mac Orlan both started publishing well before the First World War, and carried on working across the whole gamut of literary activities until their death in 1958 and 1970. In 1937 Mac Orlan made a series of radio programmes about the sound of the accordion, which carried his poetic documentary over into the mass media. And towards the very end of his working life, in 1965, in the radio interview, *À voix nue*, he was saying the same kinds of things about popular culture as he had in the 1920s. His view that a woman can never be more than an empty sign in poetic discourse, and can have no voice other than that of the poet who makes her speak, above all sing, endured from the 1920s to the 1960s without inflexion. Men like him sat at the centre of a network of definitions of the popular that took a position of formal opposition to and difference from the Académie Française, and if certainly more diverse, it was neither less rigid nor less powerful in its spheres of influence.

The duration of their group membership over the first half of this century is remarkably long and stable and their connections between each other and the types of writer that they favour were incestuously close. Lucien Descaves was a member from the foundation of the Académie, in 1900, under the Goncourt Will, until his death in 1949, and his son Pierre was member in his turn. They were only once seriously disrupted – inevitably, – by the flow of suspicions and accusations that accompanied the intellectual *épuration* after 1944. The status of their masculinity was never up for grabs, even if, as the novelist Michel Tournier puts it, they were monogamous rather than purely misogynist. Before the First World War, a highly qualified woman, the vastly successful romantic novelist Lucie Delarue-Mardrus, was unable to get elected to the Ten. And Colette, the second female member and the first woman to preside over the Académie, had a long wait. She was elected only in 1945, towards the end of her life, when she had become another name for France. Her joke about taking her new status as an 'old boy' as a 'feminine pleasure' would ring less hollow had she not already been so important a member of their circles.[15]

As a figurehead Lucien Descaves was the crucial connection with the social bohemia of the nineteenth century, whose histories he wrote and rewrote in theatre, novel and reportage, reworking its radical sympathy for popular politics through the naturalism of the Goncourt brothers and the urban poetic. In 1888 his novel of military life, *Les sous'offs*, had been unsuccessfully prosecuted for obscenity, but in 1885 he had formed part of the 'Group of Five' writers who had issued a manifesto against Zola for his supposed degeneracy in *La Terre*. In 1905, he appeared to be in sympathy with the Ligue du Relèvement, communicating some post-cards to them that he had found, and which 'confounded the friends to whom I have shown them' (*Proceedings*, p. 39). His work *Philémon* plays off the whole range of literary devices inherited from naturalism, and, at the same time, underwrites their political credentials, their belonging to a radical social history as well as to a perception of city life. Philémon is not only a history of the Commune but the process of the author's enlightenment by its authentic voice, the witness of the working man.

As a trope of authenticity a witness turns up in the lightest of anecdotes and city tales. Eugène Dabit – whose popular origins should on the face of it have equipped him to speak for himself – has recourse to this voice to confirm his observations. He wants to be a city writer, and reported speech is a crucial element of such a writer's power. It's a masquerade of oral witness, a taking rather than a receiving, in which the only usual terrain of equality is the sharing of a masculine identity.[16] Pierre Descaves gives away this game of enlightenment in his memoirs, *Mes Goncourts* (1948). He recalls his childhood in Paris, evenings at his father's house in the Thirteenth Arrondissement, the courtyard cottage with a tree in the wastelands of cheap worker habitation which is described at the beginning of *Philémon*. Every week the Goncourt crowd, the very first Ten, come round to talk, and the house becomes a pool of light generated by the presence of the writers, a light that discloses the dark city around it. In this theatrical and photographic metaphor, Lucien's formula of 1913 is inverted, and the city becomes the projection of a literary consciousness. However in either version the structure of dependence remains intact. It is the ability to reveal that counts.

The thread that runs between the anthology presented by Descaves père, *The Colour of Paris*, a panorama of the city's life and social structures, published in 1910 under the patronage of the Académie, and *Les Grands Jours du premier arrondissement*, published in 1945 under the patronage of the Liberation Committee of the First Arrondissement, and written largely by Goncourt men, is woven both in the private luxury of the editions and in the populism of their texts. The imaging of a being-Parisian that can survive the effects of history, albeit two wars and thirty-five years of radical demographic change, depends upon the continuity of the 'Goncourt' ideal and its embodiment in a stable grouping of men and their succession. In 1913 Paris can as well be typified through the society lady as the *midinette* or the image of the courageous little clerk:

> For she is a Parisienne, too, in the best acceptation of the word, this little *souris* of the railroad-company, the bank or the great store, who earns her living courageously and carries home regularly her meagre wages ... (*Colour of Paris*, pp. 139ff )

It can be problematised, though not defined, through feminism, by those women who:

> do not recognise any mental inferiority on their part, and they laugh to scorn the so-called wisdom of man – a wisdom which has never shown itself in relation to woman, except by a tyranny alternately crafty and brutal: and they consider it absurd in the highest degree when they are advised to reign by the strictly feminine gifts of grace and beauty. (*ibid.* )

In 1945 and even in 1962, in the Académie's collection of essays *Regards sur Paris*, the integrity of this androcentrism can still be guaranteed in the discourses of the gallant – in *Les Grands Jours* by the overlapping of an anecdotal history of the Ancien Régime with memories precisely of the period before the First World War, when the authors – Mac Orlan, Warnod first practised on the tropes elaborated by Descaves or Billy. This compulsion to repetition, even at the fêting of the Liberation, is indicative of yet another passage: a passage through a structure of memorisations that connects the populism of *Les Enfants du Paradis* to the collaborationism of *Paris 1943*.

For 'Goncourts' their disabused yet interested attitude is one that they share with other men of significant social status, such as the high functionaries of the ministry of justice. For if it is true that the policeman and the moralist share the error of mistaking the text of the law for its meaning, this does not seem to be the case with the Parisian *procureurs* or *chefs de bureau*. On the contrary, they find themselves all too often at odds with the moralists, refusing to follow up their leads or to push for a prosecution.

They are constrained by a habit of their outlook that makes them want to see the complexity of the context of a *délit* rather than its content in the letter of the law. So, unlike the moralists and the police, who have their noses buried in their expectations, they can tell at a glance if the obscene is merely gallant, if the magazine really can't find its way into the hands of children, or if the dominant cultural mores are such that a particular text or image represents their real outline rather than their forbidden underside. The archives of the Justice, the 'banal dossiers', reveal a state of mind far removed from the dominant and readily caricatured image of moral repression in the 1920s and 1930s, conventionally represented in the powerful figure of Prefect Chiappe.[17]

These *fonctionnaires* are bombarded with pictures from magazines, postcards and reproductions of salon paintings, novels and sex-instruction manuals, rhymes, advertisements for penis strengtheners or condoms, *annonces* for 'encounters', posters for the music-hall and complaints about nudity on stage, Malthusian propaganda, nudist and artistic journals, volumes of the most learned art history. Many of these form part of those quintessential definitions of French culture as gallant, some come from the world of scholarship or classical culture and others represent a quite serious political nuisance – the left-wing agitation for contraception of the neo-Malthusian groups.[18]

To distinguish between them calls for a labour of definition and re-definition which can be followed across the correspondence of the *procureurs*, the *parquet* and the minister. How to draw a line between a salon nude and its reproduction? Between *Die Frau in der Karikatur* – Eduard Fuchs's great work and *Lady Chatterley's Lover*? Between an amusing double-entendre or a visual pun in an advertisement for cognac and a sex-manual from Germany? Such problems do not even surface for the moralists and the police, though it might register in the contradictions of their discourse. In 1938 the Ligue rebutted an accusation that they were 'attacking the French Genius' as a ruse of the "pornographers" who enjoy a scandalous impunity in our country'. Before the First World War a clever lawyer in the south-west had called their bluff in his defence of an offending newsagent, prosecuted for selling postcards that displayed 'half-nude' women. Surely, he claimed, nude must be worse than half-nude, and is there not plenty of nudity around? But it's not pornography: 'It is Art ... So then, is immorality promised to artists and to no one else? It were as if you told me that only pretty women had the right to be virtuous! [laughs]' (BB/18/6168).

But for the *fonctionnaires* the stability and movement of the culture are more important. They have to decide how things get to be seen, where, from what angle, with what mode of access. A music-hall poster in black and white might be no more than an invitation to legitimate pleasure for the gallant male adult – while in two lurid colours it might outrage good manners. The display of the news-stand with its open and sealed items hung at different heights, and ordered by their price and appearance, is itself a version of the social space of the city, of its day-to-day circulations and crossing tracks of physical proximity and social distance. Circulations whose rules the Pères de Famille and the Ligue refuse to obey. The same lawyer, realising that this was a strong point in favour of his client, had gone on to point out that the defendant had in fact obeyed the rules of social propriety: 'M. J*** had his postcards in a box, carefully wrapped up. At the theatre everyone can get in without knowing what they'll hear' (ibid.).

All of this confronts the officials with two weighty problems in the application of the law. One is the complexity of the industries of pleasure and their continuous multiplication and growth between 1900 and 1940; the other is the nature of their own pleasure in the city. The stages of this development of new means of diffusion is uneven and complex; early on, the colour postcard, the gramophone, the cinema. And then from the cinema to the radio and the second, belated take-off gramophone that accompanies it at the end of the 1920s. Dealing with 'obscene' radio or gramophone records was a new problem (BB/18/6172). And all along this is doubled up by the explosion of specialist magazines and the increased variety of places of entertainment, the invention of pin-ball and then electric pin-ball machines, of one-armed-bandits and juke-boxes and promotional games for goods, the increasing popularity of horse races and betting, the use of middle-class *cercles* and billiard halls as covers for unregulated betting or other pleasures, and the mapping of all these and other phenomena on to each other in fiction and daily life alike. Elaborate decisions had to be taken over profoundly trivial matters. A proud café owner in 1936 installed an up-to-date pin-ball game *cum* promotional device, the 'Jeu Tol-Boul' (BB/18/6128). He set it so the player could accumulate free turns by making high scores. But to get back more than you lay out, however small the sum, was to gamble, and gambling was forbidden in cafés. Hours of effort, sending a policeman out to get a precise description of the thing in question, of the exercise of judicial skill over the philosophy of gambling, and the exchange of letters between departments were needed to decide that one 'free turn' and only one, could be seen as conforming with the law. The law really did have to be remade from day to day, even if nothing changed at all as far as the essential justness, integrity and wisdom of its drafting were concerned. If doubt were admitted, then each act of its implementation became an ethical debate around the relation of the everyday to the codes of social values.

The law of 1882 controlling the civil and criminal infractions of outrage to public decency and obscenity provided a baseline and a framework of moral and legislative truth. At regular intervals it had to be rejigged, with major revisions, pressed for by the moral groupings, in 1898 and 1908.[19] It cast its net wider and wider through decriminalising an ever-increasing number of potential offences that were to be dealt with through the *justice correctionnelle*, but preserved its rigour for the most serious crimes that were still to pass through a trial by jury. While a contentious development, then, this can be seen to reflect as much the exponential growth of the urban pleasure markets that provided the terrain of infraction, and the need to cope with it through administrative suppleness, as it does the interests of the moralists. But more than that, the changes to the law represent how the overall social transformation of entertainment entailed the emergence of mores that could less and less convincingly be seen as criminal, yet which must, none the less, be accounted for in a language of both bureaucratic convenience and moral probity. After all the crime surrounding a new game might itself become a legitimate spectacle – in the film *L'Entraîneuse* (1938) a magnificent American-style brawl breaks out over a protection racket run round some pin-ball machines. The problem for the *procureurs*, then, is that the wider the field of legitimate pleasure becomes, the more loosely that the mores of the day open up, the more the Pères de Famille and policemen on the beat bombard them with materials that infract the letter of the law.

In opening up possiblities of offence that social change is tending to deny, the law confronts the *fonctionnaires* with the modalities of their own pleasure. This is their other unspoken problem, which brings them under the constant criticism of the moral groups. These no longer believe that the *parquet* itself is prepared to take the law at its face value. At the first conference in 1905, M. L. Comte, the general secretary of the Ligue, made what proved to be an ill-timed joke in his final address. Replying to those who doubted that pornography could be defined, he made the famous declaration:

> Well then, my dear fellow-citizen, let all that be declared pornography which is of a nature to make blush a public prosecutor of the Republic. (*Premier Congrès*, p. 293)

But they were to come to see the Parisian court as the very instrument of the toleration of decadence and vice. They could hardly believe the prosecutions or 'corrections' that never took place. They saw only decisions deferred, and refusals to accept provincial cases as precedents for Paris: 'it is certain that the Parisian *Parquet* has let numerous, offensive illustrated journals get through without prosecuting them, but which have been prosecuted by the provincial courts' (BB/18/6172). The ministry's most obvious excuse, and a reasonable one at that, 'We can't prosecute all these publications every month', amazed them. For *their* rooting around was quite well organised, and took place on a national scale. (At an International Conference in Paris in 1908 the French mustered forty-two organisations against one from England.)

From their own point of view they had a point. In 1922 public opinion, in the form of a presidential decision, had vindicated them in a manner that was as remarkable as it was unprecedented. Victor Margueritte, one of the great social novelists of his age, had been struck from the Légion d'Honneur following the publication of his scandalous tale of a liberated woman, *La Garçonne*. The parliamentary and mass pressures for the raising of morals seemed at last to be crowned with a national triumph. Alas, all, it must have seemed, to no effect. As far as the *fonctionnaires* were concerned this was not to be the start of a new and rigorous regime.

In 1920 the minister of the interior drafted a letter to the Garde des Sceaux – there can be no higher level of exchange – about a police report of the showing of pornographic films in a *maison close* in Marseille (BB/18/6172). In his reply, the minister is quite clear. *Maisons de tolérance* are what they are called for a very good reason. Officially they do not exist. They ward off a greater vice with a lesser one. You can't prosecute a film shown at a place that doesn't exist, and if you were to do so it would open up a host of sempiternally irresolvable social questions. And what about the tax status of a *maison*, and the question of any rights due on the films? No, he concludes, if the films are imported, then seize them as an 'administrative' measure under the international convention of 1910. If not, do nothing, but above all, nothing.

In the case of Fuchs's work, the letter of the law won the day. After several appeals around the technicalities of distribution the *Cour de Cassation* took it off the market. *Lady Chatterley* got a smoother ride. The *procureur* clearly liked it quite a lot, and even if the translator had used trivial words to render the English, they were anyway 'French words known to everyone, currently in use in the faubourgs as in the *corps de garde*'. To turn down the municipal councillor who had lodged the complaint on the grounds that it was just fine to swear like a trooper was a nice turn in the relation of the popular to elite culture. And he went on, 'I don't want to argue that it is altogether free from obscenity or insult to good manners.'

> but one must be careful not to give, in this respect, over absolute affirmations. As far as it goes, it is sufficient to evoke certain works of sculpture and principally painting that are displayed in great numbers, to all eyes, in public places … (BB/18/6175, dossier 44.Bl.387)

Arguing that the law must represent the spirit of its age he quoted *all* the reviews *Lady Chatterley* had received in the Parisian press. All, with only one exception, praised it. All were written by that certain class of men, of whom even André Billy – in *Femme de France* – was not the most distinguished of the roster. The one exception was a young Robert

Brasillach, who found the novel 'boring'. Here the deliberations of the *procureurs* and the *parquet* in their own way read like those Goncourt texts that grant a permission to enter a world that is beyond control. And that, in this instance, is anyway not as it was before, and will never be this way again:

> In literature, in painting, in sculpture, in music, manners are no longer such as reigned in the period preceding the last war, for example ... tomorrow everything will have changed again ... (*ibid.*)

Nor from the 1920s onwards had these functionaries much difficulty in bringing the same arguments to bear on the music-hall and its new fashion for nudity. A risqué-version of *Après-midi d'un faune*, presented at the Palace in 1920, got off on the grounds that no one could really tell where art ended and where the 'stirring up of the public to lascivious ideas' began (BB/18/6172). Least of all the three police officers sent out to inspect it, who had all given in different reports. One had said it was obscene, and noted gestures akin to the wiping of a penis after intercourse. Another said he had seen it before, but in this version the lighting gave it too lurid an air. And the third said only that it was more fit for a fairground than a music-hall. (The Ligue, needless to say, wanted fairgrounds to be patrolled as well.) The affair took years to deal with, the promoter Oskar Dufrenne getting exculpation in 1924. (Eight years later he was to die murdered, by a sailor–lover, it was rumoured.) Likewise in 1924 an official made a margin note in a police report to 'check up on the nudity' in a performance of *Lysistrata*. A further note reads 'daring, but not obscene'.

In 1934 a distinguished senator dumped publicity and reviews for the two shows at the Concert Mayol, *Le Pays des femmes nues* and *Naked Adolescents*, with the police, where they languished, never to be dealt with (BB/18/6173). Indeed ignoring this stuff was a long-learned skill. Even before and during the First World War there was a certain embarrassment at the enthusiasm of the moralists. Of some unfolding postcards that look like scenes of imminent intercourse when closed, but reveal domestic scenes when open, the *procureur* wrote to the Garde des Sceaux:

> are they really obscene? Unfolded they present a certain inconvenience. Opened out, they are more or less irreproachable, and, if I might say so, don't fulfil their promise. (BB/18/6172, 1916)

What would fulfilment have been? Possibly the front page cartoon on one number of the 'private' magazine *Amour*, 'Vengeance d'un apache'. This showed a *mauvais garçon* seated on a park bench, buggering a police officer whom he has tied face against a tree, while his girl pees on the victim's feet. Or perhaps its more elaborately lithographed scenes of priestly orgies and its finer reproductions of some of the more overtly erotic paintings by Boucher. But what of the fine illustrated editions of French classics, from Diderot to Verlaine? Their failure to deliver could also be ironically compared to the moralists' own inability to discourse precisely on the unspeakable, or the confusion of a sexual expert in the face of the object of his study:

> In this study which, as I am well aware, demands courage, I will be as discreet as possible, and, even at the expense of my case, I will avoid a mass of examples that would be painful for me to lay before you. (*Problèmes de sexualité*, 1937, p. 177)

In addition, the *fonctionnaires* had every reason to be cynical about the respectable middle classes. Were they not keeping a watch on their *Cercles*, that pre-eminent social form of the bourgeoisie, to check that they were only all that they seemed? Even in Passy there was a hint of betting, of bridge parties and tea-dances where the stakes and entertainments were not strictly legal (BB/18/6126). No, the authorities opined. It was up to heads of families to take their own precautions to stop children from getting their hands on the wrong kind of reading, such as some German nude studies, on sale in 1930, which could hardly be seen as obscene: 'in terms that we understand today ... even the most scrupulous examination fails to reveal that the editors might have criminal intentions in offering them to the public' (BB/18/6175). It might be reasonable to ban the occasional issue of *Détective*, *Paris-Sourire*, *Frou-Frou* or some other magazine from open display on the news-stands, but that was already an administrative monstrosity. The *Chatterley* file finished with this bitter little aside:

> M. XXX affirmed that 'The Devil alone knows where pornography begins and where it ends. At one time or another, the magistrates try to find out, but regularly they are in error.'

The curious turn in things is this: that if the *procureur* of Paris had recourse to Billy to justify the official attitude to *Lady Chatterley*, Billy was much more circumspect. His book reviews in *Femme de France* are a rather special intervention. For example, reading a biography of the famous seventeenth-century courtesan Ninon de l'Enclos, by Jacques Dyssord (January 1937), he extols her disinterested sexual freedom at the expense of 'our modern feminists'. Like the moralists, he stands between his readers and a potentially negative image of woman. The difference between Billy and the Ligue or the Pères is that he modulates access to the erotic rather than represses it. He attenuates the thrill of vision, the sight of the forbidden women with whom lies the risk of misrecognition. It is gained over his shoulder, so as to speak – as with the narrator in Gérard Bauër's *Recensement de l'amour à Paris* who takes his aristocratic lady companion to a low dive and shows her the forbidden of both sexes. She trembles at the sight of the wildlife, but she also senses some utopia of unaffected sexuality. She looks at a *voyou* – 'Would he hurt me?' she asks, from the safety of her escort's arm.

Systematic in its severity, the Ligue excluded this viewpoint. The 1938 programmatic pamphlet by Daniel Parker was very clear about the crucial issue with pornography, that it was a problem that linked street-life to the wider field of social training. Parker echoed what the Senator Bérenger had concluded thirty years before, 'the way in which the street teaches immorality is one of the most fearful anti-social machinations of our time':

> The reading of these publications doesn't only stop adolescents reading! IT DRAGS THEM INTO THE LOSS OF RESPECT FOR THE DIGNITY OF WOMAN, who becomes in their eyes nothing more than an object of gross pleasure, because all true love is banished ... (BB/18/6173)

Yet, if the principal figure in this degradation was the nude woman, then it is all the more important to know that many of the magazines that crop up in the Ligue's blacklists after 1919, *Beauté, Paris-Plaisirs, Pages Folles* were in fact addressed to women. They typically include pages of letters from 'nos lectrices', artistic nudes, adventure tales and picture stories of female sexual pleasure, advertisements for 'male' contraceptives – condoms – which, as protectives, were not as such illegal. These magazines would seem to aim at a lower middle-class public of single women, women not dependent on men, or lesbians. In sum, the lower ends of the social strata of 'feminists' caricatured in *The Colour of Paris* twenty years before. This rising class had risen. The bank clerk's wife in Vautel's *Amour à la parisienne* belongs to it. Used to independent sexual pleasure during the war, now, years after her respectable marriage, she frequents a brothel for her tea-time entertainment. Vautel was editor of *Sourire*.

Even with the finely crafted gallant writers, like Vautel or Dekobra, the tone of their work is very different from that of *Chéri* or a small, luxury edition volume of 1931, *Conseils à l'homme nu*, by M.-F. d'Yverchen, where the woman's gaze is turned on man. Colette's images of Chéri insist on a female pleasure other than that of narcissism, and a control of social space which also suggests a complex formation of a new subject – one that is not easily available to a mass public, and may be no more than a line of fracture in the perception of pleasure. D'Yverchen expresses it like this, before she goes on to recommend for men beauty treatments like body shaving – depending, of course, on the taste of their women:

> If, as M. Roger Allard has said, the naked woman is a site that men have in common, then for us women the naked man is in the process of becoming the same ...
>
> Gone is the the idea of us as game for these gentlemen, for them to feather, prepare and eat according to their fantasies ... we have become doctors, lawyers ... (p. 8ff.)

CONSEILS A L'HOMME NU

férence entre les hommes et les
femmes. J'en avais cherché le pour-

Though this is, of course, an ambivalent strategy, as we can see in *Un Lupanar aux hommes*, a work by Le Nismois, one of the most prolific pornographers of the late nineteenth and early twentieth centuries.[20] Here the spread of male beauty offered to the wealthy women clients of the *lupanar* starts out as a witty inversion of the conventions of the sex markets, and a refutation of *bérengisme* – the prejudices he attributes to the Senator Bérenger. Women can at last free their hearts by freeing their bodies for perfect pleasure, enjoy sex and read the works of Le Nismois or Fuckwell in the elegantly appointed library. Their lives will be happier and more moral, even if they must sacrifice the feelings of the young men who do tend to fall in love with them. One of these women, Luce, explains the matter to the 'stud' Alexis who wants only to give her the 'whole of my being':

> I can love no man with a true love. I have a voluptuous temperament that you satisfy marvellously. Of my heart I give you all that I can, and I happily abandon you my body for your pleasure and for mine. (p. 12)

But Le Nismois is enslaved to the conventions of pornography and the book soon enough becomes a paean to male sexual prowess and a rerun of the classic, voyeuristic fantasy of lesbian seductions. In *Pages Folles* or *Beauté* too, things are rather more simple. A young woman might tease two men on a local train, before going off with the handsome driver, or an adventuress badly treated by a pirate in the South Seas puts a bullet through him when pleasure turns into risk. The beach and the beauty parlour provide ready images of a conventionally idealised self, an unsophisticated dream. But one that, while it cannot readily be framed by the moral conventions of the Ligue, is all too readily available on the news-stands as a challenging convention of sexual diversity. At the same time as the illustrations to the stories of *Pages Folles* skilfully combine the artistic nude with conventional flirtatiousness and daring and an occasional hint of sadism, the magazines almost certainly also opened up an easily available 'pornography' to men.

This meant that while 'pornography', in the Ligue's designation, had really changed its address from before the war, its members were not constrained to recognise the implications of the shift. They were able to stick to their pre-war analysis that, while the naked woman was the subject of pornography, adolescent males, idlers and travellers made up its public. Women were to be protected from its image of them, not simply from consuming it. On the contrary it was assumed that even prostitutes did not enjoy pornography. At the 1905 Congress M. Lecomte declared:

> She [the common prostitute] prefers an honest novel, one of those novels full of killing and rape, without a doubt, but where virtue is always rewarded ... one does find obscene postcards and engravings amongst these drudges of love, but they are nothing but instruments of work ... (p. 51)

Ironically, if this reading of the magazines is correct, then it does suggest that the associations were right to go for them rather than for more unspeakable, 'hard-core' materials. For they open up a world of pleasure and self-gratification for women, as loosely free from their smokescreen as from the staying and protective hand of a Billy. And that precisely at the interface of male power with the most banal form of men's fantasies.

The glance on the city is structured through gender as well as by it. That is, both by the relative social positions of men and women of different status and by the social and sexual imaginary of the generally male preserves of the journalistic and literary institutions, the state offices of law and justice, and the cohorts of moralising groups. But if the identity of 'man' coincides with the whole field of the generation of imaginings in this way, then the relation of subject and object in the culture is utterly polymorphous. Expertise and sex, for one example, coincide unevenly in the relation of author and reader – and belief in their equivalence depends upon accepting the common confusion of experience with sexual experiences. Man and woman have to look across the same shoulder, without any guarantee of the right degree of complicity or distance. In the passage from Bauër that I have just cited, the narrator gently reproaches his companion for her longing for the voyou, but even as he does so reveals more than a hint of his own. The voyou and the narrator clearly share a freedom, but maybe the narrator and his companion share a desire.

So each sex is as classed as classes are sexed, and class and sex often stand in for each other in relations of power and desire. One of the problems that the Ligue had with the magazines, but which such men could only articulate naively as one of the nude, must have been the opening up of their ranks to a type of literature that, while it was uneducated, was complex in its address. Or, too, the knowledge that there existed a kind of woman who could enjoy or even live out this literature for her own undegraded satisfaction. The *débâcle* over Victor Margueritte's *La Garçonne* suggested as much and, as I have noted, the Ligue counted on this success to legitimate further prosecutions of gallant literature, stepping up their pressure on the *parquet* after 1922.

*La Garçonne* indeed is a key example of these complications in a way that makes it form a pendant to its twin contemporaries, Colette's *Chéri* and *Fin de Chéri*. If Colette, through the figures of Léa, Chéri's lover, and his mother Mme Peloux, was to construct an informed female sexual gaze, together with a social and financial skill that removed the traditional economic need for men, she did so out of successful courtesans. However, the modern, young, bourgeois woman of impeccable family, who finds her independence and eventually love, was the literary invention of a man: a vastly successful social novelist from a tradition related to that of the Goncourts, but more consistently militant in his radical political and social objectives, in which the liberation of woman held an important place.[21] Margueritte confected his heroine, Monique Lerbier, out of a tradition of political feminism and out of male sexual fears and fantasies of uncontrolled female sexuality of the kind we find in Le Nismois. When, at the beginning of the novel, Monique discovers that her fiancé is unfaithful to her, to revenge herself, and without pleasure or desire, she gives herself to a complete stranger: 'She had no shame, no remorse. The act she had accomplished was logical and just' (p. 86). Afterwards, she recounts the event to her mother, and finds that she has once more to confront the undiluted hypocrisy of the bourgeoisie to which she belongs:

Mme Lerbier, to Monique – If you keep quiet, the harm can be undone.
Oh, maman!
What? Scruples for Lucien? The man who tricked you the first? You've had your vengeance ... aren't you satisfied? Tell yourself this, my little one, once and for all. In this world, and, in consequence, in this life, what matters is less what you do than what you say – above all, what you say.
Maman! Maman! (p. 99)

Again, from its viewpoint, the Ligue was on the right track. Mme

Lerbier seems to share more than a little of the opportunism of the *procureur*. But in turning her back on her mother's advice and after scandalising Lucien, who only wants to know who the man was, Monique sets out for a feminist world, for a life as a successful stage designer in Paris, for a life of sexual adventure in every possible form and combination. The scenes that follow, before she finds the love of a man who is her equal, would fill volumes of *Pages Folles* with exotic picture stories. Monique's refusal of a middle-class world of double standards unleashes an exponential explosion of the narratives of pleasure: an outcome that gives reason in their different ways to the *procureur* and to the Ligue alike. The outcome that is the worst imaginable. As Paul Bureau, speaking from a moralist position, had pointed out, feminism could raise women's status, but also 'she might be promoted to the enjoyment of liberties and rights until then reserved for the "chief"'. 'But', as the *procureur* lamented, 'in these times', nothing can stop it.

If the terrains of social freedom and sexual fantasy are so wholly mapped on to each other, then the relation of identity and knowledge is fraught with its own undoing. Each new phenomenon has to be brought into coherence with the known as well as with each other discovery, imaged within a counterpoint of different and contradictory uses and understandings. The nude woman on the stage of the Folies is as ready to undo the saint in the Louvre as the saint is to redeem the stripper. This discussion even appears in a little, anonymous booklet, *Nuits d'orgie*, about a provincial man up for good times in the big city. He progresses from the classical beauties of the Louvre to a charming session with two girls in an hotel, losing en route his companion, a homosexual priest. As Kiki de Montparnasse, the mythical, everyman's model of the artistic bohemia of the 1920s and 1930s was reputed to have joked, 'I'll become a museum girl, like the Mona Lisa.' The pretentious, socially mobile *pute* gets to the top, as a masterpiece if not as a countess. The gap between the stylishly sleazy image of Kiki in a Kertesz photograph and the aspiration to the immortality of the art museum could not be wider. While Monique Lerbier might have fallen on one side of that imperceptible middle road, a fallen woman rose on the other in Mistinguett's review of 1931, *Paris qui brille*, the shimmering image of the boy-hunting *grande dame* singing 'Dans les bouges la nuit'. Here, Bauër's companion not only gets the boy but gets addicted to him, and all that for the pleasure of no less a company than the nightly tourists at the Casino de Paris.

> Près des mauvais garçons
> Mon coeur est en délire,
> Un air d'accordéon
> Et mon être chavire ...
> Une Java violente ...
> Me fait ... (sung to a sinuous waltz)

If there is to be a space left for harmony, for some cohesion, then it is to be discovered in the way that the lists are made over into grammars, the grammars of conjugation and montage, of viewpoint and sightline, seen, for instance, in the pool of the spotlight on the stage, or of the view over the reporter's shoulder in *Détective Magazine*.

This image can be seen as the beginning of a trail that sets out from the codings of the glance, hers and ours alike, and which ends by revealing them as narrativity. As in the murder scene of the *Little Old Man of Batignolles* the reader can take it in, here with a glance so commonplace that the snap provides the basis for collusion with the author. This elegant disavowal of the author's expertise lures the reader into the unequal collaboration that is the stratagem of the detective story. *Détective Magazine* excels at this empowerment of the reader's glance to follow and find out with a fresh act of cognition.

In *Détective* the unlimited susceptibility of city life to lexical inflection runs wild, exhausting the possiblities of montage as a means of conjugating a plethora of differences. The page montage of *Détective* records both the omnipresence of the freelance enquirer and the spontaneity of his glance. In the foreground it raises the barrier of his shoulder, and the reader peeps over it as he shifts around his networks. His activity is basic, one of following tracks, as you might in a scouting book where every sign has its prescribed meanings. Telling you who has gone before you, turning on and off the lights. As Mac Orlan noted of Atget, he uses light purely as a technique of seeing in the dark, and in *Détective* the snap or candid shot not only is a lighting up of the unseen, but also provides a metaphor for its invisibility in the transience of its flash. The montage, on the other hand, provides the means of instating the glance in the system of the known, which has anyway directed it, finding not only one but a number of positions for it in the criss-crossing mnemonics of city life. The montage allows for the shocking as unexpected, forgetting its predicatibility, yet at the same time, in fulfilling the conjugation of the mnemonics, makes shock read like the simplest of common sense.[22]

However the pages of *Détective* have a certain sophistication that makes them stand in contrast to the imagery of the photographic 'masters'. For they realise and accept that no single image can contain a sufficiency of mnemonic meaning without slipping into a maudlin and sentimental view of city life; that looking up never includes enough to be going by, unless you look up and what you see has already been completed by its relation to other icons of cultural value. In some of Doisneau's or Cartier-Bresson's most favoured images, the moment is supported by the idea of the 'gamin de Paris', by the race-type of the poor immigrant (which Bresson shares with Mac Orlan's brothel in Grenelle), or simply by the idea of the Parisian rain or the accordion/people connotation.

Nº 457 — Jeudi 29 Juillet 1937 — 1 fr. 50

# DÉTECTIVE

commence
cette semaine

## LES MEMOIRES D'UN PLACEUR

Ce qui n'a jamais été dit

# SUR LA PROSTITUTION

*Détective*, on the contrary, often has to tear things apart to put them together again. It visibly works the lexicon, whereas a Brassaï in his images of 'Paris by Night' already, thanks to Manet, glances with the worldliness of art. Francis Carco, in his volume *L'Envoûtement de Paris* (1938), uses Christian-Jacques's photographs to confirm each insight and image of his text, as if it were the writing that is the image and the image its caption. In *Détective* we find the frenzied re- rendering of mnemonic for a fickle and and greedy market-place. There the buyer must be lured into active complicity, rather than relied on for the habitual and common knowledge of the equal. And there too the same authors, Mac Orlan, Carco, Montarron, Danjou, ply their craft in another milieu, stepping easily through the different types of literature and public. Ironically, this gives their work a new twist, an almost ingenuous encounter with the expressive vocabularies and techniques of high modernity.

It is not difficult to work out the middles and the ends of the reportages and photo-montages of *Détective*, though the photo-clue puzzles – some of them were set by Simenon are sufficiently elliptical to cause a moment for reflection.[23] After all, it was not a magazine of the literary avant garde – though it was in some ways an important institution of literary bohemia. It provided a site for the intersection of different points in the career of the city poet or novelist, the international reporter, the adventurer and the professional moralist, which it maps on to a market for the literature of excitement, of prurience and of shock. But the means that it finds to do this turn out to be closer to a principle of aesthetic modernity and to the representation of the modern as a system of displaced orders and anarchies, worked through the open constitution of narrative and the revelation of its possible grammars, than does the fraudulent mastery of the informal in the 'decisive moment' of a Bresson or in Kertesz. It takes off from the usual collections of places and types, but goes on to reorganise them into ever more dramatic conflict constructed through the codes of the serial novel and the documentary reportage. Crime becomes, as it were, a necessary condition of city life and its social relations, rather than their symptom.

If Atget's photographs come to look like the scene of a crime this is a result of the habit of remembering a place through the crimes that have occurred there: of the ways in which criminality comes to be figured through its association with place: and of the development of police photography itself. Crime is a relationship of social classes, strata and sexes, whose places interrelate through it as only one of many mediations that include tourism, pleasure and entertainments. Its revelation permits the glancing of an indefinitely modulated range of types and typographies of difference, a modulation that is itself a source of narrative. And in the place of its greatest frequency, which is not the street or the living room or the factory but crime fiction itself, it is a powerful vector of social space, in the sites of its occurrence, in the psychological topographies of known and unknown, admissible and inadmissible, desire and impulse. To represent crime, in the first place it is necessary to have a space and to configure it, like the corner of the Rue Tournefort and the Rue Lhomond in *Détective*'s reportage on the suspected murder of the young baker's boy Léon Lijour – whose lover, as it happens, was a young dancer performing in *Au Pays des femmes nues*.

Here, you might say, a crime begins to look like the scene of an Atget. The scene is first drained of people. The streetlights, burning the emulsion, carve out a space for something to take place. Mouffetard has the the worst connotations of Parisian crime, antonym to the innocence of provincial life. The twist of the montage from the equivocal illumination and concealing shadows of the street to the revealing glare of the ceiling lamp is the artifice that demonstrates the formal elements of the narrative and their moral weightings, but neither its truth nor outcome. The gap between the sensible and coherent speculations of the text and the overcoded evidences of the image strains the relation of the carefully gathered information and the processes of its representation, offering a space for the reader that is as fresh as the opening of the eyes and as entrapped as the ligamented corpse. Here the simulation of shock is a condition of city life, not shock itself, which is merely an incidental routine of the pavement.

It does not make much sense to refer *Détective* to a simple history of popular horror, charnel house novels and flysheets on crime and executions, for it writes one spectacle against another in the language of the city mnemonic. Thus the reports on the great political–criminal affairs of the moment, of the Stavisky affair, the trade of the Corsican drug gangs, the terrorist bombings of the right-wing CSARS or the persecutions of Nazi Germany, are linked through those same narrative grammars that also give a form to everyday life as the narrative basis of the extraordinary and the spectacular. The trajectories through cities and the suburbs, between the quartiers and social echelons, between the champagne and the cheap red wine, the Metropolis and the colonies, stabilise the spectacle as a condition of normality.[24]

In the sophistication of the ways in which its methods of representation and its narrative referents interchange and replace each other *Détective* is inevitably much more than a report on the city. For if the space that it creates with its montage of so many glances is made up of the interrelatedness of different kinds of history and political and social presents, then such narratives of crime or vice are as much a part of the coming to know and to handle the urban as are health statistics, grand plans for worker housing or the projections of ideal garden cities on to its teeming archaeologies. The city slips between the roles of being a heuristic tautology explaining that life and itself are like each other and that of a reason for deliberated action and social change. Although *Détective* frequently berates the administration of the law and justice and offers its own services to improve them, its problems differ from those of the *parquet* in that it has nothing to administer. In this way it stands in the same kind of relation to the administration as do the Pères de Famille, though it proceeds through exposure and they through concealment. Again like the Pères, the magazine makes everyone into police, but by employing the city author it also invites them to take pleasure in the look that reveals and censures.

In its pages the parts of the montages and the individual snapshots always lead towards something else, they always mark the beginning of a trail, like the clues at the scene of a crime: but the homology is not so direct. Rather the scene of the crime is like something else, like other means of narrative mappings, like the magazine itself, a point of confluence. The scene of a crime is not really like an Atget, both because Atget's images take care to leave few clues and because the following of trails (like scouting) can never begin with an irony. This is the key to the pomposity that dogs the Surrealist (re-)discovery of the urban marvellous, the Passage des Princes in Aragon's *Paysan de Paris*, his hysterical reading of the scraps and paper of the *déchets* of daily life for a significance that transcends the transience of their use, like André Breton scouring the fleamarkets in his 'taciturn and prodigiously attentive walks' and probably finding no more than the couturier Balmain in search of a rare colour of silk.[25] In investing the end of useful life – that is the character of any object of daily consumption – with psychic value, the Surrealist or the city author forgets to ironise the transience of his own subject. Rather he endows it with the romantic aura of finding its permanence in what has been thrown away. The simile is too trite. The revealing glance, the chance discovery, actually become the masquerade for fear of the aleatoric.

In a more banal rhetoric of the *délit* and justice the photo can itself become a crime, like the dramatic image that appeared on a front cover of *Détective* in 1934 (BB/18/6492). It showed a rag-dressed youth labouring on some terrible punishment of a mechanical tool, over the dramatic caption that read 'THE EXPLOITATION OF YOUNG PRISONERS IN BACK-BREAKING LABOUR'. The mother of the young lad happened to see the cover, for the magazine's success ensured its visibility on the news-stands. She appeared before the police and complained. He was no delinquent. He was a good boy and he had been photographed at his normal work. Someone had filched his image and exploited it to his detriment and their advantage. The police debated the case with the Justice, the question of the right to one's own image, the point at which this is intentionally or unintentionally renounced in the public place, the damage done to the prison's reputation, and so on. They concluded that this poor, widowed mother had a good case. The magazine had lied. Only

she lacked the financial means to take it to the court. The image of the boy, the crime of its theft and the false trail it set off, the imaginary or real crime that the trail was used to lead to, the crime of poverty, Léon Lijour's strangled corpse in the no longer private space of his little hiding place, the narratives that they nourish in the imagery of crime, get tangled in the legal status of the truth and the right to an identity. This is harmonised by the glance.

These have all been situations without intended irony, or in which such ironies as those of the crossed lines of justice, money and status are concealed. For, I insist, with irony the power of the mnemonic begins to fail, as it does in Atget's Paris. There the crafty misconception of place throws light back from the expected reading of the surfaces of historical luxury or poverty – that is, from the decor of the Grand Siècle or from the rag-picker's hut, from the social glory of the actress's boudoir or its absence in the prostitute's smile. But it does so not as an illumination of the scene but as a blur in the viewer's eye, and substitutes puzzlement for astonishment, doubt for pleasure and recognition. In this, irony shortcircuits the conventional predication of the unexpected, which usually proceeds through the conversion of connotation into a naming process and of naming back into an efflorescence of attributes. Irony does not just expose the grammar of mnemonics. It neither names nor connects. Objects are made strange in terms of their established connotations, without being provided with new ones. The eventual price for this may be the shortcircuiting of irony itself, in the recuperation of its work as a version of the marvellous, as a means for the dysfunctional consumption of the objects that it represents.[26] Still, nothing could be less ironic than the Surrealist reading of the city of the commonplace, worked out as if unconscious of its own overdermination.

An irony that really corrodes the ordering of mnemonic must be one that shifts the structure of its reading as a social process, even if the proposed reading is far from ironic in its intention. One such reading might be that of a feminist *flâneur*, which would shift the parameters of value and their conjugation as imagery, rather as we saw in *Conseils à l'homme nu*. D'Yverchen's narrator, seeing a pretty man on the Avenue Gabriel, calls to her chauffeur – 'Jules, please tell the gentleman without a hat that Madame would like to speak to him' (*Conseils*, p. 89). Such a project might be of the greatest difficulty or solemnity, but Chéri's untimely death in Colette's *Fin de Chéri* laughs at the certainties of the historic regimes of woman's suffering. Sidestepping, masquerade or reappropriation can be traced as well in the novels or the beautician's work of Colette as in the bravado of Mistinguett, her ability to control the way you're caught by the glance, to return the fulfilment of expectations while slipping behind the image. As if the young woman in 'New

Types of Murder' had coolly stepped out of the frame, and let her trackers smash themselves on the wall. Or as if the frightened face of 1934 either smiled, or looked indifferent. A slapstick joke and a subversion.

For what is this woman's face staring out in fear and horror at 1934? The terror in her eyes is the reflection of the year looking at her, not seeing but being seen in the varieties of narrative that *Détective* can weave for women's lives. Aimless deaths in the street or home, the wanderings or enclosure of the prostitute, imprisonment for a presumed crime or for living at all – the fatal love meeting that follows the pleasure of the 14 July ball. The light in her eyes is like the blinding glare of headlamps in 'New Types of Murder', where the car drives up on the pavement to kill this tormented sign of the fatality of city life. It's in a way surprising that this look should be so frightened, just to register such humdrum *ritournelles* as 1934 might hold in store like any other year. After all these *faits divers* mark only the precarious dividing line between fiction and everyday realities, the accommodation of the bizarre, the brutal and the unfortunate to the narrative forms and the confirmation of the expectations of the city mnemonic. Maybe it is an expression that is assumed really to amuse, just as the audience for a horror film assume a certain kind of expression as a part of the process of their amusement, or the singer takes on a tormented look as the spotlight shines into her eyes. The motor car has as much to do with it as does electricity in the availability of new forms of entertainment. The light falling in the eyes of the woman of 1934, then, does not just blind but illuminates the fate that may be encountered in the *faits divers*. Just as the spotlight that falls on the singer not only dazzles her and stops her from seeing her audience, but frees her to fulfil their expectation of her, which is to give up the *faits divers* of her life. The projector or the headlamp are the neutral arbiter of an unequal process of exchange between these individual women and the possible idealities of woman, and they also reveal a certain kind of utopia in which woman is the space for the polymorphous identities of Paris.

The spotlight look is not a look returned, but nor is it subjected. It is one that sees out over its viewer, or somewhere else, a displaced look at the forbidden or fantastic which is within the fissures of the viewer's subject. These fated women are the vision of an imaginary freedom, whose imagination compensates for the childlike character of the repeated manipulation of the typologies of literary culture, the failure of the odyssey of man to realise the complexity of difference.[27]

These possible ideals form a part of a continuum of images out of which the associations of moralisers and 'fathers of families' wanted to abstract women to ensure another ideal – that of women's monolithic and simplistic dignity. No doubt in seeking this they risked undermining all and every ideal, including those that they set out to protect. They

# MACHINES DE MORT

Avec la vie moderne, un nouveau genre de meurtres est né : on tue maintenant à coups d'auto. C'est le procédé dont vient d'user, cette semaine, un industriel de Lyon.

Page 14, le début d'un étonnant reportage d'Albert SOULILLOU

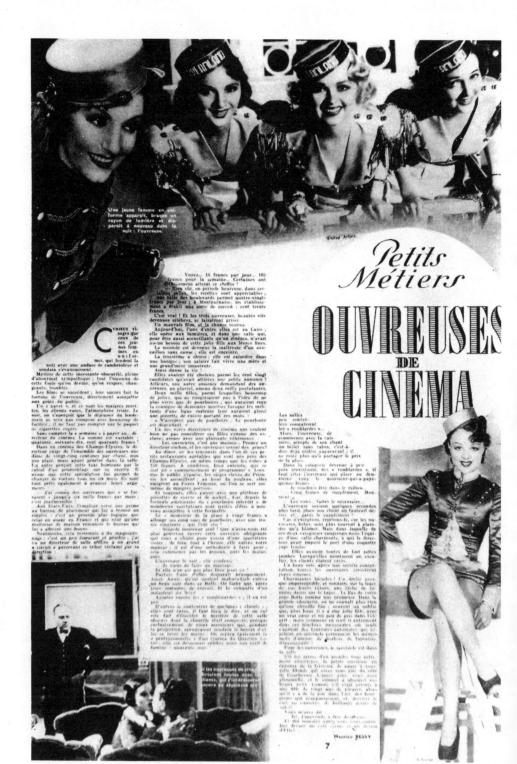

Une jeune femme en uniforme apparaît, braque un rayon de lumière et disparaît à nouveau dans la nuit : l'ouvreuse.

*United Artists*

## Petits Métiers

# OUVREUSES DE CINÉMA

**C**urieux visages que ceux de ces jeunes femmes en uniformes, qui fendent la nuit avec une audace de cambrioleur et soudain s'évanouissent.

Métier de cette incessante obscurité, pleine d'anonymat sympathique ; tout l'inconnu de cette foule qu'on devine, qu'on respire, changeante, troublées.

Les films se succèdent ; leur succès fait la fortune de l'ouvreuse, directement assujettie aux goûts du public.

Un « navet », et ce sont les maigres recettes, les clients rares, l'atmosphère triste. Le soir, on s'aperçoit que le dépanneur du lendemain ne sera pas composé avec beaucoup de facilité, il ne faut pas compter sur le paquet de cigarettes espéré.

Sans compter la semaine à payer au directeur du cinéma. La somme est variable : quarante, soixante-dix, cent quarante francs !

Dans un cinéma des Champs-Elysées, le directeur exige de l'ensemble des ouvreuses une dîme de vingt-cinq centimes par client, non pas place, mais ayant pénétré dans la salle. Un autre perçoit cette taxe honteuse par le calcul d'un pourcentage sur sa recette. Si avoir que cette spéculation lui permet de changer de voiture tous les six mois. Ils sont tout prêts également à avancer leurs arguments.

J'ai connu des ouvreuses qui « se faisaient » jusqu'à six mille francs par mois. C'est inadmissible.

Aux Etats-Unis, l'employé verse une prime au bureau de placement qui lui a trouvé un emploi : c'est un procédé plus logique que celui en usage en France et qui veut que la maîtresse de maison rémunère le bureau qui lui a adressé une bonne.

Néanmoins, rien ne ressemble à du maquignonnage ; c'est un peu écœurant et pénible ; j'ai vu un directeur de salle afficher un grand « ... à circuler » percevant ce tribut réclame par sa direction.

Voyez... 15 francs par jour... 105 francs pour la semaine. Certaines ont effectivement atteint ce chiffre !

Bien sûr, en période heureuse, dans certaines salles, les recettes sont appréciables ; une salle des boulevards permet quatre-vingt francs par jour ; à Montparnasse, un établissement a établi une sorte de record : cent trente francs.

C'est vrai ! Et les trois ouvreuses, beautés vite devenues célèbres, se laissèrent griser.

Aujourd'hui, l'une d'entre elles est au Caire ; elle opère aux lumières, et dans une salle qui, pour être aussi accréditable qu'un cinéma, n'avait aucun besoin de cette jolie fille aux lèvres fines.

La seconde est devenue la maîtresse d'un avocaillon sans causse ; elle est enceinte.

La troisième a choisi : elle est caissière dans une banque, son salaire fait vivre une mère et une grand'mère impotente.

Ainsi danse la vie !

Elles avaient été choisies parmi les cent vingt candidates qu'avait attirées une petite annonce ! Ailleurs, une autre annonce demandant des ouvreuses au pluriel, amena deux mille postulantes.

Deux mille filles, parmi lesquelles beaucoup de jolies, qui ne rougissaient pas à l'idée de ne plus vivre que de pourboires, qui auraient reçu la consigne de demeurer muettes lorsque les militants d'une ligue curieuse leur auraient glissé une pincette de cuivre portant ces mots :

« N'acceptez pas de pourboire ». Le pourboire est dégradant.

Un des rares directeurs de cinéma qui veulent bien ne pas considérer ces filles comme des esclaves, assure avec une plaisante véhémence :

— Les ouvreuses c'est ma maison... Prenez un directeur cochon, et les ouvreuses seront des grues !

Au dîner, sur les restaurants dans l'un de ces petits restaurants agréables que l'on voit près des Champs-Elysées, au même temps que les robes à 150 francs à condition, bien entendu que ce soit au « commandement de programme »... Lorsque le public s'épuise, les sièges élevés du Prisunic les accueillent ; au bout du rouleau, elles émigrent au Foyer Féminin, où l'on se sert un même de maigres portions.

Et toujours, elles paient avec une pléthore de piécettes de cuivre et de nickel. Car, depuis la formule américaine du « pourboire interdit » et de nombreux spectateurs sont irrités d'être à nouveau assujettis à cette formalité.

— Et à monsieur de la place à vingt francs qu'allonge ces cinq sous de pourboire, avec une ironie cinglante, peut-on dire : « peu cru » ?

Stupide monsieur sait ! Que n'avez-vous été plus généreux envers cette ouvreuse obligatoire qui vous a choisi pour voisin d'une spectatrice de loin, tout à l'heure, elle suivra votre mouvement ; et d'une orthodoxie à faire peur ; cela commence par les mains, puis les mains...

L'ouvreuse le sait, elle confesse :

— Je tiens de faire ma musique...

Et elle n'en est pas plus fière pour ça !

Parfois l'une d'elles disparaît brusquement. Jouait. Aussi qu'on appelait maharadjah enlève un beau soir dans sa Rolls d'un clafa qui après trois semaines de travail. Et la conquête d'un industriel du Nord...

Ajoutez encore les « combinardes » ; il en est peu.

D'autres se contentent de quelques « clients » et à vrai rare, il faut bien le dire, si on rai vite fait d'élucider le mystère de cette salle obscure dont la chaleur était compacte ; presque caoutchouteuse ; le vieux monsieur qui, pendant la projection, éprouvait soudain le besoin de se laisser les mains, on outre faisait l'objet d'un... professionnel ; il est l'ennui du Quatrième Art... elle est désormais célèbre pour son tarif de femme... maraude aux...

... les ouvreuses de cinéma... tiraient toutes avec bienveillance, qui s'intéressent au septième art.

Les salles peu comblé, les connaissent les « roublardes ».

Alors, l'ouvreuse, de connivence avec la caissière, accepte de son client un billet sans talon, c'est-à-dire déjà utilisé apparaissant ; il ne reste plus qu'à partager le prix de la place.

Dans la catégorie devenue à peu près inexistante, des « roublardes », il faut citer l'ouvreuse qui place au deuxième rang le « monsieur-qui-a-payé-quinze-francs »

— Je voudrais être dans le milieu...

— Cinq francs de supplément, Monsieur...

— Les voici, faites le nécessaire...

L'ouvreuse revient quelques secondes plus tard, place son client au fauteuil désiré, et, gentille le supplément.

Cas d'exception, répétons-le, car les ouvreuses, hélas, sont plus souvent à plaindre qu'à blâmer. Mais dans laquelle de ces deux catégories rangerons-nous l'équipe d'une salle charmante, à qui le directeur avait imposé le port d'une coquette jupe fendue.

Elles avaient toutes de fort jolies jambes. Lorsqu'elles montaient un escalier, les clients étaient ravis.

Un beau soir, après une secrète conspiration, toutes les ouvreuses croisèrent leur jupe cousue.

Charmantes insides ! Un éclair presque imprévisible, et soudain, sur la trace de vos bas tibians, une flèche de lumière mauve sur le tapis. Vos pas de votre jupe fuite comme une promesse. Dans la grande obscurité, on ne connaît plus rien qu'une pacotille fine, souvent au oublie que, plus haut, il y a une jolie fille, avec un vrai cœur et un peu de gris dans l'œil, mais continuant en suit à autrefois dans ces ténèbres mouvantes où seuls s'agitent des fantômes ambulants qui se perdent et, derrière le spectacle personnel, les dominantes d'amour de jalousie, de fantaisie d'insouciance.

Pour les ouvreuses, le spectacle est dans la salle.

S'il lui arrive d'en prendre trop nettement conscience, la petite ouvreuse en extrémité de la fenêtre de sortir à cause jolie blonde qui vivre son jour du côté de Gaulhers de l'autre jour avec plaisanté, et le sourire a ailleuré vos heures très lointaines... Il était présent, la jolie fille de vingt ans ne pleure, alors qu'il y a de la boi dans l'air, des fantômes qui réapparaissent, et, derrière le spectacle, de brillants éclats de soleil !

— Vous avez dit...

— Je l'approuvais, à être abordonné...

Et dix minutes après, vous vous resstiez dîner devant un café crème et un dessin d'Eisi...

**Maurice Bessy**

7

threatened to deprive the housewife of the meaning that cannot but be embodied in the values produced by the scales of difference. The fatal perception of 1934 or of the headlamps as the car mounts the pavement provide the housewife with an identity as surely as do her husband's presents. In the end it was the laxity of the *Procureur* and his staff, buoyed up by social transformation, that ensured that the dialogue between the prostitute of Tunis, the *Môme* Piaf, the shop-girl and the housewife would continue: the dialogue of looking and listening that enabled entertainment to produce identity out of the diverse and irreconcilable differences of their lives as the points of their coincidence expanded into the popular press and novel, into the airwaves and the gramophone. If irony is to be found, it must be through the lapsuses in structure of social relations, in the look that is not returned.

This irony would be something very different from the mere adoption of an ironic tone or style, another means of delicately evading recognition of the loss of self implicit in the uncontrolled urge to mnemonic activity and the pretence of intimacy with the city. Henri Béraud, right-wing, dyspeptic and hung over, provoked by the klaxons of the cars in 1927, hears the horn calls of Charpentier's *Louise* in their deafening noise:

> It seems that the whole of life turns round your armchair – the horrible whirlpool pulls you and the nasal honkings of its cars carry into your prison the imperious horn-calls of *Louise*, – Paris, Paris! (*Plan sentimental de Paris*, 1927, p. 9)

The sound empowers him to recover, overpowers him to go out once more into the city and to trace on to it his Sentimental Map. Yet another grid of sights and sounds, but also a bitter admission of an unextinguishable urge, the temptation that overcomes the *flâneur's* resistance, that leads him from the music hall and the *ouvreuses de cinéma* to a night-time mass at the aristocratic Sainte-Clothilde. He overhears the city sounds with particular care, the look of a sound in an image:

> they [the ticket collectors] wear expressions of boredom that come from hearing without end, for a century, famous people uttering their names with those white and featureless voices that dream figures use in their interminable confidences. (*ibid.* p. 31)

Béraud's scale runs from the lower depths of the gutter to the Faubourg Saint-Germain and, while memorising Balzac, foretells the circuits of arms deals and financial corruption in *Détective*, from the chic and wealthy avenues of the Eighth Arrondissement to the squalid hideouts of the Eighteenth. Charpentier himself had said that he listened to Paris when he composed his opera, leaving his doors and windows open to hear the cries and songs and plaints, writing down only what he heard: Julien's city of cries and songs:

There came to me through the open door the cries of the street-sellers of the old faubourgs: and so I could confront these far away music(s) with my young efforts. After a hard night of labour, while the dawn threw its blue light on my paper, the songs were like the smiling 'good-day' of friends who cared about my task, knowing that I was trying to write their story, and so wishing to encourage me.[28]

In Bruant and Charpentier, at different points in the structure of the entertainment industries, hearing discloses a means of representation for the noises of the margins. Hearing admits their sounds, to make the impersonal professionalism of the travel writer or musician over into a private *jouissance*. And the private *jouissance* into a public peep-show. Thus the evolution of the forms available for hearing, like those for looking, becomes crucial to the reproduction of the city lexicon, which imposes itself upon them even as they prove to be the ideal structure for its repetitions. The witness of the Zonard in the enquiry into hygiene (chapter. 1), the engrossing structure of the operatic score, or the endless repetition of the strophic song and the inflections within these make up a space for hearing, and ways of doing it. The repetition of the *ritournelle*, which is both a musical form and a casually pretty, meaningless kind of thing to say, can move as fast as needs be for people who hardly listen as they chat or dance, or who ask to be carried along on the crest of excitement in the touristic music-halls.[29] Or as slowly as is required to hold the attention of the public for the select *tour de chant* in an expensive club. Thus the same glimpses of the woman fallen to drugs or dangerous young men, the mortal plight of the city sparrow, drift across from the stage of the Casino in Mistinguett's 'Gosse de Paris' or 'Les bouges la nuit', which move like a mechanical ride, to 'Comme un moineau' in its limping pathos in Fréhel, or its broken near arrest in the close spotlight of the night-club in Piaf's 'Quand même'.

In Béraud it is the motor cars that give away the unconscious irony of a redefinition. One that turns the noise of this exclusive commodity into the sounding of the people's Paris. In 1927 the streets of Belleville, Ménilmontant, of the Bièvre or the Butte-aux-Cailles were barely disturbed by motor transport. Nor had they been changed beyond the recognition of their appearance in 1880 by rows of parked cars[30] It was possible to go to a *quartier populaire* in mid-winter and photograph every street under a thick snow that rested undisturbed by vehicles. It was an image still close to nature, needing none of the artificial light that is essential to the capturing of an accident, a murder or an entertainment. It allowed a long, sentimental way of looking, up and down streets in search of their timeless decor, a sentiment disturbed only if one notices the motor repair shops that flourished in working-class quartiers. *Détective*'s fantasy of an everyday, individualised form of power that throws its own light on its victims was as much a prophecy as a reportage. Even the crowds of cars at the Opera or Chaillot were sparse by today's standards and as late as 1937 the Salon de l'Auto was still little more than an exclusive fashion show.

In his essay, 'Advertising and the Romanticism of Commerce and Industry', Mac Orlan tried to rework the mnemonic with the efflorescence of modern technology; the new forms of lighting, the mechanical women in the shop windows, the speeds and movements that were halfway between the poetry of adventure and the charm of drawing or painting.[31] The problem was to hold the essential image in place across this new range of potential signs, without having at one's disposal any other means than the *récit* or the documentary moment. An author who, in his way, had pioneered the popularity of photography, the diffusion of the recorded song, was eventually to lapse back into the old images of light and dark that the war made so easily available once again. In 1951 he eloquently admitted the nature of the problem, reaching for some of the same words as he had used in 1930:

> When Villon spoke of the Rue Saint-Jacques, and he perceived the poor glimmer of a calel under the door of an oven, he used the word light. Then, this word revolved at 150 rotations – If I can put it like that. To describe the lights of Broadway in 1950 we use the same word, that now has to 'revolve' at 2000 rotations. Very rapidly words lose their practical, that is to say, their every-day signification.(Images lyriques, p. 178)

It was the popular media themselves, like *Détective* and *Voilà* the radio and the gramophone, the early forms of juke-box, and their overlapping sounds in the café and the home, their interweaving with each other and with other noise, the collectability of their products and their redundancy, which had already achieved this speed, in a way that was not easy to author.

In this complexity the cinema too occupied an uneasy and ambivalent position. The camera could follow the already coded *trajets* – the change of woman for each arrondissement in *Souvenirs de Paris*, the lamplight in *À quoi rêvent les becs de gaz*, or work from the reconstructed film-set of urban mythologies as in the *Hôtel du Nord*. But ultimately it had to remake this imagery, for its market, rather than transform it on account of its own technological potential. This evolution then ends up inverting the relation of art and technology that Benjamin observed with Futurism. With the exception of Surreal film imagery, which was really doubly parasitic on the urban marvellous, and particularly through figures like Prévert, film amplified the space for the elaboration of mnemonics, and their international markets. The ensemble of means of seeing and hearing, and the choosing between them, were more opaque than their components. Thus the 'New Types of Murder' remains part of a particular construction of the relation of woman and city – if only for the banal reason that the motor car represents a change registered within social relations rather than on them. This is nicely concentrated in the very rapid passage of the gramophone from the cutting edge of mechanical innovation to becoming a relic of the fleamarkets. More than a relic, indeed: a defining characteristic of the markets, an old instrument blaring out an old song, a retroactive access to the present like an old photograph. The very consumer culture that jettisons the new invention at an increasing rate of redundancy is rolled back out of view, it is the repressed or concealed in its image as a *déchet*. Inversely, the accordion, another relatively recent invention and a newcomer to the gamut of popular instruments, comes to be seen as a timeless attribute of the people, each time it is seen or heard offering an access to permanence. The look of things, in the space between metonym and the transferred epithet, is one of the links between the *procureur* and the poet, the policeman and the *père de famille*. And out of this space the diverse forms of entertainment and social pleasures acquire their appeal for and their affront to the publics who, unwittingly, enjoy them in common.

### Notes

1 See, for example, Barabara Johnson's 'The Frame of Reference: Poe, Lacan, Derrida.' in *Literature and Psychoanalysis – The Question of Reading: Otherwise,* ed. Shoshana Feldman, Baltimore and London, Johns Hopkins, 1982, pp. 457–505.

2 Charles Baudelaire, 'Richard Wagner et Tannhäuser' in *Curiosités esthétiques – l'Art romantique,* ed. H. Lemaitre, Paris, Garnier, 1962, p. 698.

3 Amongst various discussions of these photographs, see that of André Rouillé in André Rouillé and Bernard Marbot, *Le Corps et son image: photographie du XIX$^e$ siècle,* Paris, Contrejour, 1986. Also, on the phoney innocence of the snapshot, see Alain Fleig, 'Anatomie d'un mythe', in Les Cahiers de la Photographie, 9. This number of the review is generally of interest for the discussion of pre- and post-war humanist and realist photography. For a useful discussion of multiplicity of vision and 'shock' as a coding of modernity see Franco Moretti, *Signs Taken for Wonders,* London, Verso, 1988, 'The Spell of Indecision', pp. 240–8.

4 See Stora-Lamare, *Enfer...,* chapters 3 and 4 for a detailed study of the growth of the antipornographic leagues and their social connections. My main sources throughout this chapter are the Dossiers Banaux of the sous-séries BB/18 in the Archives Nationales. Longer quotation will be referenced in the text.

5 *Proceedings of the Premier Congrès National contre la Pornographie,* Bordeaux, 14–15 March 1905. Bordeaux and the south-west were the stronghold of the leading moralist, E. Pourésy, a frequent correspondant with the Parisian *parquet.*

6 As Stora-Lamare underlines, the culture of legal enforcement is not necessarily very developed. Diderot's *La Religieuse* continued to be referred to the *parquet* into the 1870s Cf. my own publication of this document in 'Cultural Movements and the Paris Commune', *Art History,* 2, No.3, 1979, pp. 201–20.

7 It should be clear that I am not using the theory of the gaze in the ways that it has generally been established. For example the relation of glance and gaze is here the inverse of that found in Norman Bryson, *Vision and Painting: The Logic of the Gaze,*

London, 1983, and I am also at odds with Mary Anne Doane in her seminal 'Film and the Masquerade: theorising the female spectator', *Screen* 23, nos 3/4, 1982. The reasons for this will become apparent in the course of this chapter. That said, I have found Jacques Lacan's diagrammatic representation and discussion of the gaze in his *The Four Fundamental Concepts of Psychoanalysis*, translated by A.Sheridan, Harmonsworth, Penguin, 1979, an essential tool in figuring the complex unfixity of looks and gazes. Tamar Garb, '"Unpicking the seams of her disguise" ... Self-representation in the case of Marie Bashkirtseff in *Block*, 13, 1987/8, pp. 79–86 is more to the point.

8 Archives Nationales, F/7/13960, 'Pédérastie', is a correspondence from the minister of the interior, direction of the 'sûreté nationale', to the Prefect of the Var. In effect it contains a more complex range of documentation, notes of surveillance from Toulon, Brest and other cities, depositions, official opinions and formal exchanges between these offices and each other.

9 Played, or improvised, in the one recording, by the composer and musician Jean Wiener, 1896–1982, one of those protean figures who made and secured the links between different levels of cultural production.

10 The details of sound effects from this and Mac Orlan's programme are taken from the studio scripts, conserved in the Bibliothèque de l'Arsenal, Paris.

11 It is difficult to typify such a well-subscribed genre, but to choose one text by a Goncourt prize-winner (for 1908), Francis de Miomandre, *Dancings*, Paris, Flammarion, 1932, combines many forms of privileged voyeurism on many forms of sexuality.

12 See my *Musical Moments* for a poetic of statistics and an anti- statistical poetic, pp. 135–6.

13 See, for example, Léon Deffoux, *Chronique de l'Académie Goncourt*, Paris, Firmin-Didot, 1929; Pierre Descaves, *Mes Goncourt*, Paris, 1949. And, for a marvellously perceptive critique by a current Goncourt member, cited below, Michel Tournier, 'Colette ou le Premier Couvert' in *Le Vol du vampire*, Paris, Gallimard, 1981. The *Répertoire* of French literary prizes gives a complete listing of Goncourt members and prize-winners from its foundation to 1965. The coincidence of Parisianism amongst both is very striking, and it is also worth noting how many of the main Parisian prizes Mac Orlan and Carco won in the 1950s.

14 See Pascal Pia, *Les Livres de l'Enfer: Bibliographie critique des ouvrages érotiques dans leurs différentes éditions du XVI<sup>e</sup> siècle à nos jours*, Paris, A. Faure, 1978, and Stora-Lamare's detailed discussion of the composition of the Enfer catalogues in *L'Enfer*.

15 See Colette, *Lettres à ses pairs* for an overview of these connections. Writing in 1918 to Carco, whom she calls the master of his genre, 'You were right to write to me, I have the idea that we think the same language' (p. 204). And to Carco in 1930, on receiving a copy of his *La Rue* of that year, 'Dear Carco, thank you for having dedicated it to me, of having dedicated *just this book* to me' (p. 231). See also her letters to Billy, Dignimont, Duvernois, Dorgelès, Larguier *et al*.

16 Eugène Dabit (1898–1936) has recently begun to attract critical and historical attention, but for the best empirical account see the two-volume *Eugène Dabit – Roger Martin du Gard, correspondance, 1926–27 & 1930–36*, presented by Pierre Darbel, Paris, éditions du CNRS, 1986. Dabit's parents owned the Hôtel du Nord of his book. This correspondence is a striking account of the polymorphous processes of the integration of a literary establishment.

17 The discrepancy between Chiappe's monolithic moralism and the ambivalence of ministerial and administrative correspondence can be measured by juxtaposing these archives to his memoirs, *Paroles d'ordre*, Paris 1935.

18 As in the wider politics of the period from the 1890s onwards, a link is made between

anarchist and secularist challenges to traditional systems of authority and the diffusion of contraception, especially as the neo-Malthusian groups aimed it at working-class families. See the work of Paul Bureau; for a recent survey of the feminist viewpoint, see Claudine Mitchell, 'Madeleine Pelletier', in *Feminist Review*, 33, 1989.

19  Stora-Lamare, *op. cit*, chapter 5. Duverger, *Collection des lois*, is the authoritative account of law-making. Where my and Stora-Lamare's interpretation of the letter of the law differ, I have favoured mine.

20  See Pia, *op. cit.*, for an account of Le Nismois and his various pseudonyms, Fuckwell, Caïn d'Abel, etc.

21. See Bibliography for works of Margueritte. Here I will just underline the themes of radical politics – the Paris Commune, sexual freedom, prostitution and prison – which form much of the substance of his plays and novels.

22  Cf. Franco Moretti's critique of the idea of city-shock, *op. cit.*, note 3 above.

23  For an account of the founding and staffing of *Détective*, see Pierre Assouline, *Gaston Gallimard*, Paris, Balland, 1984.

24  It is in laying out the materials for these connections that Louis Chevalier is at his best in *Montmartre* – but then Simenon is just as good; see *Maigret and the Enigmatic Lett*, London, Penguin, 1983 (originally Paris, Fayard, 1931).

25  From J.-M. Campagne, *Les Week-Ends*. For an important discussion of the relation between Surrealist vision and the everyday see R. Krauss and Jane Livinston, *L'Amour fou*, London, Arts Council, 1986, especially Krauss's essay 'Photography in the Service of Surrealism', pp. 15–54. Of general interest for this chapter see also her fascinating essay 'Nightwalkers' *Art Journal*, spring, 1983, pp. 33–8.

26  The systematic, perhaps too relentless, critique of the marvellous is Henri Lefebvre, *Critique de la vie quotidienne, l, Introduction*, Paris, L'Arche, 1958, chapter 1. Also on the Surrealist aporia, T. W. Adorno, *Notes to Literature*, translated by S. Weber Nicholson, New York, Columbia University Press, 1991, vol. 1, 'Looking Back on Surrealism, pp. 86ff. For Atget, see Nesbit, *Intérieurs*.

27  For a discussion of the Odysseian myth of male identity, see Muriel Dimen, *Surviving Sexual Contradictions*, New York, Macmillan, 1986, pp. 34–8.

28  From Erato, *Louise*, complete recording introductory notes.

29  I have found the chapter 'De la ritournelle' in Gilles Deleuze and Félix Guattari, *Capitalisme et schizophrénie – mille plateaux*, Paris, Minuit, 1980, pp. 381–433 useful in thinking through the relation of form and boundary here and throughout my book.

30  Bibliothèque Historique de la Ville de Paris, volumes of photographs from the series NA Divers etc. under titles such as the wonderful 'Paris sous la neige' by the Seeberger brothers.

31  In the comemmorative book of the Gala du Commerce et de l'Industrie, held in the Théâtre des Champs-Élysées, 9 June 1937.

# Neighbouring states (soldiers and sailors)

Entre nos coeurs quelle distance!
Tant d'espace entre nos baisers!
O sort amer! O dure absence!
O grands désirs inapaisés!   (Théophile Gautier, *Absence* )

Dans la chambre encore fatale
De l'encor fatale maison
Où la raison et la morale
Le tiennent plus que de raison ...   (Verlaine, *Hombres* VI, 'Rendez-vous')

When the officers of the naval vice squad went into the pissoir in Toulon they did so on the authority of the Prefect of the Var. But they fixed the time and place of surveillance through the personal columns of *Frou-Frou* magazine. The self- same columns that the Paris police were so anxious to clean up provided them with an assignation in the places of encounter, in the sites of moral outrage and unnatural acts. So they had an official reason to go out into the side-world of the illicit circulation of sexual pleasures that was abetted by an unofficial access. Sometimes however, for a different public – for night-clubbers or for record collectors this access could be obtained through another route – through an image so current, so banal in the *ritournelles* of entertainment, that no one without a 'special' interest need notice its possibilities.

Songs were full of signs, signals, which, taken at the face value of their place in a story, were no more than the background noise of daily life, the repetitions of the culture industries, incitements to routines of mood and feeling. Yet when they appeared elsewhere than in the song or found diversity in the listening of its many publics, their meanings ran wild. For almost any sailor or soldier hero of a popular song could just as well open the way into the enjoyment of the male body as of the suffering of the city-street woman, time and time again left abandoned by him. The abandonment, this stock tragedy of the tearful–popular, could stand in for another desire, another way of suffering. One that was heavily po-liced. The more so that it was not illegal but that its fulfilment was an obvious and straightforward case of offence to *bonnes moeurs*.[1]

These signs had many possible locations, some of them worlds apart yet pointing in the same directions. They were as likely to appear in a police report as in a radio programme of new records. In the reports of the Prefect of the Var, for example, who had organised the squads to investigate and clean up the naval scandals. In his final report to the Minister in Paris, he concluded four years of strict surveillance in Toulon with ten pages on the social and psychological pathology of homosexual-ity. The Prefect quoted from some medical reports on sailors:

> thus it is that in the No. 3 of March 1929 of the *Annales de Médecine Légale* M. le Professeur Balthazari, of the Paris medical school, and technical counsellor to the Judicial Identity Service, signals that, amongst 'pederasts of the social dregs, the frequency of the tattoo in the form of a sheaf on the prepuce is symptomatic'. M. le Médecin GOUREAUD of the Navy ... signals the fre-quency amongst pederasts, and in the region of the deltoids, right and left, the tattooing of a 5 or 8 pointed star, marked, or not, with 1 to 5 blue dots, with, sometimes, the word 'love' positioned as a caption. He adds that these tattoos are accompanied by signs drawn on the visible parts, whether on the face (a blue dot on the eyelid) or on the hands (the existence of blue points positioned in the section seperating the thumb and the index) ... (F/7/13960, from the Report of the Head of the State Police Service of Toulon, December

Such an effort to collate and understand the meaning of these signs, when made to facilitate the control of naval mores, stands in touching contrast to the failure to do so of one of the great successes of late 1930s song-writing, Raymond Asso's and Marguerite Monot's 'Mon Légionnaire':

Il était plein de tatouages
Que j'ai jamais très bien compris
Son cou portait 'pas vu, pas pris'
Sur son coeur on lisait 'personne'
Sur son bras droit, un mot: 'raisonne'.

This poem, which, according to Monnot, Asso had brought back as part of a collection he had written in North Africa,[2] was like a shortcircuit of tourism, nationalism and the literature of the exotic, echoing Mac Orlan's *Poésies documentaires*:

Le cri aigu des ouled-Nails annonce, avant l'heure des minarets, la rentrée au quartier et décroche la mélancolique sonnerie du clairon de garde devant le mur bleu de lune de la «taule»

Joyeux, fais ton fourbi
  Pas vu
  Pas pris
  Mais vu
  Rousti
  Bat-d'af

('Palais des danses orientales', p. 215. Bat-d'af is Bataillon d'Afrique)

'Mon légionnaire' takes place in a cinematic decor of the colonial desert – 'il sentait bon le sable chaud', which fills out the essential quality of the fantasy in its distance from military reality as in its closeness to a literary tradition. From here it is a short drift to the North African boy of Gide's desire in *Si le grain ne meurt* (1920) that was the ratified, literary expression of homosexuality, backed up by that acme of modern sexual politics, his *Corydon* (1924). It is in the slippage across the common ground of the literary *imaginaire* of North African sexual pleasure and the popular jour-nalistic literature of the Légion that this whore-figure of the anonymous soldier can emerge and stand in publicly for the 'special' cultures of the city. His signs merge with theirs under the camouflage of incomprehen-siblity. They reduce the distance between the desert and the steps of the Parisian Métro station:

The other more important traffic of the place is more special. The type you see over there, by the counter, is a specialist of this other kind of pick-up ... in the coming and going of the strollers, [you see] equivocal groups in mysteri-ous, secret meetings ... (*Détective*, 10 May 1934)

*Détective*'s reporter, in juxtaposing the prostitution of Les Halles with the male prostitution of the Boulevard Saint-Denis, 'this *other* form of *racolage*', makes the very inaccessibility of its codes the sign of its a-normality and of its allure. 'When the police move in on one place of assignation', he writes, 'instructions, mysterious pass-words warn the initiates of the new meeting places.' And as the reporter quotes these words they take on an alarming mood, the mood of mystery. This is a form of narrative tension as well as a reaction to the thing: both a transition from the facts of the reportage to the persistant invisibility of its subject and an emotion compromised the by complicity of its knowing. Likewise, in 'Mon légionnaire' the coolly descriptive tone of the Professor Balthazari, 'pederasts of the social dregs', is surpassed in a sensual wonder at blue eyes and sun glinting in the hair, in the wild excess of epithets. But in this way the 'special', which is more often than not represented either through a specious medicalism, the worldly novel of titivation or a marginal sociology, is made general. But only in the song of the singer-*pute* and in the assumption of its subjectivity by the artiste who sings it.

The homosexual magazine *Inversions*, on the contrary, which chose a public and a normal language, making an open forum of itself, could never enjoy such an equivocal and unstable status.[3] After only a year's existence, a few, earnest numbers that dealt with pressing issues and tried to elaborate a homosexual literature, it fell foul of the authorities. Following a complex and humiliating trial, it was suppressed in 1926. In the equivocation of the song, the multiplicity of its publics, this fate could be sidestepped.

The strategy of a 'mainstream' masquerade was all the more necessary as even negative and satirical images of homosexual desire ran the risk of repression. They could not be matched to the worldly disinterest that sheltered gallant literature and spectacles of femininity. A poem, 'La Tante', for example, from a very minor, satirical journal, the *Cri de Bordeaux*, in 1919, was scored all over by the *procureur*'s pen: 'she works in feathers', or 'Bouguereau pleases her, because his name seems full of caresses' (BB/18/6172). Here, at least, the judiciary seemed sensitive to a language that, while it pathologised and mocked, failed to utter a formal condemnation. On the contrary it made the reality of other sexuality tragically banal but present in the vulgarity of double entendre or common erotic language. In some of the judicial files we find the most crudely descriptive passages of a popular, gallant novel lovingly typed out, underlined and discussed and attention drawn to their already obvious content with a pleasure that is emphasised by the conclusion that we have now come to expect – that there was nothing much to be done. But the relatively innocent doggerel of the *Cri de Bordeaux* received a formal warning. So, despite the distinguished literary profile and social status of

# MARCHÉS DE MINUIT

*Le métro proche est devenu une annexe pour ces équivoques rendez-vous*

fureur, retourne sa colère contre les agents. Un de ses amis vint lui prêter main forte. Un autre spectateur, — un de ceux qui, à l'occasion des moindres incidents de la rue, veulent toujours, au nom de la justice immanente, prendre la parole et prendre parti, — un autre spectateur, donc, prit en scandale et à l'abomination. Il n'en fallut pas plus — en un temps où les gens du public sont particulièrement sensibles pour mettre en défense passagère des représentants de l'ordre. Ils furent d'abord vingt qui, se précipitant sur les agents, tentèrent de leur arracher leurs prisonniers. L'un des gardiens, se dégageant, sortit son revolver de sa gaine et tira en l'air. D'autres agents accoururent. Les assaillants reculèrent. L'un des blessés de la rixe fut conduit dans une pharmacie de la rue Sainte-Appolline. Tout paraissait s'apaiser lorsque des groupes, se reformant, vinrent cerner l'officine pour délivrer le blessé. Toute l'étrange faune du boulevard Saint-Denis était là, se heurtant du coude, se poussant des clameurs. La samoa dalarme de Police-Secours alerta le renfort. Il fallut l'arrivée de trois autres cars de police pour disperser ce petit foyer d'émeute et éviter les pires désordres.

Il n'était point besoin de ces curieux incidents pour attirer l'attention sur l'étrange faune qui, chaque soir, se rassemble au tour des lumières du bar « Tout va bien ». Mais jamais peut-être comme ce soir-là, où le prétexte d'une rixe banale avait tout à coup remué d'un inquiétant bouillonnement les groupes stagnants du boulevard, je n'avais eu le loisir d'observer le mystérieux marché nocturne qui tient ses assises.

Par quel pacte secret sont-ils liés, tous ces désœuvrés, tous ces buveurs attardés, toutes ces épaves de la nuit ? Et de quel nom doit-on désigner leurs louches et traînants conciliables ?

Combien de fois m'était-je arrêté là pour consommer parmi la foule laborieuse qui, aux heures d'affluence, prend d'assaut l'immense comptoir, ruilant d'éclairs sous les molles fumées d'un « perco », sans discerner, comme ce soir-là, les équivoques personnages qui, de toutes parts, semblaient m'épier.

Tout un monde secret naissait soudain devant mes yeux, dont je n'avais jusqu'alors que mal soupçonné les pratiques et les excès. Et déjà, sans en avoir franchi les frontières, sans m'être aventuré dans les voies obscures, j'en pressentais le fait d'arrière-détresse et de désenchantement, où le vice, sous tel aspect, vous conduit tôt ou tard.

L'ami qui m'accompagnait s'était chargé de m'initier.

— Il y a ici, voyez-vous, deux genres de trafics, deux sortes de marchés. On chasse ici, à cette terrasse et sur ce trottoir, la jeune fille et le gosse sans travail. Côté démolisseurs, ce sont en général des petites bonnes fraîchement débarquées à Paris et qui déjà ont perdu leur place.

Certains individus, que vous rencontrez ici, se sont spécialisés dans la chasse de ces jeunes oiseaux sans cervelle. Ce ne sont pas des placeurs professionnels. Ces placeurs tiennent leurs assises dans les bars d'en face et derrière la Porte Saint-Denis. Ceux qui « travaillent » ici — et qu'on a surnommé les « raclettes » ont pour tâche que d'engager les premiers qui ont leurs. Si les jeunes donzelles mordent à l'hameçon, la « raclette » prévient le placeur. « Ce soir, je serai avec elle à la terrasse. Vous passerez devant nous. Si elle vous convient, vous me ferez signe. » L'affaire conclue, l'intermédiaire touche sa commission. Combien de jeunes boniches ont-elles, de ce trottoir, pris le chemin de Dakar ou de Buenos-Aires ?

Mon compagnon but son verre, fixa un instant, dans la foule qui cernait le comptoir, un individu dont je ne pus discerner le pâle visage sous la large casquette, et dont le cire noir, trop long, pendait jusqu'aux talons.

L'autre trafic — le plus spécial de l'endroit — est plus spécial. Le type que vous voyez devant le comptoir, là-bas, est un spécialiste de cet autre genre de racolage. Cette chasse aussi est fructueuse. Le trottoir du boulevard Saint-Denis, la gare du métro qui s'ouvre sous ce trottoir, sont devenus des lieux de rendez-vous de tous les initiés.

Mais qui leur indique ces endroits ?

Ceux qui les ont précédés.

L'homme du boulevard Saint-Denis me désignait encore, parmi le va-et-vient des promeneurs, des groupes équivoques aux mystérieux conciliabules. Ce qui frappait et qui créait bientôt un trouble malaise, c'était la perverse insistance de tous ces regards et leur complicité.

Qu'avaient fait ces jeunes gens — des Alsaciens pour la plupart — qui avaient quitté leur village natal pour venir tenter fortune à Paris ? Ils avaient regardé dévot les vitrines où sont affichées des demandes d'emploi. Devant ces vitrines, il ne s'agit pas des gosses qui cherchaient du travail. Un homme avait surgi :

— Tu cherches du boulot ? Je vais m'occuper de toi. Veux-tu gagner vingt francs ? Je te donne rendez-vous pour le lendemain, devant...

« Tout va bien », là il y a un « Jésus » de plus sur le marché. Il y a encore un meilleur truc, conduit tôt...

Au terrasse du « Tout-va-bien », se presse une foule innombrable.

que mon compagnon, c'est le recrutement pour les photographes. Tel, dans le bar même, un individu recrutait, il y a un an, des jeunes adolescents sous couvert d'une œuvre philanthropique. Il s'intitulait « Président de l'Aide » (!) et sa carte de visite passait de mains en mains. Ceux qui se laissaient prendre croyaient venir à quelques uns dans une sorte de chambre secrète ouvrant sur un studio. L'aide à l'enfance, vous le devinez... L'homme se disait aussi photographe d'art. Et, en fait, pour des sommes modiques, les jeunes garçons bouchers, de jeunes commis en rupture de comptoir, posaient devant l'objectif dans le plus singulier appareil, isolés d'abord, puis en groupes. Séduits par le travail facile, ils revenaient voir le providentiel amateur à « poses artistiques ». Et cette fois, ce n'était pas ces poses qui étaient monnayées. Naturellement, depuis longtemps, le scandale a été repéré par la police. La brigade du commissaire Priolet est venue faire ici, aussi bien dans le métro que dans le bar, de nombreuses rafles. Traqués, ces habitués émigrent alors à la kermesse du Palais-Berlitz, puis s'enhardissent à revenir. Les marchés de minuit changent avec les hasards de la surveillance policière. Des consignes, des mots d'ordre mystérieux avertissent les initiés des nouveaux lieux de ralliement.

Nous restâmes longtemps à bavarder cette nuit-là sous les lumières de ce bar où, sans cesse, les hauts récipients nickelés versaient, par leurs tubes recourbés, des jets noirs et fumants.

Les groupes se dispersaient. Figés devant des cafés-crèmes, les buveurs solitaires poursuivaient de rêveries pensées que le vin faisait pâlissantes. L'heure approchait où de nouveaux visages allaient remplacer les blêmes visages de la nuit.

Aux surveillants matinaux, allaient se mêler les ouvrières des maisons de plaisir de la rue Sainte-Appolline...

**Marcel MONTARRON**

Gide, Cocteau or Proust, it is easy to get a sense here of how much the everyday of homosexual desire was hemmed in. In one of *Détective*'s picture stories on the death of Louis Leplée there is a photograph of a street known for its popularity with homosexuals: the mere presence of men in the image is taken to suggest the proximity of crime, and their backs to indicate furtiveness, the sinister and the evasive. They dare not face the camera.

Therefore the very real value of an appearance neutral enough to escape coding is not to be underestimated as a strategy. In the 1930s, if the witness of Daniel Guérin or André du Dognon is to be accepted, outside the restricted subcultures of the Café Graff in Montmartre, the best dissembling remained the semblance of 'normality'. It was a *faux-semblant* that certainly seemed to offer the freedom of a disguise that had neither a name nor a precise identity. The lack of a current, widely accepted definition of a homosexual identity was itself seen by some as the space of a considerable liberty. Guérin circulated round the bars of Pigalle or the dancings of the Rue de Lappe in search of sexual pleasures that, for his interests and those of his partners, best remained unlabelled: pleasures that implied a commitment by neither party to a given sexuality-as-such. A young worker could even claim that to go with Guérin was a proof of his virility, of his indifference to anything other than the adventure or the inevitable and much-needed money gift or other present:

> These night-clubs [in the Rue de Lappe] were sexual, not homosexual, but in them there was enormous permissiveness – people didn't kiss though, as the 'lads' stuck to their virile image. (Guérin, *Paris gay,* pp. 43ff.).

Certainly the skilfully handled escape from coding looks like a utopia compared to the caricature published by the magazine *Grand Guignol* in 1927. It was picked out by the Paris police as a potential problem, before being dismissed as harmless, as 'too crude a treatment' of the subject. 'The pederastic Octopus, its suckers, its pansies, its tentacles and its temptations' runs the title. The police comment:

> the drawing represents two individuals of a special allure, of whom the one, seated on the bed, holds the other, who is standing upright between his knees, by the hand, and appears to pull him towards himself. The legend is conceived in these terms ... 'Prout! – *ma chère,* money has no smell.' (*Grand Guignol*, Supplement, summer 1927, BB/18/6172)

What would have been required to make this a 'serious treatment' of its subject? Clearly not, in this context, a text by Magnus Hirschfeld or by one of those liberal medical experts with their 'intolérable odeur de clinique', as Gide railed in *Corydon* (p. 30) – though plenty of such writings did get denounced to the authorities. And the insistent double-entendre of 'La Tante'? Would the change of gender to the masculine 'mon cher' have been enough to merit repression, enough to shift the tone from the abstract realm of stereotype to an unacceptable reality? The stereotype at least left matters in the realm of the non-normal, the comic or the ludicrous, in a masquerade that could be read indifferently with innocence or disgust.

In these circumstances those great moments of the Parisian homosexual calendar, the annual drag balls of the Magic City, were less than an escape to freedom, far less than a carnivalesque uprising against 'normality'. Their dependence on the *travesti* was as much a trap as a release. They were little more than a riotous moment of surveilled and imaged remission, taken at the price of making a spectacle for all of Paris. 'All the concierges of the Avenue de Clichy stayed up untill three in the morning to offer themselves the spectacle of these divine creatures,' reported Jean Weber, in a later interview (*Paris gay*, pp. 62ff.). Strangely this is in agreement with the erotic but homophobic novel *Notre-Dame de Lesbos* (1924) by Charles-Etienne. Its hero, an eminent young literary critic, begins his descent to sexual uncertainty and suicide through a visit to the Bal Magic City. Invited by a friend, he demurs – 'And if I'm recognised?' – but his objection is refuted:

> Do you believe that you are the only Parisian who has come to treat himself to the heads of our aunts? Curiosity is never healthy. The well hung odour of forbidden game attracts there all lovers of scandal, types with *blasé* nostrils ... (p. 63)

Homosexuality here was hemmed in with utter negativity, its 'frenetic, demoniac, make-up-laden figures' loaded with every sign of femininity as misogyny. It had no choice but to accept insult in the masquerade of the elaborate ball gown, a pleasure that, even while it was chosen and enjoyed, entailed a voluntary submission to parody. Maurice Chevalier's song, 'Quand une marquise' (by Mireille and Jean Nohain), harassed this caricature from the secure masculinity of the singer – lover of the woman – city. It took the same tone as the *Cri de Bordeaux*. 'When an aunt chats to another aunt, what do they do? ... tell stories of *frou-frou*!' It was a great success. Colette, writing in 1931 though recalling the *fin-de-siècle*, recorded this stress, even in her bohemian circles:

> A débutant in his diplomatic career one day had the unfortunate idea of bringing to us his intimate friend, Bouboule. Dressed in a gown of black Chantilly on a sky-blue background, sulking under his lace bonnet, ill at ease like a country girl at a wedding, his cheeks like nectarines – but should one be surprised that a seventeen- year-old butcher's boy should be freshness itself? – Bouboule froze us with astonishment, had no success, and noticed it. Treading the lower fold of his dress with his enormous feet, he left us. Nor did he go far, only a few days away, to the unexplained suicide of a clumsy, chagrined, unsettled child. (*Le Pur et l'impur*, p. 152)

The insistence on the picture of the drag-queen has a peculiar quality to it at this point in time. It is as if it represented the ultimate and eventually subversive development of the sign of woman as the narcissistic representation of male desire. That is to say, the image of a woman with the phallus at last restored to her, literally, in the shape of a penis, as an interface between the discrepant discourses of gender and biology. A woman who wears a dress solely to hide this fact, who can, then, never be nude. The man-in-drag is the return of the repressed meaning of the narcissistic sign, and it cannot titivate without putting the whole game at risk. In this double role the man-in-drag invited both the most intense gaze and the most systematic scorn at the level of its image in mass cultures. Importantly he is doubled by the image of the *grande dame* or respectable woman, whose sexual appetite has condemned her to the world of the *voyous*. For her this fate, which for her (heterosexual) husband is an adventure, a rite, a possession of the freedom of the city spaces, is a fall from social grace that opens her too to sniggers and pitying glances. She underpins the element of self-doubt or hatred in the parody figure of homosexuality. In stark contrast, but less well known, was the relatively utopian if objectifying revelry of, let us say, Cocteau's private stories and drawings of sailors in the *Livre blanc*.

As, for that matter, but for different reasons, have these photographs – these everyday attempts to give oneself an image, which ended up in the Prefect's files in Toulon. Unlike Cocteau's sailors, they escape the controlling skills of the aristocratic poet, the formal devices of the bohemian poetic. The young Englishman who had himself photographed ecstatic, contented, got up to look like Barbette, the great, androgynous music-hall acrobat of the 1920s. Less refined than Cocteau's and Man Ray's celebrated book on Barbette, this effectively anonymous trace no less sings of a utopia, a dream of being the sign you choose to be, filling it out for pleasure and identity. Freed from the codings and formalities of the artists' eyes and pens, here it is humdrum, provincial, strangely full of hope. Or at the other possible extreme the simple assumption of a normality, the conventional album photo of an affectionately happy couple. I offer these documents from the archive of the five-year inquisition because it is necessary to underline the livings out of social difference within the sexual. Unlike Cocteau, these men were hunted. Unlike the victims of a major crime, they had no story.

Yet when secrecy was blown or disaster struck, the Prefect's men moved in with a charge of moral outrage, or *Détective* probed. It made fun, blamed and moralised. Its narratives of murders of homosexuals – of Léon Lijour, of a young false-count Italian, of Oskar Dufrenne the director of the Palace music-hall assassinated in 1933, probably by a sailor and, in 1936, the killing of Piaf's patron, Louis Leplée – followed a track that paralleled that of the helpless woman victim of her pleasure in the city –

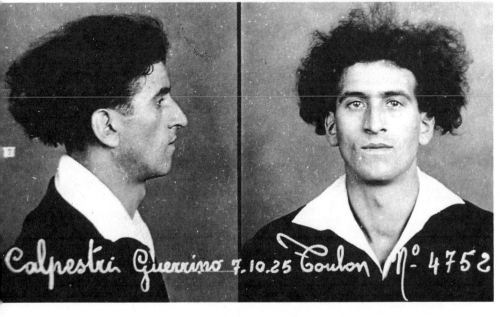

Calpestri Guerrino 7.10.25 Toulon Nº 4752

# LES PLAISIRS DANGEREUX

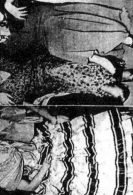

the girl who 'brings it on herself'. The predominant image of men got up in lavish ball-gowns provided the most succinct vision of a dysfunction in the rounds of pleasure and crime, the starting point for a narrative of retribution.

This not only permitted the moral parody-critique of homosexuality within the traditional imagery of glamour, but also permitted making a distinction from the young woman's fate. It reinstated hers as natural, its narrative as normative of the city. Here, in July 1939, *Détective* investigates the mystery of a young woman found stabbed in the Métro after leaving a open-air dance on the banks of the Marne:

SHE LOVED THE *BAL* TOO MUCH
The assassin was never found, nor did the motive come to light, for such an unusually audacious and rapidly executed crime … People rich in imagination saw a mystery everywhere, and gave all sorts of absurd explanations; it was the *cagoulards*, a matter of spies or the Gestapo.… The police tried to look for a pimp, but got nowhere. Loetitia Toureaux died a victim of her own haunting a *bal musette*.…

Only so far: Loetitia's death was really little more than an excuse for the reporter to take an amusing *flânerie* round the suburban *musettes*, to taste the tango, the rumba and the Lambeth Walk, and so to sniff out some entertaining anecdotes as well as clues. The investigation allowed his readers at least a double thrill! And this despite the fact that there really was some suggestion that she had been the mistress of a Cagoule leader, and that the murder was politically motivated.[4] Nor was *Détective Magazine* itself averse to spinning its own elaborate stories around the right-wing *cagoulard* terrorists, the CSARS or the Gestapo. They made excellent copy, their weapons and bombs could be montaged as dramatic fantasies of the technology of urban crime.

For the murdered homosexuals, however, it was not so much the wilfulness of routine, normal pleasures that destroyed in the randomness of urban complexity as the tragic inevitability of inversion. Inverted sexuality, with Léon Lijour or the Count, was signalled by their foolish and discordant aspirations to a better life, by an attempt at a social inversion that was to provide the reason and starting point for a storyline of fatal misadventure, 'The Crime of the Rue Labat' and 'The Mystery of the Rue Tournefort'. The young Italian with a fancy visiting card was strangled by two *mauvais garçons*, an easy prey on his own, cut off from his family and roots. The boys who killed him are arrested only two days later by the detectives, and we can recognise them, pure Parisians, Piaf's boyfriends, Warnod's pale young men. Lijour, the little baker's boy up from the provinces, who hid himself in the Rue Tournefort, the old quartier of 'Villon's ruffians', hoping to find safety and secrecy for his sexual adventures. Almost certainly he knew nothing of Villon. The designation of a quartier as 'villonesque' was a privilege of the urban poet or sophisticated reporter, a poetic licence, a literary convention. For them the name could not slide from formality to fatality as it did for Léon. Ignorant of the dangers that he ran, he made himself a pretentious little love-nest. He filled his room with too many bibelots and objects of popular luxury. Not least among them the elaborate art-deco lamp, whose cord served to strangle him, and whose dramatic, graphic light lights up the narrative of the magazine page, if not the mystery of the feeble corpse:

> Will we ever know the name of the *bel-ami* who strangled Lijour, at his own desire, during one of these abject erotic crises – of which the shameful effect, alas!, manifests itself more and more frequently in all classes of society …

And *for* all classes, you could add, in the record or the night-club and music-hall. In de Fleurigny's and Daniderff's song of 1929, 'L'Obsédé', the ambivalence in the pursuit of sexual obsession and adventure and its outcome of violence and social hatred takes on the same abstract completeness as marks the narrative montage of *Détective*: the piling together of effects that pass by in the formal routine of the *ritournelle*, as they do in the spirals and angular conjunctures of the pages of the magazine:

> J'y planterais dans ton sein nu
> Qui tous les tente
> La lame rouge et tremblotante

Du premier coutelas venu,
Et je crèverais de piqûres
Tes yeux aux regards caressants
De fille appelant les passants
Le long des ruelles obscures …

Recorded by Fréhel, and so riding on the well-known details of her drug-worn life of sexual adventure, the song loses the male-gendered 'I' of the 'obsessed' so that it can offer up either a key-hole spectacle of jealousy between women or the image of self-abuse and self-destruction as the essential being of the woman singer. Indeed nothing is more normal than this sliding of the subject from one gender to another through the asymmetrical authorship of the song's writers and of its singers'. A structure of the institutions of entertainment that permits an endless round of the *travesti* of the 'I' of the song and the 'You' of its publics. The potentially excessive specificity of the writer's sex and status is mislaid in the atmosphere of the night-club, the radio or the contention between rival recordings, which, in their ensemble, come to be the true site of identification.

The urge to self-destruction and destruction too are supposedly at the heart of homosexual desire, in its vampiric thirst for youth. With Leplée and his colleague from the Palace, Dufrenne, it draws them into the masquerade, the *faux-semblant* of love. Or in the social downfall of the distinguished or famous man, a general or an industrialist, as, like the

*grande dame*, they step into the world of the *voyous*. The prey of their own desire, these men invite their death in the very texture of their daily life, in the need to realise a desire that of its nature cannot be fulfilled. And in all these cases, the story is the same: that of the evasion of having a name put to a life of which the moment of its naming must necessarily be its end. An end to a life that makes the beginning of its narrative in the annals of crime, the law courts and the *faits divers* of the magazines and dailies. Luc Dornain laid out Leplée's death like a song, round and round from one to another closure. He picked up a young man. He brings him to his smart club, Le Gerny's, in a Spahi uniform. The young man refuses him, and goes off with Piaf, Leplée's new singer, whom he has also just picked up from the street and named. The publicity over the murder, Dornain argues, even as he contributes to it, thus hides a deep, hidden, interior drama of 'infinite sadness'. Here the drama is of Leplée's loss of affectivity – the useless pursuit of love. Or there it is one of the exposure of the eminent policeman arrested soliciting in a bar by his junior officer, or the general found outside a cheap hotel by his ex-batman. Hemmed in in this way the old homosexuals hate each other. The young men on whom they prey are not profoundly homosexual and hate them. Naturally they want to rob or to kill them. Logically many old men are killed and few killers found. Every day Leplée plunged into this world, the night-clubs of the Madeleine or Pigalle, the Turkish baths. Dornain's text reaches its emotional climax:

> He was caught up in this terrible machine, and this old man, who had never known tenderness, who cynically railed against his depravity to forget his terrible solitude, knew well that these cruel faces that he wanted to take for the face of love hounded him and hated him and that one night he would see the gleam of the murderer's knife.

It is as if Warnod's mirage of the *voyou* in the Belleville dance hall has been solidified, if only through the inversion of taking him for real in the annals of inversion.

In André du Dognon's autobiographical memoirs, *Les Amours buissonnières* (1949), the same themes appear in another guise. The first-person voice of the literary artistocrat foregrounds a class conflict, and the fantasy of the gulf of class difference lying at the heart both of desire and of the desire for self-destruction. Systematically he reconstructs his memories through an imagery of the social space between him and his lovers. It becomes clear how the exchange of sex was in part a phenomenom that grew out of the power in social relations that was built around a world of unemployment and poverty, of the displacement and homelessness of young men, often recently released from prison. This conjuncture works at the service of that acute need for social alterity that would confirm a place in the historical tropings of Paris. 'Pigalle was bursting with types crushed by hunger, who stood six foot tall and had formidable shoulders' is how du Dognon sums up the street- life of those years of economic crisis, when there was no form of social security.[5] *Les Amours* opens with a disturbingly androgynous grammar as André goes out for the night, dressed up to the nines in furs and rings. He attracts a *mauvais garçon* in a night-club, and even as he does so glimpses another, the young ex-sailor and newly released convict from the naval prisons, who will be his lover for a year and a half:

> To show his good will he came nearer to me. His right hand sought mine, counting my rings as he did so. I let him do it out of politeness, but now my eyes were glued to a big lad with broad shoulders, immobile and half turned towards us. His cap with the peak pulled down, the thin lips lit by the cigarette stuck to the corner of the mouth, the white scarf round his neck, and, above all, that waist, that squareness overwhelmed me, I who dreamed from time to time of getting myself murdered ... (*Amours*, p. 14)

Of course this almost seigneurial longing mingles guilt with pleasure. There is an implicit acceptance that it was the privilege of the intellectual, the young man *de famille* or the aristocratic consumer to make the boy buy his living in this way. René Crevel imagined the near innocence of the cocaine- and tuberculosis-ravaged – and therefore beautiful – ruffian in a *bal*, before he reminded him of his place by picking him up. But, 'for men like me, who loved soldiers and simple types' (Guérin), the whole décor of the Rue de Lappe, its sound of accordions and the traditional sirop drinks, made up the ensemble of passion. A passion long before worked out in its literary outlines in Carco's novel *Jésus la Caille*, and cutting across the whole scale of gradings and genderings of the people. Unlike the *fille publique*, the *voyou* was worth at least the decor that surrounded him. He made it real, the reality of memory, the textures and lighting of the cheap hotels of Montmartre or the Rue du Départ in Montparnasse, the possession of a satisfactory coding of the masculine. Conversely, the cost of pursuit was the greater, the relation of attraction to self-renunciation more intense and the value to a literary career less easily realised. The sum of such tensions inevitably leads to a dispersion of the personality across the compartments of social life.

Du Dognon, although he is clear about the force of the conflict with his family, equally is satisfied to benefit from the freedom that is accorded to his stratum of upper-class and aristocratic youth. And so while he experiences this sense of a splitting of the self between integrity and loss, he attributes it to a dual femininity in his personality, a conflict of two tragic heroines of opera – Carmen and Marguerite in Gounod's *Faust*. The struggle between them regulates the risks that he runs, his submission to pleasure and the will to fight, to die or to submit. Whatever the balance, the outcome is a self-annihilation that can be read as a need to kill a social and sexual personality that is badly articulated through the conventional systems of gender and class – and that is torn by the displacements between the forms of loyalty that they call for, whether social or sexual.

Age too plays a role, in the fear that the passing of youth will lead to the same lack of choice that confronts the Leplées and Dufrennes. It is not possible for a young homosexual to imagine himself as a *vieux beau*, that privileged category of older man who still swans in the gallant city, who often passes on his knowledge to young acolytes. From the beginning, 'Grand Marcel' makes it clear to André that 'had you been a day over twenty-six, I wouldn't have looked at you', and the threat of time hangs over the whole narration that begins when he is twenty-two. So, although du Dognon's love story is in some ways idyllic, a utopian

## Comment ils lisent...

Le marin en permission

*Auprès de sa blonde, qu'il fait (*

defiance of social boundaries, it ends with his attempted suicide, with this bleak little report in the *faits divers*:

IN A BAR IN LES HALLES, A YOUNG MAN TRIED TO KILL HIMSELF IN THE PRESENCE OF A FRIEND ...
A sudden drama, of which it is difficult to grasp the origins, unfolded yesterday at 4 o'clock in a bar of the Rue Pierre-Lescot....
However a manuscript sheet was found in one of the pockets of the suicide bearing this unusual title: 'Aide-mort'. Daniel de V... had jotted down there, in a romantic and broken style, his wish to die young, and he added: 'Marcel will always think of me because I died for him ...'(*Amours*, p. 285)

At the same time the inexhaustible power of representation lies at the heart of the memoirs, a power that du Dognon shares with the city poets, with Cocteau or the *Détective* reporter. He can figure his own fate through the city tropes, even turning himself into the *faits divers* that pad out the daily press and make the substance of the crime and scandal weeklies. André remains the writer, not a reader; he authors his own death. And, as it happens, one of the crucial signs of Marcel's being of the people is that it is he who is an ardent reader of *Détective*, just as is Divine in Jean Genet's *Notre-Dame-des-fleurs*. More than once André comes back from a night out to find Marcel asleep in their hotel, with the magazine by his bed. It's a taste of the people, but also, for Marcel, one that goes with roaming the streets, with his life of petty crime and selling himself cheap that enables him to buy himself a sandwich, a night in a hotel rather than on a bench, or a copy of a magazine. In writing himself into the *faits divers* André offers himself for the consumption of Marcel and his like. Suicide is the surrogate for 'getting myself murdered', an alternative way of writing himself into the popular.

Throughout his book the reader is made acutely conscious of every inflexion of André's emotions, of the conflict of Carmen and Marguerite, whether making love, at work or setting out for an evening at the Rue de Lappe. Necessarily, this is a characteristic of the *récit de vie*. But if Marcel manifests powerful feelings, they are registered mutely, only through gestures or actions. A pathetic letter to André on holiday when his family drag him away for a week, signed 'le Grand Marcel, qui t'aime-pour-la-vie': a tearful threat against a woman who has killed their pet cat: or some gesture of passing happiness or resentment, like a moment of showing off in a new suit that André has had made for him. He is read, but he is not subjected to the literary conventions of a 'rounded character'. Subjectivity remains the privilege of the narrator, Marcel is an ordering of the city tropes.

In the *Livre blanc* Cocteau meets a marvellous young sailor with the words 'pas d'espoir' tattooed on his chest. He crosses them out and writes in their place the single word 'amour'. How can anyone with those eyes, those muscles, have no hope? Certainly for Cocteau the sailor needs no more than his beauty. For Cocteau and du Dognon, as for Carco in his love of *la crapule*, the wordless prostitutes, the silence of these figures they admire or worship protects the integrity of their own longing for alterity. André is shocked when he finds out not only that Marcel is disgusted by the constraints of domesticity and family life, but that he doesn't even love his mother, as he must have done had he come from song of Fréhel or Berthe Sylva. From André's ethnocentric viewpoint filial piety is a defining character of that race of *mauvais garçons*, a crucial marker of the interweaving of softness with danger that makes its members so fatally attractive. The treatment of Marcel is less detached than that of Cocteau's sailor, but is marked in the same way by its social relations.

This inequality is the more striking because really it is Marcel who releases André from the restrictions of bourgeois codings of homosexuality, from the social rounds of the young men of good family, the *beautés d'azur*. It is Marcel who pulls him into the open spaces of the night-time streets and the Bois de Boulogne, an outdoor life of necessary but unchosen resistance to the bourgeoisie, to its domestic stability and to its social paragons. For Marcel punishment in the navy was an experience of social domination by the officer class, and he cannot sell himself to an officer, while for André the military uniform only intensifies his desire. The sentimental education that he offers to André is ultimately one of social difference, which is secured through an identity of sexual passion. If André tries to kill himself, it is because this difference cannot be dealt with when each interweaving of their lives and spaces risks a loss of otherness. If he has his lover at home, it is only for him 'to be treated like a pet dog every day, rather than spoiled twice a week'. Wearing the gift of a hand-made suit Marcel comes too close to losing his wildness and to a phoney similarity with the friends of André's own class. But when André meets him in those informal places of homeless rendezvous, the steps of the Métro station, the end of the platform, the edge of the Bois, he can sight him first, envisage him, give him a shape. That this adds up to something more than the necessities of the literary form of the memoir is underlined in in its occurrence as a convention of power across a whole range of fictional and documentary practices, as we have seen. Marcel is held in a web of controlling city images:

> when Marcel was standing at the corner of a corridor in the underground, I looked at his violet ears, his reddened cheeks – but nothing could make him ugly, as his features were hard and handsome – and I asked myself how I would ever warm him, nourish him, dress him … (*Amours*, p. 158)

And André's desire for a sense of distance from his class is also achieved through Marcel. It is secured when he sees a well-dressed woman on the Métro hungrily gazing at his lover's ragged fly buttons.

The confrontation in their relation to the military caste, which emerges when Marcel refuses to embark on an adventure with an officer in the Café Select, suggests how much the deep difference of *principle* that separates them is born of class experience. A principle that, for Guérin, was to lead him to communist politics, 'The search for flesh had delivered me from social segregation. Beyond the handsome, work-hardened chests and velour trousers, I had gone in search of comradeship. It was this that I hoped to find a hundredfold in socialism' (*Autobiographie*, p. 218). And his and du Dognon's tastes throw some light on another fashion of the period, and a recurring theme in the troping of homosexual desire, the soldier's and the sailor's uniform. Along with the legionnaire they formed element of an imagery that was both a parody, a ridicule that held homosexual desire at arm's length – and that was lived out through the experiences of social difference, of bourgeois or artist and the deck-hand or engine-room boy. The fancy dress or masquerade was a way of getting inside the skin of another class, and the sailor look was an alternative to the evening gown at the Magic City. This transference stands in an odd and partial symmetry to another myth of the transcendence of social difference – actual membership of the Legion, which was seen as a sinking of class distinction in a common hardship of pure masculinity – even though on the return to civilian life this history could only endow men of different classes with a distinct mystique.[6]

The very wide diffusion of the imagery of the military–exotic ensures a diverse market and an inevitable success for a song such as 'Mon légionnaire'. And so it caught on in the recording industry, with a surge of follow-ups and imitations, some by Asso and Monnot, that played on the same visions of hard, scarred flesh, endurance and anonymity in the field of sexual desire. Alone of the singers who sung them, Piaf stands out as an oddly inverted *travesti*, a figuring through the crushed body of the city-*pute* of a missing element in masculinity. Her recording, made just after that of Marie Dubas – an institutional figure of French family entertainment – was the more striking and sold better. It must have seemed to make more complete sense coming from the mouth of a singer whose recent emergence from the ranks of 'low society' left her untainted by the recital of nursery rhymes and ditties from operettas.

Piaf's emergence from street singer to the world of smart night-clubs, recording sessions and radio-diffusion, was on the one hand from the milieu of the mythic *voyou*, and on the other into that of a notorious but none the less discreet circle of wealthy homosexual men. The class relation between them was already established in the free purchase of sex that could be made across its frontiers of wealth and poverty, in the obsessions of crime reportage, in the anthropology of the people. For a while almost the whole repertoire that Asso supplied to Piaf recounted transient encounters with tough men, fleeting contacts with soldiers and sailors, a half parodied, half sentimental gangsterism. It is not surprising that so many legends grew up around her songs. The legionnaire was her lover, met outside the barracks of Romainville – this is the version sanctioned in her autogiography and which survives today. Or perhaps it was Leplée's boy dressed up. Or, again, for Edouard Roditi, a regular of the Rugby Bar in Les Halles, he was a boxer, an ex-legionnaire and lover of men, who one night quit his friends out of pity for the street singer to assuage her frustrated desire for him (*Paris gay*, pp. 78ff.). All this is the stuff of myth, recurring in its variations from site to site, each variant preserving only the crucial element of the transitory satisfaction of enduring desire. The poem itself disappears from sight in this melée. It is only when published after the war, alone, without Piaf, in Asso's *Songs without Music*, that it finally looks like a song from a man to a man, but even so the whole collection was disguised in the trappings of a doleful sexual humanism.[7]

Piaf was saturated with the tropes of old Paris as they had been elaborated by Carco or Mac Orlan, she bore the marks of poverty and hardship that outlined her singing with a permament decor of fascination. It was impossible to sort out the real from the mythic in her image, and this fusion permitted the perfection of empathy without its attendant guilt. Her 'truth' could be admired by Maurice Chevalier, by Ambassador X or Mme. de Y when they went to Le Gerny's and they could fill it out with a gift like the white scarf. It could satisfy the crowds of working women and men who listened to her, collected her records, turned out for her weddings and funeral. Like the elderly lady following the cortège for her controversial wedding to the young Théo Sarapo in 1962, who waves through some railings to the TV camera to proclaim, 'Moi, je suis contente! Paris vingtième!' A quarter of a century before, for men like Leplée or Cocteau, she legitimised access to the *voyous*, who were her own class. For them, the B side of alterity was oneself, the marvellous that Piaf represented was a self-discovery.

The (historic) betrayal of Genet was that, in sliding from synecdoche to metaphor, he became (like) himself, the living, literary image of the authentic people. The essential shifted from the streets to his human soul, burdening it with new freedoms and the responsibility of literary power. Genet only dissembles power in his plebeian personality, but with his canonisation by Sartre his sexuality becomes an act of faith. Yet he is neither less of an anthropologist than Carco or du Dognon, nor is he less maudlin than Colette. When he discusses the importance of atmosphere in the *éclosion* (blossoming) of a crime (*Querelle*, p. 261), he treads the same route from the grim naval port to the exotic as had Mac Orlan before him.

A few of the music-hall critics found the legionnaire fashion something of a bore, but with Piaf and Fréhel it was possible to multiply its meanings through the different connections of their images for example, to pass off a brutal colonial sentimentality to the streets of Paris through the transfer of the subaltern camaraderie of the working-class city boys into the conquerors' superiority of the clique of the colonial army that recruited them.

Derrière la clique
La bataillon d'Afrique
le Gratin des pavés de Paris ...

Belleville and Ménilmontant are written in blood on the desert sands. Or to parade them as a whole range of samples of different tempting, possiblities of class and place, the boys from all over Paris, reduced to the common demoninator of soldier. In 'Où sont-ils, tous mes petits copains?', they are sung by Piaf as a roster of pleasures from Saint-Cloud to Ménilmontant and La Villette, a redemption of the male working class as sex object. As lightly as a feather the song brushes against the memories-to-be of du Dognon's *Amours*. The musical forms too, from the slinky semi-jazz of 'Mon légionnaire' to the vigorous march of the 'Clique', suppose a difference in ways of listening and ways of dancing. Dancing through them all, the codings of homosexuality, safely hidden in the spotlights ...

In this way a polyvalent coding of masculinity is discovered to paper over the inevitability of the limited tropings of inversion and effeminacy, but it can both feed off and back into the *voyous* and *marlous* of the city poets and the day-to-day hearings and dancings of entertainment. It sings for the unconventional precisely through their more than well-worn conventions. This overlapping of adventure story and colonial glory, or brutal masculinity and female longing, of the special codings of homosexual desire and catchy, commercial music, amplifies the social spaces of misrecognition. And this is needed for the city to offer experiences which can be shared and yet invisible to each other, like the visibility and meaning of the sailors' tattoos. Uninterpretable because to admit to even seeing them was to own up to knowing their secret. They kept their Eleusinian silence, and as they did so saved these popular cultures from their own hammer blows of endless repetition.

For if you can say that the flux of the city is a significant form of stability, with its regular and repetitious production of complex relationships, a trap, then in trying to break out of the routine, or to particularise a place within it, any sign that is illegible or difficult to decipher is likely to become valued. Obscurity provides a glimpse of alternative trajectories and senses, and none more so than signs that are clearly ones neither of denotation nor of connotation. Empty, like the enigmas on the legionnaire's limbs, 'pas vu, pas pris' tattooed around his neck. For these inscriptions at least may appear to escape from grammatical rigidities, from the ascription of meaning by repetition. They offer themselves as a personal possession of their site, as an unmediated access to desires.

The blank wall and blind windows of the *maison close* have something of this potential. Behind them lies a storehouse of values of the social imaginary, from the worldly madame to the accordion-playing *pute*. The very threat of abolition of the *maisons* in the late 1930s disclosed the passion for these essential picturings of woman, which appeared alongside the self-same articles exposing her exploitation, or calling for a more effective control of the *traite des blanches*.

But the plight of the mundane rounds of cheap female prostitution approaches so closely to the alignment of (hetero)sexual relationships and industrial production that its excitation is as liable to wield a dull blow of confirmation, of the existance of a certain lower depth in society or in the mind, as a magical insight:

> Malgré toutes les combines
> Que l'on peut inventer,
> On n'trouvera pas d'machines
> Qui puissent nous remplacer …
> … Et pour gagner notr'vie
> le dimanch'comm'la s'main'
> On travaille en série
> Tout comme chez Citroën. ('Les Mômes de la purée', Veber/Kroger, 1933)

At the well known *maison de tolérance* of the Rue de Fourcy, in the 1930s this song, a more cynical contemporary of Scotto's 'Mômes de la Cloche', which made Piaf famous, takes on an air of documentary. The inmates had sometimes to do over seventy *passes* every day – the reason that it was known as a *maison d'abattage*, a slaughter-house. This kind of human machine could be used in the figuring of social distance and class voyeurism, and, perched on a street corner, by the iron grille of an old cabaret, she made an excellent illustration.[8] This abstraction through the decor might open a door into the social fantastic, or perhaps only to the self-satisfaction that could be got from recognising the depth of the gulf and picturing it as well. Or the combination of the two as in Brassaï's prying and worldly record of 'Secret Paris'. Francis Carco read the meaning of the street out of the brothel and back into literature, to and fro, each movement a glimpse of the marvellous that lived only through its vagueness, its imprecision, its investment in the act of its perception, in the movement of the self through the elements of its assembled identity:

> So, I had wandered right through to the evening under the fallacious pretext

that I was in search of Villon, when really I was giving way to the fascination that houses of debauchery have always held for me. (*Envoûtement de Paris*, p. 5)

The brothel and the *fille* were indeed a part of the decor of the marvellous, even if they were worth only the decor that framed them. The literary convention of certain aspects of the city space, its times and moods and weather, could not be sustained without them. They were there to suffer from the rain and half-light, from exclusion, marginalisation or imprisonment. Yet, more often than not, the marvellous, which repeatedly enacts transformations in the author's text between the levels of observation and epiphany, can act as no more than a momentary transfiguration for his human materials: 'Reality is the apparant absence of contradiction. The marvellous is the contradiction that appears in the real' (Louis Aragon, *Le Paysan de Paris*, p. 248).

> J' rêvais pourtant que le destin
> Me ramèn'rait un beau matin
>   Mon légionnaire
> Qu'on s'en irai loin, tous les deux,
> Dans quelque pays merveilleux
>   Plein de lumière. ('Mon légionnaire')

For it reveals something beyond and not in them, something other than the well-known, outworn but ever present codings of the reality of the social abyss. Something that cannot move if they move, but only traverse their puppet-fixity:

> Ell' fréquentait la rue Pigalle,
> Ell' sentait l'vice à bon marché
> Elle était tout' noir' de péchés,
> Avec un pauvr' visag' tout pâle,
> Pourtant y'avait dans l'fond d'ses yeux
> Comm' quequ'chos' de miraculeux
> Qui semblait mettre un peu d'ciel bleu
> Dans celui tout sal' de Pigalle. (Asso)

In the narrative of this song, the 'miraculous' is sufficient to get a man to say 'you're beautiful', but not enough for her to survive for anything longer than a very brief sortie from her natural decor. 'He' takes her to Montparnasse, where his love perishes in its fashionable light. 'Thought you were more pretty', he now says, 'It's better we go our seperate ways.' The literary trajectory from Montmartre to Montparnasse, which was a social phenomenom of the 1920s and 1930s as the one declined and the other rose in status, has little place for her baggage of realities outside the duration of the song. This sentimental, part-conscious confession of the invalidity of a culture can be backed up by a more vulgar idealisation of the broken prostitute. Her degree zero of servitude can be offered up as a joke in a gallant 'enquiry' into prostitution in the pages of *Guignol*:

Old woman, scrutinising her ledger, to young prostitute: 'Have you been up
    sixty times today?'
Young prostitute: 'Word of Honour!'

Also, these rows of dismal figures, trailing up and down the slopes of
the magical Butte, might just as well be replaced by the strass and the
rhythmic routines of the Bluebell Girls – another approximation, as
Benjamin and Kracauer noted, to the nature of mass production. But the
Bluebell Girls, chosen for their machine-like similarity were even less
likely to trigger the marvellous than the inmates of the Rue de Fourcy.[9]
The tourist industry moves too fast to catch the moment of a lapse. To
achieve that, the object had to fall out of its series, like a used bus ticket
or a blue-eyed whore.

The *merveilleux*, as it was practised by the Surrealists or the city-authors of
the 'social fantastic', really worked so effectively as a passage in and out of the
everyday because it might just as well belong either to the most ordinary
repertoire of objects as to the order of the exotic – which itself is in part a
vulgar form of the marvellous, though the marvellous is not necessarily
present in it. The psychological potential of the marvellous lies in its being
endogamous or exogamous at one and the same time – between places
and states of mind, between serial production and precious objects. And,
as a word, in this way it can just as well describe the most banal love or
seduction as the literary sightline through reality. So many songs play
round the word, 'it's marvellous when we two ...' , and so on and so on,
and their commercial *ritournelle* is thus married to other levels of culture,
while endowing with a special value the interior of the territory they
define.[10] The marvellous in love becomes both an exotically unattainable
fantasy of social otherness, a moving consolation for all kinds of social
lack, and an alibi for the pleasure in the spectacle of suffering. The marvellous thing is that, even after the seventy *passes* a day, *they* still believe
in love, for love fills the core of feelings dried out by involuntary losses:

les filles qui la nuit
s'offrent au coin des rues
connaissent de belles histoires
qu'elles disent parfois,
mais aux phrases crues,
les chers souvenirs
que gardent leurs mémoires ...
C'est bien les plus mauvaises
et les plus tristes rôles
sans se révolter un seul jour
et toutes cependant
dès qu'un espoir les frôle,
toutes croient encore à l'amour.

7ᵐᵉ Année - N° 339
CHAQUE VENDREDI

17 Septembre 193
PRIX : 1 fr. 50

L'HEBDOMADAIRE DU REPORTAGE

# VOILA

NON!
VOUS NE CONNAISSEZ PAS

## LA LÉGION !

*lisez*

# Légionnaire
### Matˡᵉ 14.762

CONFESSION D'UN DUR

Crucially, then, the grammars for the articulation of the city complexities are equipped by the marvellous, together with the exotic, with a means of reading and integrating the extra-territorial from both within and without their boundaries. They are enabled to layer on to each other possible combinations of the difference of class and the difference in sex, of sex and foreignness. This is brought into play by the newspaper, travellers' tales of far-off countries or of the east-side of Paris, novels, the gramophone or radio, medical reports, military conquest and foreign trade.

One of the peculiar abilities of *Détective* is to open up the vistas of the glance between the spaces of the city and beyond, so that the distant seaport, the Spanish bordello or the colonial deserts can be mapped back on to it – a collapsing of cartographic distance and its problem of inaccessibility into the topography of city mnemonics. A rendering of the exotic in a daily common sense, integrated and available, but maintaining a necessary distance. Inevitably the thematics of here and there overlap and coincide, in the *maison close* and the *quartier réservé*, the circulation of drugs by the Corsican gangs, and the opium dream of the imaginary east. For Mac Orlan the simple resonances of the one word 'java' link together the waltz of the *menu peuple*, the quays of Limehouse, Marseille, Grenelle and the colonial fantasy of the east.[11] A world that is both a projection of the mentalities of the French or English dockworker or colonial soldier, the mind of the poet–reporter or of a Kipling in his 'Road to Mandalay', and of the unconscious exoticism of the banalities and routines of local life and the *ritournelles* of the music-hall and its magical technology, the gramophone. A means of getting inside these others, yet maintaining the seamless unity of the masculine subject of cultural pleasure.

The sailor and the legionnaire are two of the characters of mass cultures who achieve this integration figures into whom even the most insistent author–reporter can sink his own identity. The legionnaire becomes the marvellous because he represents the self-estrangement of the metropolitan country in the very act of its own self-aggrandisement. He is white, and strong: his identity and nation are effaced by his membership of the legion. But he is ever overcome by the enormity of his tasks. For him the foreign is meaninglessness and it produces boredom and *anomie*. And boredom in turn fathers the will to destroy. The construction of such pure masculinity engenders the total subjection of woman in the body of the colonial prostitute, who is hidden from any eyes but his in the *quartier réservé*, and over whom he has rights that make the collective slaughter of seventy *passes* a day pale into nothing other than their dully mechanical rhythm. The legionnaire possesses in their most bloated form the power over life and the knowledge to dispose it that characterise the city connoisseur. He has the independence that comes from perfectly trained misogyny, an integrity of body that parallels the integrity of the poet's gaze. Because the most ordinary and practised subject 'I' is the I of the male narrator, its projection into a male object is the most artlessly self-effacing of disguises.

For the legionnaire is really a part of the fauna, he has no self-possessing distance, he remains an object, buffeted at the mercy of his emotions, his boredom, his needs, which he does not and cannot understand. Or why else is he in the Legion? Why else on the run, from his crimes or his emotions, from his nation or his identity? In the concealed reasons of the legionnaire the colonial situation is doubled back into becoming the exemplar of the city itself, now exaggerated and magnified in the colours of the desert, the blood, the boredom and the sunburned, tattooed skin stretched over male flesh. The legionnaire provides the model of man who exercises the conventions of power, but can be consumed. He combines identification and subjection. In the gallant women's literature of *Pages Folles* the *képi* is the most rudimentary metaphor for sexual adventure, a bathos that underlines the improbability that 'Mon légionnaire' was a song for women. The phallus is never up for deflation by men in quite this way. This is underlined in the treatment of the theme of a 'stranger on a train' on the one hand by Asso in the song 'Paris-Méditerranée', solemn, tense, hidden, and by *Pages Folles* – a lighthearted teasing of men by a young woman. Also in the same magazine we find the sentimental and sympathetic treatment of the colonial prostitute – who in one story is taken back from men, cared for and protected by a well-meaning woman traveller. Another subversion on the part of this 'pornography'?

In this object-state, the legionnaire is an exiled and reworked form of the *voyou*. The latter excites disdain and hatred in the writers who most depend on him. Mac Orlan, Béraud or Warnod seem compelled to hate precisely to the extent that they cannot otherwise escape their fascination for him. Very often the act of their worship is terminated by one of brutal renunciation, their praise for his strength or mysterious viciousness withdrawn by a declaration of his weakness, his vanity and his femininity. The passage already cited from Warnod (p. 32) first builds up the terror of the pale-faced boy. Is he a criminal, a *souteneur*? After all these were a youthful group in the poor areas – of fifteen pimps arrested by the police in 1910, for example, the oldest was thirty and six aged between nineteen and twenty-one.[12] And then, abruptly, the tension is discharged:

> Meanwhile our pale adolescent comes to a table where a woman is already seated. She has a little child in her arms ... which she seats on the table, its little bare bottom between the glasses and bottles. The baby laughs at the big, pale thug. Perhaps it's just his father ... (*Bals*).

Each description or anecdote becomes a display of the expendability of the young man as a material for the author's memories, thrown away even as he is worked up, this *petit peuple stupide* of Mac Orlan, these men he has drunk with, and of whose puerile stories he has had enough:

> The great mistake of Milo, in my opinion, was that, one evening, he discovered the mystery of the Rue Saint-Vincent. There he learned words that he should never have known, such as painting, sculpture, poetry and literature ... (*Rue Saint-Vincent*, p. 73)

The omnipresence of danger and of death, the ready disposability of the human characters as they are gathered, processed and discarded, the renunciation that follows use, bring the work of the city-poets into a homologous relation with the parodies of homosexual *racolage*. The Midnight Markets are a model for a form of power, or a type of desire, that disguises itself, its structures and its continuity, in fatality and fleeting renunciations. So it is possible to discern elements of a whole culture of social and sexual differences that reproduce themselves as metaphors for each other and of their different forms of marginality, from the bohemian author to the sexual outlaw. The legionnaire is one of the crucial links in this chain of ambivalence.

The reportages of *Détective* on the North African brothel, then, are a glimpse into the world of the legionnaire and at the same time a representation of Paris. In his *Légionnaires* (1930) Mac Orlan hides this doubling at different points. On the one hand the military music played in the garrisons of Paris drifts even further than one might think and:

> Montmartre is reborn in the heart of the Parisian legionnaires. The names of streets, the names of women, are written in the wine that spreads across the heavy, iron tables. (p. 128)

This absence produces the most intense *cafard*, the boredom that induces a man to cut off two of his fingers and fry them as sausages, the boredom that can be graded in its intensity through from the 'normal',to the 'fantastic' or the 'inexpressibly sad'. But at the same time absence is chosen as an escape from a crime or an insupportable responsibility, or to heal a wound, of love or its lack: 'Ah, legionnaires, you almost all come from those equivocal little bars, born in the shadow of the Streets where the poverty of Europe drains men of their colour' ... (*ibid.*). Literally, the Legion brings back colour to the skin, to the city streets where the story is to be told. And, at the same time, not only does a memory linger in the boredom of the legionnaire, but a configuration of Paris can be found in the colonial landscape itself:

> it [the *quartier reservé*] is a short distance outside Casablanca in a small, closed town, such that the young regulars of the *bals* of the Rue de Lappe, who are not illiterate, could imagine a little dream village dedicated to a prostitution that is picturesque and African ... (p. 114)

The *pute*–singer is the woman who has sample the soldier as readily as he will sample the prostitutes of Tunisia, but the knowledge and the pleasures that she sings could never come from the mouths of those victim–slaves of a colonial culture. The singer and her pleasure anchor themselves in the metropolitan city as she offers a taste of his flesh: 'il sentait bon le sable chaud'. She pulls the exotic back into the spaces of the unfulfilled or the inadmissible desires of Paris. And if the colonial prostitute remembers his violence with a scar, a 'memory that will only efface itself, little by little, in the solitude of the tomb', the singer's wound seems to scar only the shellac surface of the disc. A curious aspect of such an industrial culture is that nothing that repeats can be for ever. Each wound is made, each drama replayed at each cranking of the disc, and while the *ritournelle* of every song produces an internal structure of repetition that holds out the hope of memory, the series is infinitely replaceable in the market-place for novelty. In a Piaf song 'Disque usé', the shellac cracks to a repeated groove before the lost love can be found – which is never.

In sum the legionnaire is the perfection of a phallic culture, a little like the skirt of bananas draped around the waist of Joséphine Baker. In consequence, he could be worshipped by man and woman in a rite that can act as a cover for all desires. The access to the marvellous through the body of the legionnaire is both ridiculous – because after all the Legion is just another army, though an especially vicious one – and effective because it is the filling out of failures in self-realisation with alterity. The obscurity of the legends round the neck of Asso's legionnaire, the reading of which is passed off as the responsibility of the Parisienne *pute* that was the Môme Piaf, is itself little more than an acknowledgement of the laws that forbid 'him' the understanding of this emptiness or its public decipherment. Which would lead to the admission of repressed desire, which can only return in this kind of disguise. The marvellous of the *pute* and the legionnaire can, at least, publicly recognise each other, even if this recognition is condemned to be a one-night-stand – and even though, as a result, the one-night-stand becomes the metaphor for the defering of desire. But more than that, he and she do it for the sake of the culture and not for the money.

Money, of course, was one of the very best reasons for doing it, and a respectable alibi. In the reports of the Prefect of the Var the young sailors who are questioned invariably say that they did it for the money, and indeed it was a reason that could be well appreciated. After all, ordinary ratings came from poor families, and the rail fare home on a *permission* could be expensive for them. Doing it for the money could also be construed in terms of a one-night-stand, with each night in the series having the same necessitous occasion – but, for his sexually necessitous lover underlining the effect of the fleeting nature of desire, the impossibility of its achievement and its representation through the one-night-stand. A young sailor in 1928 explained that many of his mates did as he had done for 100 francs, when he was picked up by a Norwegian diplomat in Paris: 'I took off my uniform to put on pyjamas, then we made love with touchings and kisses, then I buggered him, I only buggered him once' (F/7/13960).

There was pathos in doing such an unfamilial thing to get the money to go to see one's mum. It was as well to say 'we only did it once'. There was a problem with the story though, if the getting took you from Brest or Toulon to Paris, when home was in quite another direction. (I have imitated the illiteracy of the original in my translation.)

> On leaving the Depot, I had the sum of 125 fr. on me. When I arrived at the station I found that I only had 25 fr. in my pocket. I don't know where I had lost the 50 fr. [sic] that were missing. Finding myself without resources and that it was impossible to get to Ivry, I stayed in Toulon and slept at the Patache from Saturday night to Sunday, inscribing myself as a sailor at the D.P. On Sunday 30 March, I met in town, towards 3.30, a civilian who asked me to go and eat and drink with him. I accepted the invitation and both of us had consumed in diverse establishments of the town. Towards one in the morning, my companion, having begged me to go to bed with him, to give the two of us up to acts that morality condemns, I again accepted, and we did go to pass the rest of the night at the Grand Hotel Giraud, situated at 8 Rue Lafayette. On reaching the hotel, my companion shook the patron of the establishment by the hand, and had a moment's discussion with him. As for me, I filled in the regulation form by inscribing myself under the false name of BERNARD, Jules, born in Orléans. On balance I signed under this false name so that they couldn't find out that I'd been to bed with a man. During the night-time, this man sucked my penis, after which I introduced it into his anus. When he left, he told me to wait in the room until 9 o'clock, when he ought to come to give me the money I needed for my journey, but he didn't come. (ibid.)

So, the young sailor also had to represent himself as something of a victim of circumstances, and of other men. Looking even today at the long, grim barracks walls of Toulon it is not difficult to imagine how quickly he might have turned for comfort, pleasure or some totally different space from the dockyard, the ship or, for that matter, the parental home. And then he was left waiting as surely as the girl left by the coming and going of her sailor boy, this ordinary hand who always dazzled her more than the officer. As Cocteau could turn him into a drawing, so Asso into a song, sung by his female alibi. First the pleasure:

> Nous étions seuls sur la dune
> Le vent caressait la mer
> Dans le ciel, riait la lune
> Et lui, mordait dans ma chair.( 'J'entends la sirène')

And then the loss and the wait, which reduce each moment of pleasure to its singularity in its absence:

Il partit sur son navire
Son beau navire tout blanc
Il partit sans me le dire
Un soir, au soleil couchant.
J'entends toujours la sirène
Du bateau qui l'emporta.
Sa voix hurlait, inhumaine
'Tu ne le reverras pas!' (*ibid.*)

The figures match up. The girls in the songs waiting for the sailors, the men seeking them in Toulon, bringing them to Paris, the arrested sailor's alibi of waiting in his turn, for money he never got for a pleasure he has to say he never really wanted. The sailor and, ironically, the legionnaire, in their status as objects of consumption, slip discreetly from their roles as the acme of virility to becoming models of feminisation of men within the codes of dominant sexual mores. They become the *ça* of popular speech, that strange subject as object, 'les marins, ça fait des voyages'. They line up along with the self-same girls who wait patiently for their men to come home, to find a client, to get drunk on hot red wine for their boyfriends' execution, and who quite often are waiting for legionnaires or sailors. This *récit* coincides with the range of alibis, evasions and curiosities that surround the predicaments of illicit pleasure. Everyone knew what went on, but the narrative form that would act both as a containment, an access and an explanation had to be worked by journalist, song-writer and prefect alike. It also forestalls the transformation of the tone of fantasy and desire in Genet's literary prose, the desciption of the man–*objet* that is Querelle.

The civil and military authorities, for one, were extremely well informed. They knew what the tariffs were for encounters in Turkish baths in Paris, with or without a dressing gown. They knew which foreigners, distinguished or otherwise, came down to Toulon or Nice or Brest, and which hotels they went to, there was the Norwegian diplomat and an Argentinian reporter. And they knew that a whole network existed for taking sailors up to Paris – though these were often artfully disguised as cultural circles or as photographic services. In Puteaux, outside Paris, was one Leboucher, who describes himself as an '*artiste-musicien* and gives mixed soirées, of which it has not been possible to establish the objective' (F/7/13960). He took sailors to a photographic studio specialising in soldiers and sailors, where they were taken in 'ordinaires, en tenue de matelot' and paid between 50 and 100 francs. The files had lists of bars. But the authorities were a little hemmed in by their own criteria, and quite able to conclude a lengthy list of sexual tourists to the Côte d'Azur by saying that their presence would upset the tourist trade. The phrase with which they blamed a well-known American *racoleur*, that he sought the 'company of sailors, and so propagates amongst the Crews a vice already, unhappily, too widespread', suggests how they could not quite catch up with the phenomenom. At times their curiosity finds an almost picturesque turn that leads straight back to *Détective Magazine*. A couple of lengthy reports follow the life of a young, upper-class officer who was having an affair with a rating, and set up house with him. Their discretion was such that no clear guilt could be established, and the only circumstantial evidence was the 'effeminate' weaknesses of the rating for perfume and luxuries, though, as it happened, he was also a communist. The reports take on something of the false mystery of the suggestive photographs of streets, filled with an empty but serviceable imagery:

> some time ago a tradesman, we don't know who, coming to deliver goods to the chalet 'Sainte Marguerite' had found De C**** and his young friend extra-lightly dressed, in a state neighbouring that of nudity. (F/7/13960)

At this point, in the late 1920s and early 1930s the morality of the navy was too easily susceptible to public condemnation. In fact the Prefect's mission to clear the whole matter up had been a result of the scandal of the cruiser *Béarn* in 1928, when it had emerged that this pride of the French fleet seemed to be little more than a floating brothel. For a moment, as the conjuncture would have it, the viewpoint of the Prefect coincided with that of the Communist Party, despite their bitter conflict over the Party's ongoing programme to politicise the navy and build cells within it. Indeed it seemed a matter of simple convenience for the Prefect to organise the surveillance of homosexual and communist bars by the same teams of officers, a procedure that definitely had more to do with administrative efficiency than any necessary or causal association between the two in the mind of the authorities. In fact it is only in the one case of the little household of Sainte Marguerite that any such association is made. That De C****'s young friend was a communist was considered to be a potential security risk at the level of lax pillow-talk. Rather the overlap occured in the way in which the Communist Party, hitting back against the pursuit of its cells and propaganda, tried to turn the scandal to its own advantage by blaming the goings-on aboard the *Béarn* squarely on the officer class. *L'Humanité* carried stories of jazz-clubs and debauch on board some ships, where music and drugs were used to undermine the ordinary, working-class matelot, who was more or less raped by his aristocratic superiors. Quoting the 'naive' report of the bourgeois press that 'these painful stories will hardly be the only ones that are the object of severe enquiries at this moment', *L'Humanité* concluded:

> Definitely no! There is even a legendary tradition according to which the sailors are represented as eternally blameworthy for these manners that have

overtaken so many of our young bourgeois, civilian and military. (F/7/13960)

On the other side the Prefect's investigators used the term *racolage* for the recruitment of sailors in communist bars, the technical term, that is, for picking up a prostitute.

In *L'Humanité*, as with poets and moralists, the language takes on a doleful note that it never really has in the police reports and the correspondence of the authorities. For the vocabulary of the law – 'acts that morality reproves', 'an act against nature', and so on – is essentially descriptive, it denotes the type and the limit of a crime, and in the sailor's confessions it is intoned as if a correct description alone will yield an exculpation. But in *L'Humanité* or *Détective* the moral connotations of the language come into play as social judgement. For the PCF at the end of the 1930s, homosexuality could be thought of as just another sign of fascism, while for the right it was Jewish, Popular-Frontist and Blumist. And so an already harassed pleasure was doubly enfolded in the the grip of moralities and political expediencies. And the double aspect of the sailor is once more underlined as an outcast and as a passive victim of the immoralities at play in the social fabric.

Du Dognon remembered the *Béarn* in his encounter in Pigalle that begins his passionate descent to attempted suicide, 'I, who would have got myself murdered':

> He [Marcel] pushed me into a dark corner, and if I could no longer see the trouble in his face, I was already no longer free to ignore the great, hard lines of a young body, impatient to play as he had done before, a game of amorous hide-and-seek on the rear deck, with the little telegraphists of the *Béarn* ... And I also, at that moment, rediscovered the emotions of seesawing together in my old [school]courtyard that was left out of bounds to the pupils so that the grass could grow. Our two such different beings continued in their life – that life of the hedge school that seems to the bourgeois to be its lowest form, where the enemy was no longer the schoolmaster or the quartermaster, but our absurd and tragic youth. (p. 16)

Like a wealthy woman who falls from social grace by going slumming alone, by prostituting herself or by buying *voyous*, du Dognon had to think about stashing his furs and jewels before pursuing his adventure. It was the only way to find some guarantee of love, but the fallen bourgeoise and the middle-class homosexual sometimes had to share a social space: another twist in the narratives of gender, in which Piaf is a man in *travesti*, and the soldiers and legionnaires are women. The shifting sightlines of gender never seem to be able to come to rest in this Parisian culture, so readily defined in terms of its healthily gallant normality. Rounding up his report the head of the Police Services in Toulon summed up the surveillance and arrests that had been carried out, and complimented himself upon them:

Pursued without respite by my inspectors and my services specialised in these researches, homosexuals, it must now be said, do not give themselves up without circumspection to the *racolage* of our plants. Certainly there are prostitutes and go-betweens, but I hope that they will soon be identified. And that thanks to a recently intensified surveillance, they will be pitilessly signalled out. However, the inverts have so well understood the difficulties in which they have been placed by the Inspectors charged with their identification, that I now find out that they receive their 'friends' in villas situated outside the main agglomerations, where, for the moment, the police services are, so as to speak, non existent. (F/7/13960)

As we have seen already, for a variety of reasons the public space of entertainment was one such no-go area, too complex a set of traps for regular or systematic policing. In the midnight markets of the Château-d'Eau Métro it is difficult to avoid a feeling that these girls and boys are waiting on someone's behalf other than their own, for some utopian vision of a freedom from the tyrannies of gender.

### Notes

Some time after this chapter was completed Jonathan Dollimore's *Sexual Dissidence Augustine to Wilde, Freud to Foucault*, Oxford, Clarendon Press, 1991, appeared, probably as the most significant work on its subject to date, and readers may refer to it for short but telling discussions of Gide's *Corydon* etc. Many of my 'sources' for this part of the book are fiction, the work of writers like Andrew Holleran, *Dancer from the Dance*, New York, NAL, 1978 and Samuel R. Delany's four volumes of the *Tales of Neveryon*, New York, Grafton, 1979 have illuminated the relation between writing and sexual politics. *Les Amours buissonnières*, Paris, Scorpion, 1948, is the middle part of André du Dognon's three-volume autobiographical novel, the whole of which is a refined and moving record of a form of sexual being.

1  See Copley, *Sexual Moralities*, and Girard, *Le Mouvement homosexuel* for these regulations.

2  The significance of this assertion of Monot's, culled from her Recueil Factice in the Collection Rondel, is that Asso's poems were written prior to his encounter with Piaf. This must be related back to the role of her 'auto-biography in securing conventional meanings for her work that I discussed in chapter 2. It is a piece of 'evidence' which predates Piaf's rise to substantial fame and which is never subsequently reconsidered as an anecdote appropriate to her image.

3  See *Paris gay*, chapter 3, for the history of *Inversions*, its trial, and an extensive anthology of its range of articles and reports. *Paris gay* remains the most substantial work on homosexuality in this period, and I have drawn extensively from it, as well as finding many lines of my own enquiry. The very recent publication of new biographies of René Crevel, Jean Cocteau, Jean Genet and others seems to have added very little to our knowledge of the time and I have chosen to ignore them. On the contrary there have been a number of excellent short syntheses/review articles in the 'Gai Savoir' column of *Gai Pied*, especially those by Nickie Cumberland.

4  See Philippe Bourdel, *La Cagoule, 30 ans de complots*, Paris, Albin Michel, 1970, for a history of the right-wing movements and material on Loetitia.

5  See either *Paris gay* or Daniel Guérin, *Autobiographie de jeunesse*, especially chapter 5,

'L'Explosion', for a fuller development of this relationship. Clearly it is a crucial congruence of class and sexuality, yet an emiprical basis for understanding it is difficult to establish, if only for the all-too-classic reason that the witness comes from the stratum of literary intellectuals alone. Copley, in his otherwise useful chapter on Guérin, ducks the issue. Interestingly enough an early Guérin typescript of a lecture on his life, given to homosexual students (undated), ends up in the *Enfer* as late as the 1960s.

6  See Mac Orlan, *Légionnaires*, Paris, 1930. For 1930s *Légionnaire* films, see René Prédal, *op. cit.*, pp. 165ff. One of the most popular versions of legionnaire heroism, a match for *Beau Geste* in its terrible racism, was Piaf's other desert song, 'Le Fanion de la Légion'.

7  It is difficult to assemble much coherent biographical material on Asso, who became President of the SACEM later in the 1950s, and thus a distinguished figure in French musical life, and I am not sure that to do so could prove the point. In 1947 he provided the introduction for a homosexual gospel, *Évangiles*, with erotic illustrations by Jean Boullet, and the *Chansons sans musique* unquestionably represent a sustained dialogue with a glamorous masculinity. However it would be wrong to think of him in the same way as Guérin, for it is difficult to see how he managed to escape any *épuration* after the war, as he wrote some quite scandalously anti-Semitic articles for the collaborationist weekly *La Gerbe* on 24 April and 8 May 1941. Here he takes up SACEM's demand for better authors' rights, arguing that they are being shared with 'deux Bloch.... un Rozemburg ... et un quatrième larron. Et hop!' He planned an article for Paris Midi in which he argued that SACEM was a mixture of freemasons and Jews, representing 'the BANK ... the PARLIAMENT ... and the LODGE ... Thick walls and an immense ditch separate it from LABOUR ... YOUTH ... and BEAUTY'. All this wartime material is in Archives Nationales,/F/17/13369.

8  For the history of the regulation and life of brothels, Corbin, *Filles* remains the best access. Laure Adler's recent *Les Maisons closes* is disappointing. As for the prostitute as illustration, see Mac Orlan, *Images secrètes*. A good example is to be found in Henry de Motherlant, *Fichier de Paris*, Lausanne, 1951, an engraving taken from an Atget.

9  On this important relation of amusement and mass production, see Buck-Morss, *Dialectic*, pp. 190–2. Clearly, from the work of Maurice Verne, we can see the issue was very much in the air.

10  See Gilles Deleuze and Félix Guattari, *Mille Plateaux*, chapter 11, '1837 de la Ritournelle.'

11  Mac Orlan, *Aux Lumières de Paris*, Paris 1946, p. 123, 'La route de Mandalay et la Java de Javelle', from Olympia to Limehouse, from the Java to Kipling '"la crapule" produces literary images that annexe different experiences'.

12  See a suggestive document in the Archives de la Préfecture de Police in Paris, D.B.411, État Nominatif des Arrestations, 1902 from which this information is drawn.

# 5 Passages of reality and the zones of bargain pleasures

... street noises, rolling of the Métro on the overhead tracks of the Boulevard de la Chapelle. Whistling of the locomotives of the trains at the nearby Gare du Nord ... (Francis Carco, *Comme aux bons temps* , indication for sound effects)

Villon, qu'on chercherait céans
  N'est plus là, ni Verlaine,
Dans ce caveau sombre et puant.    (Francis Carco, 'Villon, qu'on chercherait',
from *La Bohème et mon coeur* , 1939, p. 182)

No more must there be souls in the open air and bodies aimlessly drifting.
  (Christiane de la Hammonaye, *Âmes en plein vent*, 1938, p. 119)

In chapter 1 I referred to Georges-Henri Rivière's wartime notes on the Musée des Arts et Traditions Populaires and the ways in which his *parti-pris* on the content of the Museum suggest a conflict in the thinking of the popular. In this respect his discussion of musical instruments is particularly interesting. At that stage of the unfolding of his plan the essential purpose of the Museum was to conserve a dying rural culture and to encourage its revivification – 'the practice of traditional song in the family, social evenings, during family, collective and employers' festivals'. The notes treat a range of topics from agricultural implements to building methods and types of clothing, mapping them through their region and history, suggesting what should be displayed and how it was to be explained. There is little to foretell the current, complex display, with its resounding, programmatic opening panel – a quotation from Claude Lévi-Strauss that defines its systematic representation of material culture.[1]

On the contrary, you could imagine Maurice Chevalier's 'Ça sentait bon, la France' as a theme song for the 1943 notes. But nothing of the kind! They are resolutely directed against precisely this kind of modern, urban culture, which is set in opposition to the rural as destructive and parasitic. A listing of threatened musical instruments goes like this:

Taking with them their musical repertoire, traditional instruments are little by little disappearing; the bagpipes and bombard resist, as do the cabrette and

Basque, Catalan and Provençal instruments; tenuous survival of the hurdy gurdy ... etc. Invasion – oil slick of the accordion, invasion of urban instruments, to finish degenerate jazz.(F/7/13369).

And to make things clearer still the brief sentences on the recording industry bemoan the fact that France has done very little to conserve its heritage compared, say, to Francophone Canada, where some four thousand records of folk music have been made. The accordion is treated as what it in some respects it really was, a modern, industrial instrument, belonging to another, completely alien culture, which was not fit to be represented in a museum of *France profonde*. Yet in urban culture the newcomer accordion held the supreme rank in the city's sound-plan. In general it was the successor of a range of older instruments, of which the violin alone seemed able to compete with it and accompany it in the decor of street songs. Carco described the scenario in his radio programmes:

> little orchestras, most of them made up of a simple violin and an accordion. They didn't always play in tune, but their presence poured a little balm on to many a heart ...

Its most immediate predecessor had been the *orgue de barbarie* (barrel organ), that had itself only been cleared off the Paris streets by an order of the Prefect round about 1902, on the grounds that it made too much noise. An alibi, in effect, for the changes in public taste brought about by the gentrification of some traditional quartiers, which had also resulted in the displacement of a number of old clothing markets. This prefectoral *arrêt* provoked the denunciation and lamentations of Lucien Descaves. He wrote an article, 'A Dying Sound,' in which he ridiculed the Prefect's reasoning at a time when 'children's roundabouts now have three storeys, electric lighting and steam driven organs'.[2] His complaint finds voice in *Philémon* as well, and reminds us again of the deep resentment against the emerging technologies of amusement, exemplified by the gramophone, and the underlying fear that the popular would be unable to resist the privatisation of the experiences of pleasure.

As it happens, the accordion did emerge on the stage of mass cultures at the same time as the picture postcard and the gramophone were presenting the police with new problems of control and consumers with new means of conserving the transitory. For a moment it acted as a sign of loss in relation to the 'orgue de barbarie', which it was replacing. This meant that for an initial period the accordion itself gave rise to some of that nostalgia of which it was soon to become the principal vehicle. However once established its hold on mass culture was complete – by the 1930s accordion orchestras were to become hugely successful as recording stars in their own right.

Through the city-poets' perception of popular life, their accounts of the pleasures of the *bals populaires*, street singers or the entertainment to be had in the lower class of *maison close* the accordion came to be closely associated with them. And so it became a crucial signifier in their imaginary ideal of popular spontaneity. Its notes, as we have seen, figured at the opening of Carco's radio programmes and a range of adjectives was deployed to describe the sound, 'tendre et rauque inexorablement'. Some of these, like *nasillard* (whiny) and *rauque* (hoarse), were specifically anthropomorphic. The word 'sentimental' was inseparable from it.

In the late 1930s Mac Orlan made a radio programme called *L'Accordéon* that used the instrument to integrate the city sound-plan out into the most far-flung images of colonial commerce. The Parisian dance hall echoes on the shores of Tampico. And, as under the cast-iron columns of the overground Métro, it stands in for the nature of human emotion in contrast to the alienation of geographical distance or of machine-made noise, in Carco; the rolling of iron wheels on the métro lines, the throbbing of a car. With Mac Orlan it is the steady beat of a steamship's engine. The story of the programme is the life of a sailor heard from youthful engineer to captain, a life of success, but also of change, dispersal and displacement. At the beginning is played a single, classic song denoting the pleasures of Parisian suburban dance-halls, 'Quand on allait à Robinson'. From now on it will be this tune played on the accordion that will alone hold together the babel of places and languages, the captain's identity as coherent and as French. On board the boat:

> – *from the crew's quarters we hear an accordion, which plays a simple and nostalgic dance. From far off we hear a ship's siren.*
> (Lieutenant) – It's Luciano, he plays quite well.
> (Commandant) – Yes, it's odd. A strange instrument. When I was young it was adventure that dissembled in its song … And still today, now I'm fifty years old, still as I hear it, it's adventure that torments me.
> – *the accordion finishes its song. We still hear the sound of the sea and the noise of the engine.*

In Michel Emer's song 'L'Accordéoniste', composed for Piaf in 1943, the instrument is perfectly deployed as the metaphor for popular sexuality, as both suffering and transient. A tired prostitute quits the pavement to dream her own dream in a local bar. She watches the 'the nervous play, the long, dry fingers' of her player–lover, 'qui sait jouer la java'. Odd, indeed, were he not to play the java, that fast, rural waltz that had become another of the key synonyms for the people, the dance that sounded best on the accordion or the 'little orchestra'. Anyway, the war will tear him away, and with him her dream of a better life. And she will dance the java with empty arms, when nothing but the music remains for her, played by yet another accordionist. Transfixed in a blind ecstasy by the sound and the memory of his image, her whirling can end only with silence. It renews the java's endless repetitions as a way of feeling a social *imaginaire* that is torn apart as it is made by the unending tensions of presence and loss. In the countless songs about the java, or javas for dancing, the First, the Last, the Last of the Last, the java of javas, the Blue Java, for better or for worse:

ça lui rend' dans la peau
par le bas par le haut
elle a envie de pleurer cette musique
tout son être est tendue
son souffle est suspendu
c'est une vraie tordue de la musique ...

A frankly middle-class and only mildly satirical dream of this kind was to be heard in 'Il n'est pas distingué', a song to the spontaneity and acuity of popular knowledge, made flesh in the figure of a working-class accordionist, 'Zidor. It had a mildly anti-Hitler twist, 'me, I've got Hitler up my nose / and I can't sneeze him out.' Written in 1934, it proved sufficiently good a runner to have been recorded by both Piaf and Fréhel. And after the war in his *Comme aux bons temps*, Carco was to set it up in opposition to the wartime taste for 'Lili Marlène'. He saw it as more typical of Frenchness and truly representative of the spirit of popular resistance. This is important, because in associating the accordion with the war and the resistance Carco reinforced its role in sounding the redemption of class difference. By the same token it became an innocent metaphor for slumming. In 'Il n'est pas distingué' the middle class indeed go slumming. Their search for the instinctive wisdom of the popular classes opens them to the risk of ridicule, but they can consult 'Zidor's pithy, delphic slang on any topic from dancing to politics, their oracle is the combination of street-tough and musician. They address him as *vous*, or as *monsieur*, while he comes back to them with the informal *tu* that places them at his service and as intimates of the city in which they are strangers as in their dreams: 'vous, monsieur ... what do you think of Hitler? – Me? I've got Hitler up my nose and I can't sneeze him out ... '

The ideal pendant to Carco's programmes is to be found in Doisneau's series of photographs of a woman accordionist. The sex of the player clouds the insistent melodies with an enigma.[3] Beautiful, yet fatigued, is she tired of being looked at, or simply of playing? Tracing her trajectory through the old, working-class cafés of Paris from La Villette to the Rue Tiquetonne, Doisneau embeds her sound in the multiple textures of popular life, almost stifled in one space, dominating another. Amongst these is the 'Café at la Villette', its multiple levels of absorption in the playing of the instrument: of the meat porters in the woman, of the woman in herself, blindly in her own playing, of the camera in the invisible plane that divides it from its scene and represents its power, whose impenetrability is confirmed by one furtive returning of a glance:

and of the viewer in the compelling silence of the accordion that fills the pictorial space. This way of seeing the city as sound is hard to imagine without the complex of meanings that flow from the sound-plan. The role of listening and hearing in the recognition of the site and the knowledge of the urban conjugates with the polymorphous forms of the culture industries to turn this into an image of the timeless popular. The geologies of entertainment preserve a life-form at the moment of its disappearance.

At the same time the accordion articulates the relation of man and woman. Eroticising the look with a sound, it connects the solemn stares of Doisneau's meat porters with the casual *ritournelles* of popular life, of falling in and out of love, of happiness or betrayal. It was something that Carco could, had to, joke about in one of his songs, 'Au son de l'accordéon':

Mais aujourd'hui je me demande
Si c'était vraiment pour Fernande
Et non pas pour l'accordéon
Que mon coeur battait pour de bon.
(*Bohème et mon coeur*, p. 243, 'à Dignimont')

This way of conceiving the qualities of a national culture was ultimately to compel the submission of Georges-Henri Rivière himself. In 1965 the Radio company Europe 1 set about opening up a Museum of Song, and they got both Rivière and Maurice Chevalier to give it their blessing. Writing in the commemorative album, Rivière fell into the embrace of the entertainment industries. His contribution was an essay entitled 'In France, Everything Begins With A Song':

Better, songs accompany everything, express everything. From religion to love, from politics to morals, from history to the *faits divers*. In the form of timeless oral songs. In the form of the audio-visual songs of our time.[4]

Effectively this museum – whose realisation was postponed until 1990 – meant a cultural rag-bag: one that melded together different types of popular song, whether *fantaisie* or realist, urban or traditional, which would together accede to the pantheon of museality precisely at the point when French economic development and the recomposition of Paris had finally begun to make the ensemble of their cultures seriously anachronistic. Mac Orlan was to give his radio swan-song in 1965 and to die in 1970, concluding a long retirement to the countryside. Malraux had set about his great programme of cleaning and scraping all those grimy monuments of historic Paris. Literally, the surface of the city began to change colour, to reflect the sunlight rather than absorb it. Sightlines passed to the television by the late 1960s, as well as to colour cinema, and sound-plans to an Anglophone type of rock-music on Europe 1. Even the idea of an avant-garde, cinematic version of the traditional urban trajet, the film *Paris vu par ...* ,was a ready-made atavism when it was filmed by six New Wave directors in 1962.

Completing a demographic trend that had already begun before the war, Barbès and La Chapelle became the centre of an immigrant population from North Africa, and this working class began to sing for itself, in Arabic.[5] The Zone became a synonym for the problem of immigration, the informal, squalid cities of the *bidonvilles* the refuge of the dark side of the heritage of colonialism. Around them grew the new, concrete suburbs. The alienation of the Zone from its traditional poetic was nowhere more strikingly represented than in Jean-Luc Godard's film *Les Carabiniers*. Here two tramps on a wasteland, where neither lilacs bloom nor french fries sizzle, are forcibly recruited for the service of an anonymous state by a couple of soldier thugs. The absence of poetry is underlined by the modernist aesthetic, and one or two critics sensed that the filmmaker was twisting, breaking something from Prévert or Mac Orlan.[6] The culture of the social-fantastic, the decor of naturalist miseries and tight-knit communities, was passing into history as surely as was the rural economy of *France profonde*.

Not that Rivière had ever been a sole voice raised against 'realist' song culture as the image of the popular. As we have seen in *Philémon*, the gramophone itself sounds the death-knell of working-class culture. In 1936 a record critic discussing the annual gramophone awards in *Le Temps* set the newly released version of *Louise* against the dirges of the 'female *barytones*' – that is to say, the Piafs, the Fréhels – who were both in the annual competition for the best popular song. For this critic the exquisite intonation of Ninon Vallin and Georges Thill was clearly the more finished representation of the popular than the vulgar products of the industries. Hailing the attribution of an award to *Louise*, he went on to support the jury in its;

> most vigorous reproval of the abuse of songs from the low dives and the phoney lyricism of the gutter that is right now poisoning French song in its entirety. We have deplored the spread of these *'barytone-women'* with their raucous voices. With their knowingly sought-out vulgarity of timbre and all their vocal tricks in the worst of taste, they are for ever confiding to us the miseries of some alcoholic whore. And this in such lamentable rhymes as bring dishonour to a genre that has produced so many little masterpieces in our country.

To write like this was to set oneself against the whole tone of the culture industries, the music and cinema magazines, the ranks of songwriters and poets, and their publics, for it was just this subject matter, the life of 'an alcoholic whore' that most readily denoted the presence of the urban poetic. Yet he had a point. If *Louise* had become a source and reference for all kinds of Parisianism, it had really been intended as a redemption and a purification of the working-class girls, to rescue them from the sex-markets and give them the right to love. Shortly after the first performance, a delegation of working girls, who had been given free tickets for the Opéra-Comique by Charpentier, presented him with a medal. Mlle Michaux expressed their feelings:

> We offer you this medal on which our hearts have placed our signature, on which an Orpheus, enamoured of the ideal, will express to you better than our words the thought of our sisters, their desire for a larger life in which more beauty shall be accorded them. The simple history of Louise, in which each one of us recognises herself, so to speak, the marvels which you realised in the stage setting, the great vocalists who impersonated us, and above all the joy of finding ourselves judged worthy, at last, of an artistic spectacle and considered as something more than labour-machines or sources of carnal pleasure – all these things made that evening, for us, a unique and unforgettable occasion.[7]

Charpentier, meanwhile, had devoted himself to organising provincial *Fêtes* like the one in his opera, the scene of the *fête* in Montmartre where *Louise* is crowned queen of the 'Free Commune'. In these, a real working girl was crowned Muse of her community to music and singing composed by him. He had no intention at all of generating a new stock of depressive or voyeuristic images in the style of Bruant, but he wanted rather to revivify the cultural autonomy of the people. To this end he set up popular music schools for working girls, the 'Conservatoire de Mimi Pinson' where, of course, the accordion was not to be heard. Yet taken in fragments, alongside so many other texts, *Louise* could not but become one source of tropes amongst them. Its great authority valorised them, it helped to give birth to *petits chef d'oeuvres* Changing mores too guaranteed that its interpretation would be made to exemplify different social relations. The demands made of *Louise* herself, as a kind of heroine, could not be same before and after *La Garçonne*. The role of Louise's parents slides from one of honest and understandable disappointment to the virulent repression of the young generation by the old. Even in the really refined 1935 recording Vallin seems to attempt a light Parisian accent that makes her sound a little like Berthe Sylva, bending the *è* of *mère* into a long 'ay' vowel. And the exchange of ecstasy between her and Julien, 'mourir sous tes baisers' is certainly no more innocent than a *louche* or sophisticated night-club song like Lys Gauty's 'Paradis de rêve', an erotic journey round a lover's body. As the *procureur* had said, 'things have never been like they are now, and will never be the same again'. *Louise* remained one of the vectors that carried the diverse forms of the social margins into the heart of the metropolitan culture and inscribed them there as a matter of its nature. It underwrote the realism that *Le Temps'* critic so deplored.

It was with Bruant's cabaret and eponymous journal, *Le Mirliton*, and his collection of verses, *Dans la rue*, that the realist song had achieved the status of a literary genre and a clearly defined form of entertainment – one that claimed a lineage that descended from Villon and down through the whole tradition of popular song which was commonly understood as an essential link between urban and rural, proletarian and peasant, bourgeois, petit-bourgeois and proletarian cultures. In certain respects such authenticity is naturally phoney and lacks historical sense. It's a fetish predicated by the objectification of the concept of the 'popular' and of the 'people'. Realism was as much a product of the nineteenth-century city as were the artistic physiognomies or the Universal Exhibitions. It made up a whole with other forms of popular fiction, whether the detective romance, the *faits divers* of bloody crimes or the political romances of the Communard bohemia. Indeed, it became more than a physiognomic representation of trades, types or stock situations: a method of working them into the map of the twentieth-century city through the complex of the relationships of performer, place and type of entertainment, and the layering and differentiation of the public.

Realist song was hardly political in the sense of having a determined objective, although it inevitably shared some of its tropes and modes of affectivity with political and salon culture alike. In their turn songs of political cultures and movements defined a separate mode, address and call for attention – though they might at some points of the repertoire completely coincide with realism or other music-hall styles. The famous anti-capital-punishment song of Jules Jouy, 'La Veuve' ('The Guillotine'), for example, was part of the realist repertoire and sung to the music-hall public by its leading exponents like Damia. Jean-Baptiste Clément's 'Temps des cerises' was widely sung both as a sentimental or jazzy romance – which it was, written for the cafés-concerts at the end of the Second Empire – and as the commemorative song of the Commune, which it had also become by association and use. But the 'Internationale' of Pottier and Degeyter, or the anti-militarist 'Gloire au dix-septième' of Montéhus either had their place in a different social formation to that of mass entertainment, or made a transient and conjunctural intervention within it.

The old Communard Pottier was rediscovered, barely living, and an edition of his poems published just at the point that Bruant had become a rising star in the artistic cabarets, and when his Communard colleague Jean-Baptiste Clément was becoming principally a Union organiser. Pottier was as isolated from the politics of the 1980s as from its artistic cabarets. Alongside Bruant's knowing mixture of racy wit and social comment his verse must have looked either chastely classic or out of date. Its outrage against injustice was systematic, but its imagery comes not so much from the 'street' as from the linguistic fantasies and social–

erotic utopias of Fourier. It took a very particular, militant engagement to popularise the 'Internationale', and it was accomplished within political circles in need of a tradition both of social action and of cultural production. Political song-writers accused the realist song of lacking true social reality, and from the late nineteenth century onwards, especially after the development of a coherent communist theory of literary realism, it was subject to many of the same criticisms as high-bourgeois literature, whether naturalist or avant-garde.

The realist song was, then, accused of one-sidedness, gloom, caricature and negativity, the indulgence of a sentimental, middle-class taste for immiseration. This line of criticism is summed up by Georges Coulonges, the official guardian of the history of Communard song, writing in 1969 of Bruant's song 'À La Roquette'. An exemplary ditty, it sings the execution of a petty Parisian crook at 'La Roquette', the best known prison of capital punishment. His girl, the sexual decor of the true *titi*, waits helplessly and she suffers:

> It's finished – her man has 'sneezed in the sack'. Tonette is alone … A frisson crosses the hall of the Mirliton which brings the house down with applause. Instinctively the lovely women draw close to the handsome gentlemen. The rich folk have just met up with the *marlous*. In Bruant's, song and in his cabaret. The meeting is useful, though made easy by the crush. High society, for its pleasure of an evening, does not disdain the lower depths, even if it will not go near the forge or the mine or the plough. It's in this way that Bruant distances himself from Pottier, and we are sure that this distancing served and facilitated his glory. And we are also sure that, as his song did achieve glory, it was more effective than Pottier's.(*La Chanson et son temps*, p. 76)

But if any factor facilitated Bruant's success it was not his 'distance from Pottier', but the narcissism of the literary establishments that framed him and the openness of his thematic materials to repetition as Parisian tropes. The girl in Daniderff's 'Sous la blafarde' (1931) wears her best dress for the execution. Her boyfriend dead, her descent from the bottom of society to a social hell is only as short as the song itself. From drinking 'red wine' to her 'heart's death to love' is a matter of two verses. Yet it seems clear enough that Bruant's club was, at that point, also a model for a form of slumming in representation. The wives of rich men would at least meet images of the kinds of women whom their donations to charity were destined to rescue from the street. Coulonges has a point here, but it is hard to think of *any* one song more effective than the 'Internationale'.

Pottier wrote it in hiding after the defeat of the Commune in 1871, and it was finally set to music by a worker band in Lille in 1888, shortly after its publication. Within seventeen years it was one of the best known songs in the world, even if it does remain a historical irony that such a *Fourierist* poem, with its images of the working class feeding in common from the earth mother, became the purest expression of Leninism. Its deeply felt, 1840s-sounding rhetoric may be nearer to the 'forge, the mine, the plough', but its difference from Bruant is as precisely marked in its use by the workers' movement as by its political purity. Coulonges's problem is the difficulty of living either with commercial success, which becomes a complicity with capital, or without it – which can turn out to be only an alibi for ineffectiveness. Still it's easy to see how the figure of the worn old Pottier, an original member of the First International, workless on his return to Paris from a decade of exile in England and the USA, stood in such stark moral and aesthetic contrast to Bruant in *his* older years. In his *Époque tango*, Georges Michel describes him swanning on the Riviera, impeccable in his handmade tweeds, chatting with the rich and titled, and admired by them, easy with his millions of *rentes*.

None the less, while Bruant could be depicted as an easy *succès de scandale* and a parasite off the misery of the working class, he could just as well be represented as the (current) true heir of François Villon and the real voice of the street. Béraud picked up bits of both of these, which enabled him to impose his definition of the terms, and to articulate that knowledgeable and ambiguous detachment that we have come to recognise. Situating Bruant, then, as the descendant of Villon, he assembled a meaning that cuts completely across that of Coulonges:

> He was the avenger of the pleb and the rabble. Did not his red shirt date from the time when the last *pétroleuses* and the prisoners of the Commune had just been amnestied? Coming in the 1880s, between the funeral of Blanqui and Boulangisme, the raised fist and the vulgarity of Bruant were a piece of the inarticulate rancour of the people: it came from the lower depths, it stank of the alcohol of the gin halls, coal-tar, prisons, the bloody basket of the guillotine, the cry of the old poverty sung as complaints – but what complaints, – instead of lamenting some dull bourgeois they psalmified the soul of the *garces* [tarts] and the *poisses* [lay-abouts] … The whole of the Paris of letters, even the good Coppée, considered the birth of this crapulous narcissism – which pushed the thugs to contemplate themselves in the gutter, with a mixture of admiration and fear. (*Plan sentimental*, p.40)

Béraud artlessly situates this idea of the narcissistic longing of people for their own image as a phenomenom of profound political and social fluidity. And there lies the frisson, in a representation of a people whose face is both that of the Communard and the *poisse*, whose complaint can lead either to Blanqui or to Boulanger, whose poverty is timelessly 'old' but whose misery is that of the contemporary 'lower depths'. If the line between a picturesque and fascinating glamour and the deterioration of the race cannot be cleanly drawn in the picturing of the people, then it becomes a minefield. In the 1900s we can also sense this particular danger in the contrast between the sentimental fascination with the *apache* or the *marlou*, fed off the inheritance of Hugo and Balzac, and the semi-official position of the police, given here in their journal, another *Détective*. Declaring the deter-mination of the police to thrash those fashionable figures, the 'Apaches, burglars [*grinches*], murderers [*surineurs*] of every kidney', it threatened that 'From tomorrow, M. les Apaches, it is a battle to the end without either truce or mercy' (13–19 October 1907).

At the end of the 1920s it was more or less the same minefield in which the first critics of Eugène Dabit's *Petit Louis* found themselves, in their inability to decide if this lachrymose *récit* of a working boy's war was very socialist, a little socialist, or not socialist at all. Was Dabit the authentic, working-class writer such as an Aragon or a Paul Nizan would have dreamed into life, had they been able to do so? Or was he, through the simple fact of being a writer, a traitor to his class in a way that a bourgeois could never be? Or was he just a nicer version of Céline? Nizan found that *Petit Louis* was petit-bourgeois realism and Brice Parain accused it of lacking class-consciousness, while Lucien Descaves backed it for the Prix Goncourt.[8]

As we can now see, this confusion is largely due to the transference and displacement that takes place around the figure of narcissism, imbricated in its different forms: the recognition of the writer's knowledge in the materials he consumes, their negation once consumed, and the attribution of the narcissism to the people as subject of these representations. Certainly in the novel and the film of *Hôtel du Nord* Dabit is the master of just that: the indulgence and gratification of being-Parisian, French and popular. Béraud, concluding his comments on Bruant, skilfully embodies these complexities, confounding the poetic canon with the culture of the common prostitute – a muse so different from that of Charpentier's working girl: 'Villon took up his quarters amongst us again, and the Muse of the Crossroads entered the Society of Letters on the arm of the man in a red muffler' (*ibid.*, p.42) He became as much an ancestor as Villon. Carco, afoot in Montmartre, sighed in his opening programme:

> (Carco): The quartier – in this corner it's not changed. It was Bruant's. They called him grand-dad Bruant. The young men touched their caps to him, as was only right. One of the grand-dad's songs, that really meant something: 'Rue Blanche', 'À la Roquette' ... *ce chef d'oeuvre*, St Lazare.
> (Morane): But St Lazare has been demolished.
> (Carco): Never mind, the song remains.

These debates and uncertainties had a genealogy in popular cultures. They continued the arguments that had broken out over the cafés-concerts in the Second Empire, already touched upon in chapter 2. At that time there had been the accusations that these had displaced an old, supposedly autonomous working-class culture of '48, throwing its authors into poverty and misleading their public with a negative and egotistical image of the people, and there had been counter-claims that they gave the people the culture that they wanted or deserved. Just as the young Clément had lamented in the 1860s that he had to sell cheap songs to pay for serious ones, that the working class was so subjected to fashion that could no longer tell the difference between Henri Rochefort, Thérésa or Louis-Napoléon, in 1900 he attacked the *cabaret artistique*, arguing that it was the kind of place where:

> Everything connected with justice, progress and humanity is made a laughing stock, and where on the pretext of realism the poor are made to speak like whores at the barriers and the working class talk like pimps. (Rancière, *Good Times*, p. 88).

It is not my intention to re-run these confrontations. On the contrary, the question can best be treated as one of the uneven compatibility of different types of representation and the mode of their production rather than as a reflection of the situations from which they came. A musician, Jacques Ferny, was clearer about this than Clément had been, when he unveiled a plaque to Bruant in the Rue Christiani in February 1929. Trying to make sense of Bruant's early years and the formation of his style, he found that he had to justify the cabarets that Clément had attacked:

> It must be agreed that, before the creation of the first 'Chat Noir', it was difficult for a singer – however great he might have been – to write for any publics other than those of the café-concert, to sing on other stages than those of the Scala, the Epoque and the Folies-Saint-Martin and the like. For there were not as yet any cabarets. Another great song-writer, Jules Jouy, also had to submit himself to this necessity, and he was undermined no more than Bruant had been. (Dossier on Bruant, *Arsenal*)

The differences really articulate unevenness in the social formation, the growing separation of the structures of amateur and professional performance and the industrialisation of entertainment; the fetishising of the redemptive power of the committed literary intellectual, the very partial coincidence of political and pleasure cultures, and so on. Thus the production of the social–political–poetic through song is a rite of intellectual authenticity for an Aragon or a Sartre, both of whom engaged in the genre. It is a finding or inventing of an organic relation with a historic, national culture that both purifies it of its commercial character, and feeds off it to make their thought popular. Or another, interim position, which can lead to mass popularity, is the appropriation of a high literary tradition as an individual style within the exigencies of a mass market – the post-war types of Léo Ferré or of Georges Brassens, who in their turn were also to be widely spoken of as the descendants of Villon.

The gradations in the lineage that lead from Villon to Bruant and *fin-de-siècle* salon culture in the manner of Reynaldo Hahn, and out again into the night-club and the music-hall, are too continuous to be well-defined. The supreme virtue of Villon in the process was the fact that he is no more than a name attached to a rag-bag of poems about Paris. Nothing is known about him that could disrupt his recruitment for one or another a-historical, reified tradition of pure, masculine, urban sensibility. Mac Orlan gave Willy Ronis the title of the Villon of the lens for his collection of photographs, *Belleville–Ménilmontant*. (1952). The images reproduced a being-the-people that escaped their place in time. 'Villon' signifies the continuity of a national-Parisianism, 'Bruant' signifies its renewal.

Thus, whatever the particular demand made for the value of a type of song and performance, in its politics, in its poetics, its musical structure and the style of its singing or dance-ability, and in its place in the cultural market, the music-hall and the refined salon can overlap for a moment, or find themselves together in a specialised night-club. In the late 1920s and early 1930s this relation was consecrated in the repertoire of a night-club entertainer like Lys Gauty who sang Hahn and Fauré as well as Daniderff, van Parys and Scotto, and who had a huge success with the works of Kurt Weill, with Brecht or without. The 'Pirate's Fiancée' was a lynchpin of the repertoire at a moment when the *Opéra de Quat'sous* was all the rage. It conjugated rather well with the more traditional, nautical elements of the repertoire, whether the hearty, fishing classic, 'Valparaiso' or with the most up to the moment, commercial successes like 'Le Chaland qui passe' – the haunting complaint of fugitive love which was added to Jean Vigo's *L'Atalante*. 'Au fond de la Seine', a pre-war poem of Maurice Magre set by Weill in 1932, reads more like a classic Surreal dream, of tears and weapons, decay, slime and death embedded in the river's mud, than a charming *nostalgie de la boue*. But this, rather, is what it amounts to, in the combination of Magre's cynical renunciation of Paris with a version of the tango that could only have come from the Second Viennese School.

From another starting point, this journey across social frontiers was made by the woman singer–sparrow, sprightly and irrepressibly the Parisienne *midinette* in Mistinguett's 'Gosse de Paris', tragic in the most everyday sense, the broken, girl-prostitute of 'Comme un moineau' with Fréhel and Piaf, and sublimely pretty in Hahn's *Ciboulette*. It could be made through the combination of style of singing, refined and artistic, with a text that is Surreally erotic and a casually jazzy piano score, all focussed through a mode of address that supposes the mass publics of the gramophone and the dance hall – Lys Gauty developed this genre with the 'Chaland' and 'Paradis de rêve'. Or the transition takes place in the reportage of a music-hall review. Here a rich couple, Freddy and Oriane, go on a 'gallant trip' from the Madeleine to the Bastille in 'twelve easy stopovers'. From the most abject luxury to the dirt and squalor in the *bals* of the Rue de Lappe, the cracked, grimy lamps over their doors, their fetid scent of 'blood and wet cyclists', laughter at Oriane's silk stockings. Like Daniel Guérin on his visits to the same places, they lose none of their assurance – and they too get something in return for their courage and their fascination. In this case, a dancing lesson.

The realist song relates to all these possibilities at one time or another, and while both sides of the debate around it constitute a form of reception, neither side effectively places a limit on the production of meaning as the types of song stray across the various languages that consume them. The realist song and the performers and publics that belong to it may never enter into the realm of social optatives, but their city map is none the less one of the very real spaces between the orders of desire and history.

As we have seen in Chevalier and Guilbert, being of or imagining yourself into the people is a crucial passage into the power of representation. So crucial that it can justifiably call for a little invention, as with the provincial bourgeoise Mistinguett, when, in Chevalier's arms for the first time, she feels herself to be a little flower-seller of Paris. Momentarily she finds a new ease in the life of her professional relationships, an odour of the 'real Paris' in the artificial world of the music-hall. But however crucial the passage might be, it remains a game of coming and going, of delicate or brutal renunciations as well as of acknowledgement, of denial as well as of knowledge. Conformity to the given narrative can prove perilous, the ambivalence of the narrative at one time its essence, at another a burden. Here lies the complicated character of the auto/biographising of Piaf's early years, the construction of her relationship with the figures in her songs, and the men and women in her life, the making of a plural voice that sounded only like a single one.

Lucienne Boyer, who launched herself as a more or less realist interpreter of the 'chanson de charme' with the enormously successful 'Parlez moi d'amour', acquired a whole entourage of tramps who were brought nightly to her club, Les Clochards, becoming a feature of her performance. But she shifted into the top end of the right bank night-clubs when she opened Chez Elle, favoured the American market, and preferred to underline her association with the lighter side of Parisianism, the sunlight of the guinguettes. Ridding herself of the tramps proved difficult, as she needed to renounce not only this well-tried Parisianism, but a painting she had commissioned that showed her with them. She had to establish her right of property to the canvas in order to dispense with it, but to do so without reneging on the commission. The legalities were complex, and the publicity around the case teetered on the negative.[9]

About the same time (1931) a critic interviewing Marie Dubas praised her style by saying 'Since you … it's been impossible to swallow realist songs with their baggage of fortifications, wan mornings and red scarves'. Hardly surprising, then, that even Maryse Damia, the greatest of the 1900 generation of realist singers, the 'Marseillaise' in Abel Gance's

*Napoleon*, insistently tried to underline the poetry of her genre at the expense of its repetitive decor of cracked gaslamps, gutters and the fortifications. Despite this, Maurice Verne noted the number of cocaine-red noses as well as bunches of violets amongst the really popular sections of her audience, the '6 sous' seats. After all, he wrote in *Aux usines du plaisir*:

> Damia, Yvonne George, Fréhel, they too knew poverty, and those deceptive sense-killers that never end up by putting in the artiste's brain the inexpressible thing, oblivion ... (p. 176)

To get more inside the deep ambivalence of this idealised marginality, it is worth looking at the ways in which the marginal is brought into the centre of the cultural field and fixed there as a value in the realist song, but dragging with it a baggage of contradictory and incompatible feelings.

An important instance is the evolution of the fleamarket as a place to go, or to come from, the fleamarket of Saint-Ouen as the immortal remains of all the types of marginal consumption of the nineteenth century. This market is both the zone of cut-price hearts, the affair with the girl who is not the daughter of a civil servant or a grand bourgeois –

> Et bien de mots qu'elle emploie
> Ne sont pas dans le dictionnaire ...
> C'est au marché aux puces
> Qu'j'ai trouvé un p'tit coeur d'occasion.  (J.Boyer)

– and the zone of popular regrets

> Les yeux clos j'revois mon passé
> Le ciel si doux, les durs pavés
> L'herbe jaune ...
> Et pataugeant dans les ruisseaux
> Des bandes de gosses moitiés poulbot
> Moitiés paumés
> L'odeur des frites et des lilas
> En frissonnant je r'trouve tout ça
> Sur la zone ... ('Entre Saint-Ouen et Clignancourt', A. Sablon/Mauprey, 1937)

– as well as of stunning bargains, of great art collections reassembled out of the *déchets* of the city. Fragonard's *Femme à la chemise* turned up there, for example. A place that can be seen as as being disgusting, as full of waste and squalor as it is with potential pleasures for the connoisseur:

> one day a man came to me and said what do you want for that heap of rubbish, an old stick etc., and I bargained and sold it to him for 3 francs, and then we found out, for we have our own 'police' that it was real gold ...
>     ... my colleague said what do you want for that sheet of canvas ... 400 francs, after all it's signed Degas' ... and an expert examination showed it to be just that. (Newspaper stories, 1920s).

Looking back from 1958 – another point at which the markets were threatened by the expansion of Paris and the impending completion of the ring-road and the sports grounds at Clignancourt – the *Petit Journal* had this to say:

> this high spot of the picturesque belonged one hundred per cent to *tout Paris*. Every Saturday you would encounter Salvador Dalí, Marie-Laure de Noailles, Jean Cocteau etc, roving across the flea markets in search of the marvellous and the heteroclite ... (*ibid.*, 1950s)

It is sung as a territory of mutually inaccessible knowledges for the *Zonard* and for the bourgeois. Consider the finding of bargains, which is a form of the restitution of connoisseurship to its proper materials and, at the same time, a recuperation of capital to its proper stratum of class ownership. For the small sellers of the Zone the encirclement is twofold. On the one hand this invasion from the city by the middle-class connoisseur, cruelly intent to get something for nothing, to turn rubbish alchemically into capital, masquerading the disdain and indifference appropriate to the displays of the pavement or the little stalls that must be made to yield their bargains. And, on the other, the installation, from the period before the First World War, in the wake of the rediscovery of important works, of branches of the city-centre antique shops: lookout posts for items of real value and intermediate points in their recycling back to the city centre. A trade that produces something that we might call symbolic capital, or cultural capital, as a form of power both over value and over its recognition. These stallholders who lose out no longer hold the power of the *fripière* of previous times, but become passive representations of the passage of time that only the rich survive. Their representation is forced into the poetic of the Zone as such, as part of a system of discriminations.

At the same time, then, the whole thing can appear repulsive. More repulsive, even, than Mac Orlan's Grenelle brothel, and just as necessary to the elaboration of city differences. So Mac Orlan himself could elegantly consign the Zone to the history of the people:

> For Paris the fortifications belonged much more to the ordinary people at leisure *petit peuple flâneur* than they did to the military authorities ... already they are no longer a street spectacle ... Now they belong to the history of Paris. (Lagache, *Ambiances populaires*, 1944)

But André Billy could only do this while trying to turn the reader's stomach in his expensive volume *Adieu aux fortifications* (1930). The accounts of his farewell walks spare the poverty-stricken areas of the Zone nothing in their militant hygienist rhetoric, which, drawing on the language of Lucien Descaves's own visits of 1910, rework the Goncourt mixture of fascination and disdain, distance achieved through knowledge. There is a very literary reworking here as well, the self-plagiarising of the professional journalist rehashing an old text but giving it an extra literary allure. If Billy sets up his descriptions of 1930 on the basis of Descaves of 1910, Warnod in his book of 1927 uses anecdotes straight out of his own volume on the *puces* of 1911 – although that book had, at the time, appeared to be scupulously contemporary and utterly realistic. Anyway, Billy and his companion walker play a game. Each is to assemble a collection of twelve hetroclite objects that will typify the *puces*. But as they upturn one object after another, they arrive not at the marvellous but at the pettily absurd and the ridiculous – the utter negation of either use or pleasure. When the two of them decide to risk a café, the Rendez-Vous des Sans Souci – 'Maison Alice', it becomes clear that his investigation is both a charity of moral outrage, a condemnation and a self revelation:

> Ah, exactly, here is Alice … slowly, almost afraid, she comes to the threshold like a toad to the edge of a gutter, she looks at us with her globulous eyes, the colour of dirty water. A mat of hair more sticky than fresh seaweed holds an enormous *paquet* to her skull. Her lips are two slugs.
> What can I serve you? murmurs Alice, with a bizarre sweetness.
> We look at each other. What can she serve us? Blood? Poison?
> Have you some white wine? asks my friend. (*Adieu* p. 95)

Their one care is not to touch the drink if they can help it, and their real curiosity is only aroused when they find that this woman is Alice's successor and that the real Alice kept a brothel in the grimy hut:

> We jumped with surprise.
> – But yes, it's so, look at the bed.
> She pointed to an opening in her lair, where, indeed, there shone the brass of a bed with an embroidered cover
> – It's there that it happened? We were prodigiously interested. Were there many women?
> – Only one, the *bonne*.
> – And the clients were who?
> – A little of everyone.
> – *Chiffonniers*?
> – Not many. *Chiffonniers* are serious folk.
> – But then who?
> – A little of everyone, she repeated, a little of everyone.(*ibid.*, p. 100)

This voyeur's interest is both underlined and defeated by an earlier description of the abject filth of the *chiffonniers'* lives. Their characteristics, their very physiognomy, flow from the appearance of their cities. Made of tin, cardboard, wood and plaster, 'fused into a new nameless material with rags and food-tins', they are the excremental condition of an excremental class. The two voyagers look at the mothers on the doorsteps 'if doors they can be called'. In fact doors they were called, for the landlords of these slums took them away as a punishment for the non-payment of rent. But this kind of detail is insignificant, or dangerous for what is to follow. As a simple, economic fact it is too much exterior to Billy's discourse, too suggestive of an order of suffering outside his fantasy. The practised look of the connoisseur–voyeur, which even in these extremes can still enjoy the young and pretty woman, if only as a transient condition of the horror – 'the robust health of a young girl fades in the mud' – is thrown into crisis by the accumulation of nameless forms of dirt. A crisis, that is, of its own modes of pleasure. 'Some of the women have a burst eye, a work accident or the fruit of a domestic battle, but what is unimaginable is the filth that covers their skin,' Warnod recorded on his walk. The entropic power of the rag-pickers' filth threatens the sexual imaginary even as the openness of their misery breaks down the privacy that cloaks the bourgeois visitor:

> they [the mothers] were sorting things – undefinable things – with their hands, hands which just before had been preparing vegetables and touching the kids, hands which this night would make love … (*Adieu* , p. 91.)

It's as if the purpose of the journey had been to confirm a neurosis, some fear of a pleasure excessively other in its sources. The worldy curiosity in the mores of the Zone henceforward seem hollow and defensive. The taking of pleasure and its renunciation can only be reconciled in the production of nostalgia.[10]

It must be supposed, then, that the conditions for this to be turned into the idyll of the song were manifold.

> Moi j'ai connu de vraies caresses
> Et pour les retrouver
> Quand mon coeur a besoin de tendresse
> Je me mets à rêver …
> Entre Saint-Ouen et Clignancourt
> J'ai connu mes premières amours
> Sur la Zone. ('Entre Saint-Ouen et Clignancourt')

The metonym of the bargain as the low price to pay for contact with the Zone, which is invested in the sector between Saint-Ouen and Clignancourt and the site of the Marché aux Puces; and the threatened erasure of the whole from the social map is both a relief and a foretaste of nostalgia in the memory of the corner café, the old chums, and the characters from Bruant becoming the names for streets or members of the Institut.

Or a sexual desire and its denial, so closely intertwined with mingled distances of charity and entertainment, roves across the bodies of its men: 'L'printemps des gars au torse nu / Dormaient dans l'herbe des talus …' (*ibid.*). Something that Billy too noted, the homeless men asleep on the 'talus' of Clichy. Their immobility disturbed him, he wondered if, in a reversal of their roles, it was they who might be watching him:

> May they not ask me by what right I come here to surprise them in their wild intimacy of the open air. I pass, I pass, I distance myself from this herd of

savage, sleeping men whom civilisation has pushed back [*refoulé*] on to this glutinous hillside. (*Adieu*, p. 83.)

Piaf's song returned them to civilisation as the misrecognition of pleasure in the nature of the urban savage. A source, perhaps, of a shudder as you passed through the rubble on the way to the restaurant Chez Louisette, which drew tourists to the Marché Vernaison. The flaunting of a worldly knowledge, which made slumming into an adventure that reinformed the relations of middle-class man and woman. And from across the fortifications, a certain knowledge of the rich, acquired from sifting their rubbish, might have been redeemed. In this balance the singer's role as an escapee from the Zone and as a woman from among its people is a conflict that cannot be resolved. It must turn about itself, facing now this way and now that, so that each turn confirms another public in what they know and feel.

The fleamarkets and the Zone can work as a dream of semi-alterity for the petit-bourgeois. Not because these are necessarily either coming up from them, or are on their way down, but because they offer an easy attachment to the longing for popular origins through a release from the courtesies of the inner city rounds of consumption. So there flourish the tales of the petit-bourgeois taking their Sunday out to find some amusing ornament, some crumbs from the hidden display of amazing bargains. These people are more clumsy than the connoisseurs, a social difference worth remarking. In both his books Warnod tells a story of how a lower middle-class woman steps on an old bicycle tyre, which she cannot even see as a commodity on offer, only to find herself treated to the fury of the offended stallholder. Such anecdotes help to purify the *puces* of their economic realities and so to confirm them in their literary status. They go along with the descriptions of the decrepitude of physical and moral hygiene, which help to warn the reader off those dangerous shoals and throw the markets into light relief. Made amusing by the possibility of a 'marvellous and heteroclite' version of everyday consumption, the purely voluntary choices of an alternative way of shopping to that of necessities from the city store or corner hardware shop, they make for a ready stereotype of an otherness that is no further away than the end of the Métro line.

Repetition works the Zone into the city's history both through time and at a single moment. If in Warnod, and other writers, the image of their reportages hardly shifts over whole decades, in the period round 1910 Lucien Descaves used the same phrases to describe the squalid alleys of the rag-pickers' city of Le Touzet as he did to delineate the streets of the Thirteenth Arrondissement where he lived. They all 'communicate with each other', 'they are all the same', they all 'lead back to the same place'. Of course the details are different. The Thirteenth is neat and clean, a last resort of a good, old Paris that is passing into history.

The Touzet is sticky, filthy, a sentence to death: 'two dark rooms, two cavities of tuberculosis, where those condemned to death succeed each other, are rented for 160–80 francs, a high price to pay for the *coup de grâce*.' But then the endless, tedious streets, the prisons and hospitals of the Thirteenth are a sentence for life, 'it's an archipelago of pain. [Suffering and poverty] take man at his birth and abandon him only at his death, saturated with the illusion of having lived' (*Philémon*, pp. 1ff.).

In Le Touzet, Descaves escapes by virtue of his status as a visitor; in the Thirteenth, in his little house that stands outside the interconnected circuits of popular life, while built within them. The literary salons that he holds there are a pool of light that reveal the social question beyond their confine. The sameness is important, for it reveals the portability of a way of seeing, of a structure of description, of a moral unity and judgement that underlies the surface of descriptive detail. In effect, in evoking a certain mood or atmosphere of popular life, in filling it out with longing or repulsion, distinctions fall into disuse as one image comes to stand in for another. Thus the sameness suggests the facticity of its apparent opposite, this making of endlessly fine distinctions that marks the Goncourt mode. Like the sameness, the distinctions are likely to represent a professional state of mind, the movements of the professional mind rather than those of its objects.

Repetition offers an access to the network of city images. Here the mytheme of the lilac profusion of the little gardens between the huts spills over into the picturing of Belleville, the country of passages and backyards. Here the chip-fryer cooks his potatoes in the bitter smell of oil and the white wine is as easy to down as a conversation with him or one of the other sages of the Zone. Apart from the *maquis* of Montmartre or the open lands of the Pré-Saint-Gervais or the Butte-aux-Cailles, no other part of the city can be so open to a dream of individual freedom. The shacks, with their trellises and vines, wisteria and vegetables, cheek by jowl with the storehouses of antiquities and the industrial plants, seem to offer the choice of independence or the refusal of the city as a popular spectacle:

> the *puces* are a city of wood that begins at the *périphérique* and finish nowhere ... from Saturday night to Monday morning Saint-Ouen becomes for its citizens by patent or by honour a true capital of which Paris is only the faubourg ... For me, all the streets of the Market could be called 'Rue de la Gaîeté'. (René Clair, in Campagne, *Les Week-Ends*)

A spectacle that leads straight back to the Casino de Paris or the gramophone with a song like 'la Rue sans nom', the little street that is not even on the map, where the kids play and the accordion plays, where life unfolds, but which has no name.

Namelessness is the outcome of an excess of naming. There is an atrophy of the language to suggest the difference between Belleville and the Zone, or that Belleville has a different fate from that of absorption into the language of the Goncourts or Montmartre, the Casino or the night-club. A culture so exclusively based on the making of fine distinctions appears to be the instrument of homogeneity. Poverty, exploitation and misery merge into each other in a single state of nostalgic grace. But the nostalgia turns out to be narcissism, its objective to articulate the margins from within the centre of its self-consciousness. At the same time the atrophy is subjected to more and more diverse readings in the mechanisms and media of mass entertainment.

Here, then, is the site of a conundrum, of naming a paradise in the cultures of entertainment: for organisation in urban planning or military strategy: in the redemption of a foul underclass for a generous God. That is, the problem of the noisome but highly developed *bidonville* for the hygienic ambitions of the inter-war governments, a place of resistance for the Nazi occupiers to overcome, an endless source of souls for the Catholic societies. For one, the *barraques*, unappealing as they were to communist leaders, anyway seem to have been a better place to live than the great industrial agglomerations of the red belt – Kremlin-Bicêtre, Villejuif, Gennevilliers or Saint-Denis. For if the Zone shows up in the health statistics of the late 1930s as a worse place to live than any of the *arrondissements* inside Paris, it comes out several tens or even hundreds of per cent better than those great swathes of the modern working class, smoke-filled and treeless, afflicted by any and every industrial pathology.[11] With its informal fabric and abundant plant life, the Zone was as much a hiding place for a now impossible idea of the people as it could have been for a *résistant*. In another of Fréhel's songs, it only needs imagination, not social engineering, to efface its miseries, and a bullying spouse can be as easily replaced by a 'photo of Maurice Chevalier' as a cracked wall can be pasted over with 'post card of the Côte d'Azur'.

One of the objectives of the Catholic missionaries, who produced a significant discourse on the Zone at this time, was to flush out precisely this image of a careless and unruly people and, with it, a more general problem in French social life:

In truth the problem of the Zone is located in a much greater problem.
    To revivify France, we need a healthy race. We need a higher birthrate. We can hope to get some result from bringing help to children in danger. in undertaking to struggle against the afflictions that are the attributes of this caste …
    We all know that it is exactly in this cell of our society that chidren are the most numerous, but they are conceived in conditions that are, as we know, atrocious. (C. de la Hammonaye, *Âmes en plein vent*, p. 116)

As with Billy, the juxtaposition of civilisation and its own detritus, 'only seven kilometres from Étoile', was unbearable and even more lacking in poetry. The Zonards were a cohort of 'beggars, without either law or faith, given over to their lowest instincts':

the greater part are inveterate alcoholics, who, at dawn, towards four o'clock, trail up to Paris to collect rags and – supreme irony – to 'do' the great thoroughfares in the neighbourhood of the Arc de Triomphe. (*ibid.* ).[12]

They pile their carts with the most disgusting objects, even 'faded flowers coming from some palace', they pile it up round their homes, with their 'barricade of planks in the guise of a door', and when the rain falls, it will turn the whole lot into 'a black and slimy heap'. As with any group of pagans, the cause of this impossible situation is that these people have been left too long in their state of original sin. They are almost impossible to reform and prefer their hovels to modern social housing built by the city of Paris. So that, while a minimal precondition of redemption is that the whole Zone is razed and its population rehoused, in the meanwhile the children can be saved. Like savages they can be won over with kindness and with gifts, and their eventual integration into the social body will save 'souls from the open air and bodies from aimless wandering'.[13] At the same time, Catholic missionaries contested the body of the unemployed sailor and tried to send him also to some imaginary fireside of domestic grace. During the war, the German authorities shot resistance fighters in Saint-Ouen, and in 1942 it was they who finally ordered the destruction of its *barraques*.

I believe that we can see a meeting point of these coverging discourses in a series of photographs taken by the Service Technique du Plan de Paris from the year that the destruction of Saint-Ouen began in earnest, and conserved in the Bibliothèque Historique de la Ville de Paris under Divers XXXV. The photographs, which number some thousands, were evidently part of a project to record the entirety of the Zone, but the precision with which the plan is executed seems to go beyond the needs of a memorial. In them the Zone is finally subjected to the rigour that had escaped the authorities' plans after the declaration of insalubrity of 1924. These were held up by financial disputes, by the conflicts and 'negotiations' over the rights and freedom of the Zonards and of the marketers in particular, as well as by the stabilisation of the market with the founding of the built and fixed section by Romain Vernaison in 1920. The Zone thus stayed in ever more sharp contrast with the building on the fortifications. Many collections of photographs of the 1920s and 1930s show a typical perspective of the uneven but low-lying hillocks and plains of the Zone against the not-so-distant cliffs of the new housing, the near conjunction of the old rubble and the art-deco brickwork. It becomes a trope in the etchings and wood- cuts of illustrated books, a source of elegy. The photographs of the Service Technique prepare the end of this conjunction and record it.

Each remaining sector, all around Paris, is first photographed from the air, with a point of view for each direction, and a map indicating the plan of the aerial view. Then each sector is taken street by street, in each

direction. And then court by court, and hut by hut, yard by yard. It's like an invasion, which drives the people back behind their doors. The streets are largely empty, apart from some groups of children, looking at the camera the odd family group caught at a meal in their yard. One or two figures stand in the gardens behind the trellises. Faces peep out from windows. Sometimes there are no people at all, or only the technicians measuring with their poles. And even the most broken-down shanty is marked on the photograph with a red number so that it can be identified from the ground or from the air. It is a strange land, which only conforms in some very vague way to the descriptions of Descaves, Warnod or Billy.

At Levallois there are large numbers of factories and car repair shops, garages and tiny groceries or hair salons. There is a sense of the demands made by the city, but without its life. There are no workers in the repair shops, and it is impossible to tell if the cars have been abandoned for the war, or if the shops are doing 'war work'. There is one warehouse of architectural details that looks like an uprooted Marais, a ghost museum of old gateways and columns. At Saint-Ouen it is back to the 'residential suburb', the bricolage of tin and wood and cardboard that we know, the odd ice-cream cart in one yard, with its cheap and jaunty decorations, an ancient torso in another. Even where there are signs of human life, no one circulates. It looks already like a set for Carné, a scrupulous reconstruction, a neat and almost fresh representation of the old and the decaying. Or, in the abounding fragments, a dream for Benjamin, angelic traces of a lost civilisation whose *déchets* are yet to be renamed and valued. After all, the authorities are not the Goncourt men, framing, moralising as they go: they have only to list or to number. Yet this deadly, neutral presentation does look like the space of fantasy, whether to consign the Zone to hygiene or to nostalgia.

If the fleamarkets struggled on during the war, for the hard exchange of rare necessities, afterwards they became a place for the exchange of its waste and minor trophies. And the project of picturing them carried on, guidebooks prepared before the war, or in its first year or so, now appearing as records of loss, memory and transformation.

In the end the 'zone non-aedificandi' was a sometime legal entity immeasurably outgrown by its acquisition of symbolic and narrative values. Its juxtaposition to the City of Light was a paradigm for the system of differences that articulate the narratives of Paris, the echo of each of them: the *beaux quartiers* and Belleville, the Champs-Élysées and the Marais, the glamour and the underside.

The municipal cemetery at Pantin is an example of a place outside the Zone, but which falls into the more generalised zone of the urban peripheries. It signals the end of the road that winds round the line of the fortifications, the tracks of what was, by the 1930s, that long extinct form of prostitution, the *pierreuse*. There or along the Canal St-Martin and the Boulevard des Filles-du-Calvaire, she wandered beyond the desire of all but the needy, outside the rounds of voluntary consumption. Her margins threaded through the city, and out to Pantin, end of the very lowest form of life, the most spectacular in the sheer nudity of its suffering, its abjection in the gaze of the barely curious public. In Lys Gauty's 'Un soir d'hiver tard', the girl's murder is bracketed in the pun 'Boulevard des Filles-du-Calvaire, calvaire des filles du boulevard', in 'Les Mômes de la cloche' they struggle in their ten-day blouses, stinking, with only the canal for a mirror, and for oblivion when there is not even a last *sou*: 'Que la mort nous fauche / C'est notre plus beau jour ....'

This, then, is the Zone that is a place of all that is marginal, that is to say, a space of the social imaginary, a store of images interleaved with the geographies of the city, which can attach to different realities and represent desires. This Zone is one of displacement and condensation as the representational process of social relations. Quite suburban or rural images like the *guinguette* belong to it: a word that, in touching up against different locations – the topographic Zone, the Courtille of before 1859, the riverside at Bougival or Joinville – allows them to drift into a single, but fractured or dispersed monologue of popular pleasures. Overlapping here and there, and having at the same time a particular physiognomy and a complex of connotations, it is always the topographic zone that remains as a source of images or as a measure. Waste-land, mud, gutters and streams, lilacs, *barraques*, the free wandering and unregulated work of the Zonard, the Zoner epitome of marginal masculinity in those sleeping men.

Acceptance of this profusion of interrelations both calls for a precise moment-to-moment redefinition in popular cultures and, at the same time, allows for a certain freedom of expression and play between elements that also frame other zones: of gender, or Zone lives like those of Piaf: zones of pleasures and fates, some of which confront woman as the object of the city and the material of its definitions and which link the lives of a Piaf or a Fréhel to an understanding of their songs that take us to the seventh floor, the servitude of class and the pleasures of authenticity. In 'C'était un jour de fête', the sixth floor of a hotel in the Faubourg Saint-Denis, 'ça sentait bon Paris', in 'De l'autre côté de la rue' the working girl's attic of love looks down on the arid apartment of the bourgeoise, in Lucienne Boyer's 'Chez moi' from high up under the roof, 'on voit Paris'. Here is the touching, false naivety of the sisters in *Faubourg Montmartre*: 'nous, nous sommes pauvres, on ne nous regarde pas', that artful renunciation of a gaze that ever confects the heart of the metropolis in the image of its countless margins.

In *Femme de France* they meet with the middle-class woman in the column on make-up, 'Académie de Femme de France' which cuts

7ᵐᵉ Ann... ... CHAQUE ... OREDI ... L'HEBDOMADAIRE DU REPORTAGE

1ᵉʳ Janvier 1937
20 PAGES — 1 fr. 50

# VOILA

# Parlez-moi d'amour...

PAR
LUCIENNE BOYER

through the sometimes scandalous particularities of the singers' lives to the peace of the middle-class boudoir and the family hearth. The preparation to be looked at, the ways in which how you look articulates your feelings and identity, the tips that can be exchanged on how to achieve the right look, and on its fashions, provide a common ground of femininity. Here the singer, who in other situations may be too much a *femme galante*, becomes a model for a kind of knowledge of the world, of the self and of men, that is suitable to be passed on. A worldly acqaintance through the mechanisms of culture that makes over Ninon de l'Enclos, the seventeenth-century courtesan, into a model of disinterested womanhood. Who, in this 'period' costume, falls into the same genre of memory as Yvette Guilbert's serious repertoire of Old French Songs, or the chaste *flânerie* of the connoisseur among the monuments in aristocratic Old Paris.[14]

Across their different moralities and ways of life a Piaf, a Lucienne, a Ninon, an Yvette or the reader of *Femme de France* share a common goal – the intersection of the ideality of woman and the ideal of France, the readings of the word *feminine* and of the word *Paris*. And the complex formation of these elements allows for any possible discord of intersection to go unheard, or deafened by the fanfares.

These representations of the singer, which hold her in a relation to classical or to middle-class cultures, or see her as an active maker of these cultures, are only partially related to those that define a being of suffering and of the negativity of life. That both these registers can work for one and the same figure is made viable by the polymorphous nature of the ideal of woman, and by the complexity of a system of entertainment that cuts across the structures of class and social position with so many different meanings to offer. The abstraction of woman and the abstraction of the city hold together differences too great to be acknowledged within the field of pleasures, but whose irreconcilability is none the less the source of pleasure.

One mode of their reconciliation, or at least of their opening up, is the nod of permission to enter the unknown or to recognise the forbidden. The young Edith nodded by Leplée from the street to the most luxurious night-club in Paris, the hapless heroine of *Grain d'Cachou* from innocence to experience by the worldly *maître d'hôtel*, the reader of *Femme de France* from the home to the salon of Ninon by André Billy. This permission comes from a man, from someone who possesses the ensemble of knowledge of the irreconcilable differences, and whose skill enables him to offer openings in an appropriate order. As we have seen, it is important in a magazine such as *Femme de France* that the book reviews should be done by as expert a *littérateur* as Billy. In opening up access to the forms of social and cultural wealth and power, the regulation of perception and point of view calls for a skill that will not only orient them in an

Fréhel bonimentant à la ménagerie Jouvian en compagnie du dompteur Hulin, à droite, qui fut tué dernièrement par le lion Choura.

Vraie fille de Paris, Fréhel se sent « dans son monde » au milieu de ceux qui prodiguent aux faubourgs une joie bruyante et simple.

La gloire ! Le « cochon d'pain d'épice » traditionnel porte le nom de la joyeuse parigote.

# FRÉHEL
## UNE CHANTEUSE DES FAUBOURGS

Foulard à l'abandon, jupe plissée, poings sur les hanches, voici Fréhel foraine. Fréhel chez Jouvian, entre deux drames ; Fréhel chez la belle géante, Fréhel chez les cochons, Fréhel déchaînant la panique du plaisir à grands coups de cloche. Bonisseurs et tâcherons de la parade peuvent se reposer quand, au profit d'une bonne œuvre, se déguise ainsi la verve populacière de celle qui, au music-hall, débite la poésie populaire avec l'autorité d'une matrone des Quatre-Saisons.

Qui l'eût dit, en 1910 ? Débutante, elle surprenait les poètes rêvant d'écrire pour elle en ce temps où l'alliance de la littérature et du caf'conc' paraissait une gageure. Ils n'y parvinrent pas et ce fut heureux. Grande artiste, Fréhel sut atteindre par ses moyens à l'étage des émotions de qualité, rien qu'avec ce qu'on doit à l'inspiration des autodidactes de l'harmonie qui composent, paroles et musique, l'oreille collée à leur accordéon ou se ravageant un cœur immense en grattant la vieille guitare. Fréhel seule, Fréhel a su se choisir, sans abus, d'autres chansons. Elle est la meilleure interprète du Petit Caboulot de Carco :

*J'ai voulu revoir, tout là-bas,*
*L'auberge au milieu des lilas...*

Avant guerre ! Douceur de vivre ! Fréhel est mince, presque mourante ! On la voit au cabaret chic et mal famé, après le vieux gîton respirant un bouquet de violettes et, d'une voix posée pour la Sixtine, engageant à consulter l'Bottin dans le Métropolitain ». Après lui, la voix de Fréhel renouvelle l'air de la boîte. Elle fait rêver de départs, quand ce n'est pas encore la mode.

Les impresarii décidèrent d'autres voyages. Il est une internationale des Variétés plus déliurée que les conservateurs de boulboui parisien. Ils exportèrent en Roumanie Fréhel à qui ni l'Olympia, ni la Scala ne faisaient un pont d'or.

Avec la reine Carmen Sylva, la Cour de Bucarest avait possédé ses grâces académiques de Loti. Avec la reine Marie, la Cour, toujours éprise d'un air français, eut la franchise parigote de Fréhel. Celle qui ne soupçonnait pas l'idolâtrie des poètes du pays subjugua les vieux chambellans. Ce fut du jour que, présenter à l'intelligente souveraine, Fréhel tomba en arrêt devant les Bijoux de la Couronne flingolant au col royal, au courage, aux poignets et aux doigts délicats. Les Bijoux de la Couronne ! Évidemment. Mais quand on vient de chez Bobette », fut-ce par l'Orient-Express, c'est, avant tout, « des émaux et des perloures ! »

Risquant une révérence, Fréhel laissa tomber ces mots dignes de figurer au catalogue des mots historiques, du fier « A moi, Auvergne ! » au futur « Lafayette, nous voici ! », en passant par la morne plaine de Waterloo et « Bah, merde, celui qui l'offre ça ne s'en fout du tol ! Garde-le ! »

Si la reine au libre esprit marqua son plaisir, le roi dut être secrètement flatté. Fréhel méritait-elle un tabouret au pied du trône ? Elle n'évita pas la justesse le camp de concentration, pour aboutir à l'hôpital au seuil duquel montait la garde un soldat ennemi, l'en abaissour...

Fréhel nous revint presque exsangue. Paris qui n'avait pas su la retenir, le Paris des directeurs de théâtre, bouda celle qui l'avait délaissé. On ne l'accueillit que dans les boîtes encore plus mal famées que les premières. Elle eut asile là où l'on pourrait graver, d'un diamant mal acquis, sur la glace du bar : Mauvaises mœurs mais bon cœur. Ses premiers admirateurs désespéraient. On allait chercher au bar des messieurs-dames quand elle venait de s'installer, devant le même Vichy-menthe, chez les dames-messieurs, muette. Il fallut beaucoup de patience. Un soir, la convalescente se leva. Elle chanta. On retrouva la voix claire percée de gouaille et qu'on croyait étouffée par les fumées de la bataille et les vapeurs du lazaret.

Fréhel retrouvée eut sa place aux boîtes élégantes. Mais un Bœuf sur le Toit n'était pas pour sa riche nature. Une Yvonne George avait eu le temps de paraître et de disparaître, hélas ! Fréhel déjoua les pièges du snobisme, tournant le dos au consortium de couturières et de duchesses protégeant les arts. C'est à vivre si benoîtement que la mince Fréhel devint une grosse mémère, à point pour conquérir enfin la scène illuminée du music-hall. Elle y triomphe devant un peuple de supporters dont une moitié ignore l'autre, ceux qui se souviennent d'une Fréhel en la douceur de vivre et le bon populo n'imaginant pas que sa nouvelle idole ait pu avoir une minceur de cigarette.

Elle n'a pas besoin des leçons d'un nouveau Sardou pour être la Sans-Gêne de la rampe. Bien des choses de l'art iraient mieux si chacun avait sa franchise. Il faut la voir, encore que si bonne fille, suspendre un couplet, dégonser du geste l'instrumentaliste qui n'est pas dans le mouvement pour, du trio, déclarer au chef : « Recommencez !... Oui, tout !... Pour se mac-là ! »

Avouez que la méthode mériterait qu'on la transporte ailleurs. À la Chambre, au conseil des ministres, est-ce que je sais !...

Du peuple, dont elle est si magnifiquement, cette grosse enfant chérie des artistes a le sens de la chine ». Elle est brocarde soi-même. Par exemple quand, blaguant l'amour (audace populaire proprement française et d'un nous sauva du romantisme), elle lâche, exprès, en tendant ses bras de Républicaine au chef d'orchestre et qu'elle s'interrompt pour dire : « Pensez un peu aux drôles de petits que ça donnerait lui et moi ! »

Combien de vilains bougres avec leurs moches petites poules, ne consulte-t-elle pas lorsqu'elle chante le refrain :

*Il n'est pas distingué !*

À « rue sans joie », lourde d'angoisse mitteleuropéenne, la Française Fréhel oppose sa « Rue sans nom » où ceux qui ne sont rien s'arrangent tout de même pour rigoler :

*On ne reconnaît les saisons*
*Qu'aux légum's des petit's voitures,*
*Dans cett' rue sale et sans traficteurs*
*Les moineaux, les gosse's, tout y piaille,*
*C' qu'on peut s'y amuser, faut voir !*

Pour elle, les musiens du Globe ont mis Coppée en chansons et arrangé la terre des Forgerons en « valse-musette » :

*Monsieur le juge,*
*Que l'on me juge*
*Sans trop d' sévérité...*

C'est sa dernière ; cela s'appelle : Un chat qui miaule :

*Un chat qui miaule.*
*J' vous jur' que ça fait drôle,*
*Quand on cambriole...*

Un chat qui miaule ! Les chats des Toits de Paris et les lions de César exhibés à la foire. Le faubourg ! La Cour ! Du trône à la Foire du Trône. Bonne grosse, Fréhel, poings aux hanches, image du peuple réduisant l'Histoire au quotidien et le lyrisme épuisé à la truculence ; le peuple, ce « donneur de sang » rouge comme le foulard de la blonde Fréhel.

André SALMON.

*Reportage photographique*
*VOILÀ-ARDIÉRY*

— Enterrez ! Enterrez ! Un franc aux populaires ! — Voix de la Foire du Trône, voix de Paris, voix de Fréhel.

appropriate way for a particular audience but that will allow a common, if internally differentiated field for men and women. The differing kinds of woman, with their narratives of damnation, bliss or domestic ordinariness, will share, if nothing else, the form of their permission. While the differences between them will also allow the illusion of the man's identity through the freedom to adventure across their boundaries and define them. A culture that is so highly gendered becomes a shared one through the fragmentation of its living out, its own margins of woman to man and of some men and some women to each other, interleaved in the unconscious of the everyday.

So, when the Môme Piaf sung that the 'gens de la haute ne sav'nt pas faire l'amour' this acted both as a consolation to the high-up women as well as a seduction to their men, a discreet hint to the women that they missed no more than they already got, and an invitation to the men to try again for a bargain affair. It made a bridge to du Dognon watching the hungry, middle-class women eyeing Marcel's shabby flies. And, at the same time, in the reiteration of the transcendent truth of popular life, in its irreducible reality, the song works the inconclusive and alluring displacements of class and sexuality. Despite the evolution of social relations since the time of Bruant, or because of the slowness of their evolution, or both these things being the case, entertainment renews itself in in such a way as to fix those relations that pass across it as affective values. The means of the overlapping of social trajectories, of desires, pleasures and their fantasies, was both very simple in its address and very rich in its possibilities.

Though it might look as if there is a very direct correlation between good sex bought cheap and an undiscovered masterpiece, a cut-price heart is not quite the same as a Degas or a Fragonard. For these paintings have a different kind of pedigree that they can carry with them. The recognition of a star in the little street singer, or of the the depth of experience in the soul of a cheap prostitute, is more precisely a transaction in the market for transient pleasure and the renewal of the markets of entertainment with fresh discoveries. But the future of the Fragonard is tied up with the recognition of a past that puts it above transience and fashion, the readmission to an aristocratic privilege as of right. For a Fréhel or a Piaf the recognition of an exceptional voice and anoriginal turn in the *tour de chant* is a predicate of the culture that she is entitled to re-enact – provided that she observes the rites of low origins for the rest of her life. That is to say, that she publicly displays, in its most piteous and generalised form, the unredeemable character of the subaltern. And that she lives it out in her own ruin, without ever lacking in the prodigal generosity of the expenditure of self that bestows a voluntary allure on exploitation.

In these women the restless life of the commodity, the uncertain wanderings of desire, the perplexing distance of the margins – those mysterious, sleeping men – and the effects of class domination are pulled into the spotlight of emotional satisfaction. It is on the stage the wandering body is pulled into social normality, the space that connects so many different lives. For Fréhel, 'Bonne grosse Fréhel', her dumpy, ruined body, her blonde hair and her red scarf make her the icon of the people, and their voice. Yet the song that goes with this may as well be despair:

je n'attends plus rien
rien désormais ne m'appartient
je n'ai que d'vieilles histoires
au fond de ma mémoire ...

## Notes

1 See G.-H. Rivière, *Muséologie*, and this quotation from the notes in Archives Nationales, F/7/13369.

2 The article by Descaves, as well as information on the prefectoral decree, is to be found collected in the dossier on the Orgue de Barbarie, PPO, DB 201, 'Chanteurs etc ... '

3 See the series Na4°68, nos 170ff. in the Bibliothèque Historique de la Ville de Paris for some of the less well known images of the accordionist, who is named as Pierrette d'Orient.

4 *Le Musée de la Chanson Française*, Numero Spécial de *Variétés de Paris* édité à l'occasion de la Grande NUIT DES MUSICORAMAS – organisée par Europe 1 en l'honneur de son 10ᵉ anniversaire, Mardi, 12 Octobre, 1965.

5 See Louis Chevalier's essay in the volume *La Goutte d'or, faubourg de Paris*, Paris, AAM/ Hazan,1988, from a collection dedicated to the archives of modern architecture edited by Marc Breitman and Maurice Culot. I discuss Chevalier's position in my essay 'French Popular Song: Changing Myths of the People', *France and the Mass Media*, ed. Nick Hewitt and Brian Rigby, London, Macmillan, 1991, pp.200–19. Michel Tournier's novel *La Goutte d'or*, Paris, Gallimard, 1985, is of primary importance in understanding this shifting of identities and cultures.

6 See the dossier *Les Carabiniers*, Bibliothèque de l'Arsenal.

7 Reported and quoted in *Munsey*, New York, May 1908. The interest of this upper class women's magazine in *Louise* is a measure of its rapid success.

8 See Dabit, *Correspondance*, vol.II, p. 488ff. Parain reviewed the book in *Humanité*, 23 December, 1930.

9 See the Recueil Factice Lucienne Boyer, Rondel Collection, and her autobiography *Gosse de Paris*, Paris, La Palatine, 1955.

10 Reading out of this material I arrive at almost the same words as Stallybrass and White, *Politics and Poetics*, p. 191. Surely a significant point in realising the long duration of this culture that they trace from the nineteenth century.

11 See Docteur G. Ichok, *La Mortalité dans Paris et dans le département de la Seine, avec une préface de Henri Sellier, Ministre de la Santé publique*, Paris, Union des Caisses d'Assurances Sociales de la Région Parisienne, 1937. This is an in-depth statistical account of all causes of death in the region, illustrated with some striking maps.

12 An interesting parallel with this may be found in a film *La Zone* made by Georges

Lacombe in 1928 for the Société des Films Charles Dullin. It opens with a dramatic cut from the *chiffonniers* to a close-up of the hieroglyphs on the Obelisk at Concorde, the camera then drawing back to reveal the confrontation of one exotic with another. This is as good an account of the *chiffonniers* as I have found.

13　To avoid the risk of taking another direction I have resisted dealing with vagabondage in this work. That said, the Dossiers Banaux have some suggestive material on the subject, BB/18/6443 etc. For a longer-term perspective see Kristin Ross's discussion in chapter 2 of her *The Emergence of Social Space*, 'The Right to Laziness'.

14　Guilbert's recovery of Old French Song could very well be compared to the nationalistic anecdotalism of the Old Paris movement, especially as it is characterised in the work of one of the most scholarly of their number, Jacques Hillairet, in his vast *Dictionnaire historique des rues de Paris*, Paris, Seuil, 1963.

# The form of a conclusion

And Colette finished her work with the most soothing phrase in the French language: 'Nothing is dying, It is I who am going away, we can be assured'. (Michel Tournier, *Le Vol du vampire*, p. 257)

Chapter 1 ended with a list. A list that can be set to music, provide the captions for any number of illustrated books, or be the raw material for sociology and statistics. Such lists are valuable mnemonics. Reiterated in a certain order, emphasising one kind of place or type of person rather than another, they can be used to represent a memory, a journey, a position: a splitting and fragmentation of city space as subjectivity. They fill the spaces of representation which artlessly and indifferently articulates all the others, whether the spaces of the law or those of music-hall.

It was montage that made it possible for this complexity to be lived out with at least the masquerade of innocence: a montage of social structure and poetic imagination that both permitted and constrained the flow of one into another order of experience. This was not so much the classic power of modernist montage, to produce a third meaning, as a facility either to escape too much meaning or to produce excess. The new Jardin de Belleville, recently opened on the hillside once latticed with the stone and metal stairs that linked the courtyards, streets and tenements of the idyllic people, retains some elements of the site's history. Stairways, lilacs, a few vines, a wall of artificial rocks that recall a quarry. Like a Renaissance painting, its iconography is charming if you know it, and charming if you don't.

In the transformation and apprehension of the city, montage is the form of the conjugation of difference and identity. It is a process in which the elements conjugated take on more or less full and convincing meanings according to the shifting of their relations in the histories of their potential for significance and their conjunctural aptness to map out a present. A process of change, be it a radical upheaval, a marginal shift or a gradual socio-economic transformation, has to have some starting point, some instatement in individual memory. This normally evacuates other possible beginnings, as mnemonic collapses into the sense of individual perception.

The memoirs of Clément Lépidis, for example, *Dimanches à Belleville* (1985), which begin their trajectory forty years after Maurice Chevalier's childhood, contain much the same tropes of loss; the long-gone lilac courtyards, the sound of suffering womanhood singing the songs of the street to console herself for her lot; the closed-down halls of collective entertainment – here the cinemas rather than the music-halls. But in Lépidis's writing Chevalier himself is already the map of a vanished configuration of experience, and if we put the two together, where were the good old days? When did Belleville really start to be rebuilt? The simple answer is – as soon as it was built, or as soon as a writer's identity detaches itself from childhood. Both of these. There has not been a moment from 1859 until today when demolition and construction have not gone on, from the hovel to charity or municipal housing, and now luxury flats; when industries have not evolved and faded, from the shoe trade to the Chinese restaurant; when the population has not shifted and moved on. Lépidis, himself of Greek parents, a family of immigrant leather-workers, is frightened by the huge number of Chinese restaurants that have come to line his old pavements. In part, perhaps, this is the common, artisanal dread of the rise of service industries. More dangerously it is the refusal of a present to those who refuse one's own tropes of memory.

Moreover, what is the value of these memories now that popular life in Paris is again very largely the life of immigrant peoples? From the 1840s they came from the deep countryside. After the last war, from North and West and Central Africa. Paris is an Arab city, an African city, a city of the Indian ocean or the Caribbean islands. The older sense of rural loss that implanted itself in Belleville–Ménilmontant, and sang their future transformation, is no longer more than a fragment in a world of memory. Or, if it is more than this, then it is a constriction on others' beginnings. Today Louis Chevalier fights against the reconstruction of the quartier of the Goutte d'Or, below Montmartre, – the heart of a new urban–North African culture. But he does so because its people suit his memories. They preserve the decor. They retain the sense of mystery of Carco's *flâneries*, the colonial echoes of Mac Orlan's imaginary globe, and the suffering of Zola's immiserated heroine, Gervaise. Louis Chevalier paraphrases Mac Orlan's Grenelle. The people of the Goutte d'Or, at least, are 'worth the decor that surrounds them'. Yet their Paris is only just beginning to take shape in literature and song.

So in the end, a lot depends on where your memories begin. The points at which the past becomes felt as loss, in emotion or topography, can be the focus for quite contradictory perceptions of the city. Eugène Dabit, in the 1930s, felt that the new chain of Soldat Laboureur department stores were the last word in the Americanisation of working-class French shopping. When I saw the last of them in the 1970s, old, dark, brown and quaint with their stock of overalls and service corduroys, give way to Franprix or Codec, it was impossible to see what he meant. Lemme Caution put it like this:

> I walk around lookin' at the sights and comparin' Paris in this year of grace – or disgrace – whichever way you may like to play it – with Paris in 1926 an' in 1939. I was there on cases both years an' it was 'good goin'. Maybe I liked it better in 1939. (Peter Cheyney, *I'll Say She Does*, 1946)

The exhilarating shift between the cheap hotels and Maxim's, the sleazy bars and the bright lights, offered Lemme as many attractions as any other normal male detective or *flâneur*. In his spy story *The Mask of Dimitrios* (1939), Eric Ambler furnished his tale of an English gentleman's nightmare descent into the arms trade and drugs of prewar Europe with a dénouement in a Paris taken directly from the pages of *Détective*. The dark underside of the city presages the final hour of all old Europe. It is there that the threads of politics and money flow from Belgrade, Bucharest and Istanbul, to knot themselves fatally together. A few months later Simone de Beauvoir sat in a left bank flat and recounted a dream in one of her letters to Soldat Sartre. It was about a popular film she had just been to see, *Trafic d'armes*:

I was having a superb dream on the theme of *Trafic d'armes* in which I myself played the role of the heroic detective, when Kos opened my door … (*Lettres à Sartre*, 11 September 1939, p. 104.)

In 'Le Cygne' Baudelaire's mind's-eye images of old Paris could be a vision of the future as if it were already a ruin, its compositional elements like so many shards. The 'huts, rough-hewn capitals and shafts' can hardly be told apart as building sites or relics – 'for me everything becomes allegory'. But the collapse of it all, new or old, into allegory, was to become the playful condition of a modern, consumer culture of the city. In the work of the city-poets, the film-makers and song-writers, the multiplication of allegorical figures is so intense that they seem to become no more than proper names. Proper names tell stories, reinstating intimacy at the heart of alienation. As the entirety of old Paris is replaced or restored at the end of the twentieth century, this dispersed and shrinking whole can only be imagined in ever smaller fragments, some of which are still names from that lexicon, and some just isolated stones.[1]

Closing chapter 2, I left Maurice Chevalier bemoaning his fate, not so much as an individual but as a type. Where are the new boys from Ménilmontant? If they were missing, it was not the fault of the music industries, which had certainly done their best to reproduce them, including a clutch of Chevalier clones. And a politically more left-wing Mouloudji or Montand, whose songs chase social problems as well as pretty girls, continued to patrol the boundaries of men's space. Was it not Maurice himself, archetypal star of the gramophone, who had long ago displaced those honest, self-entertaining workers of Philémon's revolutionary memory? The division of labour that once undid the one now undoes the other. Perhaps, after all, it is the economy that is relatively autonomous. Be that as it may, Daniel Guérin, with his own, special interests, was to put to himself much the same question as Maurice. Where were all those working boys? As we would expect, he was more apt to find an answer:

> How can I use my pen to revive the young Parisians of that epoch? The type has died out, just like the mammoth or the dinosaur: muscular work has been replaced by the machine: ways of dressing and comportments have become more bourgeois: long hair de-virilises the apprentices and they look like any schoolboy or student: the cost of living and the blow that family allowances have inflicted on the state of celibacy have, Saturdays excepted, emptied the streets of their young men: last, and most important, the real, true ones live no longer in the capital, but far off in suburban subsidised housing.(*Autobiographie de jeunesse*, p. 162)

So, it seems, modern industry and its social world wiped out a whole historical stratum of sexual manners as surely as the gramophone drowned the sound of 'Cherry Time', and social housing stamped out the street corners of Belleville. Some of Guérin's memories will reappear, dimly, in suburban rock music.

In the 1950s and 1960s he became a militant of the movement for homosexual rights, taking up the unfinished work of *Inversions* in the review *Arcadie* and elsewhere. The going was hard in a way that Sartre's *Saint Genet* could do nothing to help. Men sought alibis for the crisis of French masculinity precipitated by the defeat of 1940. The satirical magazine *Crapouillot* poked fun. The notes of a lecture on homosexuality that Guérin gave to some students ended up in *Enfer* at the Bibliothèque Nationale. Frédéric Hoffet, in his *Psychanalyse de Paris* (1953), for example, argued that the very femininity of Paris had turned men into a kind of woman. Not only were the 'pédérastes' everywhere – like Jews – but more:

> [he] is the most characteristic representative of the Parisian man of today, of whom he offers us the caricature. (p. 91)
>
> The 'pédérastes' are, if I may put it like that, Paris in its pure state, the essence of Paris (p. 167)

Yet, ironically, Guérin came to regret the winning of some of the freedoms for which he fought in those grimly homophobic decades. Looking back, a label once won, being 'gay' turned out to be no substitute for the old days, for the *flâneur's* freedom to drift behind the codings of occlusion. A singular identity was less than the lost paradise of semiotic confusions.

After the closure of Les Halles in 1972 and before the building of the Forum, that great network of underground shopping arcades, old Paris lost its unconscious. One could give a date and a time. The day that 50,000 nightworkers moved out to the new markets at Rungis, leaving behind their cafés and prostitutes, the little stallholders who lived off the market's abundance, and a quarter of a million homeless, hungry rats. The severity of this loss is registered in many of the films and novels of the 1980s whose task has been to replace the unconscious of labour with the unconscious of consumption, to frame the *ritournelles* of designer culture with a profundity all of their own. Continuity with the past is sustained in the sound of that voice, the male narrator or magician, who reveals the new decor and guides us round it.

Jean-François Vilar's inner-city thriller, *Bastille-Tango* (1987) offers the imitation of Atget by its photographer-narrator as if an active presence of the past. He tracks round the streets of central Paris on his motor-scooter in search of mystery and its images, making mnemonic lists that have nothing to recall. He collects relics, making over into oblivion objects that the observant reader can still find on the pavements. But the street-names that he iterates have not as yet gained new meanings to replace those that they once had in Simenon. So the plot recruits the torture of an Argentinan woman refugee as the background of authentic suffering for a new stratum of tango-dancing gentry in the Rue de Lappe.

With films like *Subway* (1984) or *Diva* (1981), the new *flâneur* goes down into the service workshops of the Métro, the forbidden spaces of the technologies of modern transport, and finds them full of wonderful, fantastic, trendy people. He loiters round the lofts on the docks of la Villette, accompanied by a soulful aria from an opera, and they are peopled with modern magicians and criminals for whom the city invents a network of connections. In this sense it is the form of the detective novel that now provides the narrative content of a culture unable to generate new tropes, frightened of finding them either too superficial or too much for real. In the film *Mauvais Sang* (1986), the characters hide out in half-demolished butcher shops, those interim spaces of redevelopment, temporary vault-tombs for a dying pattern of consumption. There, a freshly imagined marginality discourses with itself and, for something to fulfil the look of the place, invents fresh crimes.

The newest Goncourt prize of all, Pierre Combescot's *Filles du Calvaire* (1991) resorts to the circus and brothel life of the 1930s to re-people a vanished city. The main character, a madame, has been given my grandmother's family name. No one owns their history.

For history as a source of the present, its pleasures and its discontents, look to the suburbs or to the Third World. Didier Daeninckx, the newest guide to the passages of urban and suburban crime that criss-cross the metropolis as swiftly and as deeply as the RER, has answered his own question, 'Since Chirac … Where are we going?' The answer is anywhere: anywhere in material history where memory can reconstruct the present. But especially into the suburbs, Aubervilliers and Drancy, with their histories of immigration and wartime horrors of the Deportation, which secretly work the everyday of the 1980s. And in Algeria, in the colonial ambivalence of speaking freedom in the language of your oppressor. The way to escape from under the tropings of an old culture is to re-examine them for other truths. Yet in his most recent novel *A louer sans commission* (1991) Daeninckx seems driven a step back from this position. Here a young couple, new to Paris, take care of an old down-and-out whose memories seem to hold the key to the history of the city, its crimes and its *faits divers*. Little by little they piece together the fragments of the old man's past, only to find that they all come from *Détective*, from thriller stories and from the *petites annonces*.

No doubt a new urban culture is in the making. Maybe its music will be Raï. Maybe it will come from Euro-Disneyland, fulfilling Daeninckx's injunction to look out to the suburbs. Moves to create a women's writing of the city have been few. Renaud Camus, diarist and chronicler of Paris *achrien*, recounts a world of bars, galleries and sexual pleasure at once so literary, at last so free of guilt that now Genet himself may be dismissed as a superannuated priest.[2]

But as yet the popular figures of a new unconscious are magical, eccentric others of the common shopper. The old song of Paris, the lachrymose songs of the later Piaf, her hands plunged in the washing-up at a cheap hotel as the lovers kill themselves upstairs, or the soundless tune of Doisneau's accordionist, find a successor. It is the theme tune of *Diva*, a limply charming aria from *La Wally*, a late nineteenth-century Italian opera about love and death in the Swiss Alps. All this is as it should be. In fickleness the city and the mortal heart run equal.

### Notes

1 For a brief but telling discussion of the sufficiency or insufficiency of the available material world for the experience of the marvellous or the social-fantastic, see Fredric Jameson, *Marxism and Form*, Princeton, Princeton University Press, 1971, pp. 103–5. On Baudelaire and ruin, see Buck-Morss, *Dialectics*, chapter 6.

2 'Tony Duparc and I concoted the word *achrien* a few years ago, so that it might eventually, and in certain cases, replace *homosexual*, which didn't satisfy us at all, any more than did its synonyms' – from the back cover of Renaud Camus, *Chroniques achriennes*, Paris, P.O.L., 1984.

# Note on sources

This select bibliography aims only to give an overview of the types of materials used in *Street Noises* other than those referenced in text or footnotes.

## Chapter 1

For the fleamarkets and the Zone here and in Chapter 5, see L. Aréssy and A. Parménie, *La Cité des épaves*, Paris, 1943: J. Bastié, *Croissance de la banlieue parisienne*, Paris, 1964: J. Bedel, *Les Puces ont cent ans*, Paris, 1985: P. Brisset, *La Zone de Paris et la loi du 10 Avril 1930*, Paris, 1932: C. de la Hammonaye, *Âmes en plein vent*, Paris, 1938: A. Jakovsky, *Paris, mes puces*, Paris, 1957: Léo Larguier, (of the Académie Goncourt), *Marchés et foires de Paris*, Paris, 1953: Aïda Louppe, *Marché aux puces*, Paris, 1943: G. Péreire, *Note sur l'utilisation des terrains et des fortifications*, Paris, 1901: Prefet de la Seine, *Aménagement de l'enceinte fortifiée et de la Zone*, Paris, 1933: André Warnod, *La Brocante et les petits marchés de Paris*, Paris, 1914. Various numbers of architecture and planning reviews, e.g. *Architecture, Mouvement, Continuité*, Paris: *Paris Projet*, Paris.

Photographic sources include the album of Denise Bellon – Na Album 4°, 1–109 (*c.* 1937) in the BHVP. For typical pictures of Paris and its margins see Robert Doisneau: *La Banlieue de Paris*, text by Blaise Cendrars, Paris, 1949 and *Le Vin des rues*, text by René Girard, Paris, 1955. Willy Ronis, *Belleville–Ménilmontant*, with a preface by Pierre Mac Orlan, Paris, 1954. The recently opened Vidéothèque de Paris is a remarkable source of filmic materials.

For *Louise* and Gustave Charpentier: *Louise, Dossier de l'oeuvre*, Bibliothèque de l'Opéra, Paris and dossiers on the opera and its author in the Collection Rondel, Bibliothèque de l'Arsenal: see the displays on Charpentier and the Charpentier archive in the Musée de Montmartre, Paris. Also: A. Himonet, *Louise de Gustave Charpentier, étude historique et critique, analyse musicale*, Paris, 1922: M. Delmas, *Gustave Charpentier et le lyrisme français*, Paris, 1931. In the Rondel dossier Ro 2040 on the reception of *Louise* the articles of Henry Gauthier-Villars and Maurice Emmanuel are of particular importance.

On the morphology of Montmartre see Emile Bayard, *Montmartre hier et aujourd'hui, avec les souvenirs de ses artistes et ses écrivains les plus célèbres*, illustrations by Lucien M. Gautier, Paris, 1925: G. Montoya, *Le Roman comique du chat noir*, Paris, 1905?: J. Grand-Cartaret, *Raphael et Gambrinus, où l'art dans la* brasserie, Paris, 1886. See memoirs of Mac Orlan – *Mémorial du petit jour*, Paris, 1955: *Poèsies documentaires*, Paris 1924: *Inflation sentimentale, Simone de Montmartre, quelques films sentimentaux, Abécédaire*, Paris, 1946: *Rue Saint-Vincent etc.*, with a study by André Billy, Paris, 1928. And of Carco: *De Montmartre au quartier latin*, Paris, 1927 and *Montmartre à vingt ans*, Paris, 1937. Roland Dorgelès, *Quand j'étais montmartrois*, Paris, 1936 and *Au beau temps de la butte*, Paris, 1963. Maurice Donnay, *Autour du Chat Noir*, Paris, 1926. Lucien Descaves's introductions to: Maxime Vuillaume, *Mes cahiers rouges au temps de la Commune*, Paris 1908 and J.-K. Huysmans, *Pages choisies*, Paris, 1916. For an overview of such literature see Jerrold Seigel, *Bohemian Paris, Culture, Politics and the Boundaries of Bourgeois Life*, New York, 1986.

The best collection of Eugène Vermersch and Maxime Vuillaume's *Père Duchêne* to consult is the one annotated by Vuillaume in the Bibliothèque Publique Universitaire of Geneva.

For a general guide to Montmartrois song see Michel Herbert, *La Chanson à Montmartre*, Paris, 1967, and for a collection see Pierre d'Anjou, *Histoire de la chanson française, XVII, Au temps du Chat Noir*, Paris, 1943.

On the general morphology of Paris, see: Jules Bertaut, *Les Belles Nuits de Paris*, Paris, 1956: *Le Boulevard*, Paris, n.d. André Billy, *Paris vieux et neuf*, Paris, 1909. Georges Cain, *Promenades dans Paris*, Paris, 1906. André Warnod, *Visages de Paris*, Paris, 1927. Jean Valmy-Baysse, *La Curieuse Aventure des boulevards extérieurs 1786–1950*, Paris, 1950. Charles Oulmont, *Paris, ce qu'on y voit, ce qu'on y entend*, illustrations de Bécan, Paris, 1931. Alexandre Arnoux, *Études et caprices*, Paris, 1953: *Paris, ma grand'ville*, Paris, n.d. See the Swiss writer C. F. Ramuz, *Paris*, 1939. Two novels that offer an alternative view of Paris are Louis Aragon, *Les Beaux Quartiers*, Paris, 1936 and Jacques Yonnet, *Rue des maléfices*, Paris, 1954. A left-wing guide is *Les Pavés de Paris, guide illustré de Paris révolutionnaire*, Paris, 1937.

On the question of the people and the people as other, see Geneviève Bollème, *Le Peuple par écrit*, Paris, 1986: Jacques Rancière, *Le Philosophe et ses pauvres*, Paris, 1983 and the essays collected in *Les Sauvages dans la cité, auto-émancipation du peuple et instruction des prolétaires au XIXᵉ siècle*, presented by Jean Borreil with a foreword by Jacques Derrida, Paris, 1985.

## Chapter 2

On the social and narrative analysis of popular song, see Louis-Jean Calvet, *Chanson et société*, Paris, 1981 and *Langue, corps, société*, Paris, 1979. The most exaustive treatment is that of Lucienne Cantaloube-Ferrieu, *Chanson et poésie des années 30 aux années 60 – Trenet, Brassens, Ferré ou les 'enfants naturels' du Surréalisme*, Paris, 1981. Using some 22,000, songs, this lacks any coherent method beyond a generalised understanding of 'context', but remains a good starting point. For a comprehensive bibliography of song, cabaret and music-hall, see this and two books which suggest more of a critical and economic perspective: Lionel Richard, *Cabaret, cabarets*, Paris, 1991: Serge Dillaz, *La Chanson sous la IIIᵉ république 1870–1940, avec un dictionnaire des auteurs, compositeurs, interprètes*, Paris, 1991. C. Brunschwig, L.-J. Calvet, J.-C. Klein, *Cent ans de chanson française*, Paris, 1981, is a basic tool. Sheet music can be found in the music section and records in the phonothèque of the Bibliothèque Nationale. 'Retro' record anthologes are readily available on compact disc.

On general questions of narrativity, A. J. Greimas and J. Courtés, *Sémiotique, dictionnaire raisonné de la théorie du langage*, Paris, 1979, and A. J. Greimas, *Sémantique structurale recherche de méthode*, Paris, 1986, Umberto Eco, *Lector in fabula, ou la Coopération interprétative dans les textes narratifs*, Paris, 1985 . The journal *Semiotica* is invaluable as was Pier Paolo Pasolini's 'Observations sur le plan-séquence' in *L'expérience hérétique*, Paris, 1989. Here and in Chapter 3, Sigmund Freud, *The Interpretation of Dreams*, London, 1976. On forms of dramatic narrative in this period, Ruth Harris's *Murders and Madness: Medicine, Law and Society in the fin-de-siècle*, Oxford, 1989.

On Piaf and the romance of crime, see Auguste le Breton, *La Môme Piaf*, Paris, 1980. A sample of singers' autobiographies are Joséphine Baker and Jo Bouillon, *Joséphine*, Paris, 1976: Mistinguett, *Toute ma vie*, Paris, 1954: La Houppa, *Promenade dans ma vie*, Paris, 1962: Line Renaud, *Bonsoir mes souvenirs*, Paris, 1963: Edith Piaf, *Ma vie*, Paris, 1964, *Au bal de la chance*, Paris, 1968, translated as *The Wheel of Fortune*, London, 1965: Maurice Chevalier, *I Remember it Well*, London, 1971. An early 'biography' of Chevalier is André Rivollet, *De Ménilmontant au Casino de Paris*, Paris, 1929? and for the development of his myth see P. Cudlipp, *Maurice Chevalier*, London, 1930 and W. Bryer, *The Romantic Life of Maurice Chevalier*, London, 1937.

For generalities on music-hall, see Gustave Fréjaville, *Au music-hall*, Paris, 1923: François Caradec and Alain Weill, *Le Café-concert*, Paris, 1980: Maurice Verne, *Aux usines du plaisir – la vie secrète du music-hall*, Paris, 1929: *Les Amuseurs de Paris*, Paris, 1932. Alain Hardel, *Strass*, Paris, 1983, for a fascinating Lacanian stab at the subject.

For Colette see *L'envers du music-hall*, Paris, 1913: *La Vagabonde*, Paris, 1911: *Lettres à Marguerite Moréno*, Paris, 1959: *Lettres de la vagabonde*, Paris, 1961.

## Chapter 3

René Bizet is an important comentator; see his *Touche à tout* articles of 1911, 'L'age du zinc': *L'Époque du music-hall*, Paris, 1927 and his defence of literary and other outrages in *L'Intransigeant*. Jules Bertaut, *L'Opinion et les moeurs. La IIIᵉ République de 1870 à nos jours*, Paris, 1931.

As well as *The Colour of Paris, Historic, Personal & Local*, by Messieurs Les Académiciens Goncourt under the general editorship of M. Lucien Descaves, illustrated by Yoshio Markino, London, 1914, see L'Académie Goncourt présente *Regards sur Paris*, essays by André Billy, Alexandre Arnoux, Roland Dorgelès, Hervé Bazin, Pierre Mac Orlan, Armand Salacrou, Philippe Hériat, Jean Giono, Raymond Queneau, lithographs by Beudin, Braque, Brianchon, Carzou, Chagall, Segonzac, Masson, Picasso, van Dongen, Villon. Paris, André Souret Editeur, 1962.

The authoritative source for pornography is Pascal Pia, *Les Livres de l'Enfer: bibliographie critique des ouvrages érotiques dans leurs différentes éditions du XVᵉ siècle à nos jours*, Paris, 1978. See the bibliography of Stora-Lamare, *L'Enfer* ... for an extensive coverage of all types of source.

An exhaustive list of detective and thriller fiction is in Régis Messac, *Le*

'Détective Novel'. For improving popular romance see the series Collection Bayard and Collection Fama, and for a mix of quality and popular fiction and drama the collection Les Oeuvres Libres. René Delpêche, *Les dessous de Paris, souvenirs vécus par l'ex-inspecteur principal de la brigade mondaine LOUIS MÉTRA*, Paris, 1955 is illuminating here as in Chapter 4.

Significant works by Margueritte include *Le Soleil dans la geôle*, Paris, 1921: *La Garçonne – roman de moeurs*, Paris, 1922, and *Le Couple*, Paris, 1937, being parts 1 and 3 of *La Femme on chemin: Ton corps est à toi*, Paris, 1927, and *Le Bétail humain*, Paris, 1928, being parts 1 and 2 of *Vers le bonheur*. Lucien Descaves, *Les Sous'offs, roman militaire*, Paris, 1890.

## Chapter 4

Masculinity is discussed in Jean-Paul Aron and Roger Kempf, *La Bourgeoisie, le sexe et l'honneur*, Paris, 198?. For a brief bibliography of homosexual fiction see Barbedette and Carassou, *Paris gay*, listing works by Jouhandeau, de Miomandre, Charles-Etienne *et al.*, all of importance in this chapter. Julien Green's *Le Malfaiteur*, Paris, 1987 (abandoned 1938, completed 1955), is an especially dramatic and finely thought-out story of abjected homosexuality. The works of Dominique Fernandez and Guy Hocqenghem are valuable in their ensemble. See the former's *Le Rapt de Ganymède*, Paris, 1989, as well as Hocquenghem's *Le Désir homosexuel*, Paris, 1972 and *La Beauté du métis*, Paris 1979. See the reviews *Types/Paroles d'hommes*, *Masques* and the *Cahiers gai-kitsch-camp* for a stream of basic research and comment.

## Chapter 5

See Chapter 1 for song and the Zone, adding Doris Lessing, *The Marriages between Zones Three, Four, and Five*, London, 1985. Aristide Bruant: *Le Mirliton, 1885–1894: Fleur de pavé* Pars, *c.* 1900: *Dans la rue, chansons et monologues*, Paris, 1896–7. Francis Carco, *Le Roman de François Villon*, Paris, 1926. On Paris vanishing and coming into being: Eugène Dabit, *Ville Lumière*, Paris, 1987: Clément Lépidis, *Dimanches à Belleville*, Paris, 1984. Didier Daeninckx, *À louer sans commission*, Paris, 1991, and in *Rue de Lappe*, Paris, 1987. Jacques Réda, *Les Ruines de Paris*, Paris, 1977. Renaud Camus, *Tricks*, Paris, 1982. Marie-Florence Ehret, *Salut Barbès*, Paris 1988. Michel Tournier, *La Goutte d'or*, Paris, 1985. Piere Marcel, *Articles de Paris*, Paris, 1989. Finally *Paris perdu – quarante ans de bouleversements de la ville*, under the direction of Claude Eveno and Pascale de Mézamat, Paris, 1991, including an essay by Jean-François Vilar.

Slang and popular speech: Charles Nisard, *De quelques parisianismes populaires et autre locutions non encore ou plus ou mons imparfaitement expliquées des XVII^e, XVIII^e et XIX^e siècles*, Paris, 185? Lorédan-Larchey, *Dictionnaire historique, etymologique et anecdotique de l'argot parisien*, Paris, 1872 and 1985. Charles Delvau, *Dictionnaire de la langue verte*, Paris, 1866 and *Dictionnaire érotique moderne par un professeur de la langue verte*, Paris, 1864. Simonin, *Le Petit Simonin illustré, dictionnaire d'usage*, Paris, 1957. Géo Sandry and Marcel Carrère, *Dictionaire de l'argot moderne*, Paris, 1953.

Broken series of weeklies and monthlies consulted for the period 1900-40 include: *Voilà, Vu, Pour Vous, Détective, Paris-Flirt, Paris Sex Appeal, Frou-Frou, Sourire, Paris Galant, Nuits de Paris, La Chanson de Paris, Paris qui chante, Comoedia, Paris music-hall, Femme de France, La Femme dans la vie sociale.*

# Appendix: translations of song lyrics

**p. 1** (Introduction)

A city changes its shape more swiftly, we know, than does the mortal heart. But before abandoning it to its memories – as all cities, self-absorbed in the fever for metamorphosis which marks the second half of the twentieth century – there are also times, and not just once, when it may have changed it, that heart, in its own way …

**p. 82**

He's a tough guy / He's a bit on the dodgy side.

But tomorrow, this evening maybe / They [the women] will come to see us in our *musettes* / And we will read in their drunken eyes / The vow they dare not utter.

**p. 119**

When I'm near tough guys / My heart feels delirious, / A tune on the accordion / And my whole being reels … / A strenuous *Java* … makes me …

**p. 137**

What distance between our hearts! / So much space between our kisses! / Oh bitter fate! / O harsh absence! / O great, unasuaged desires!

In the still-fatal bedroom / Of the still-fatal house / Where reasoning and moralising / Hold him more than is reasonable …

**p. 139**

He was covered with tattoos / Which I never really understood / On his neck was 'Out of sight out of grasp' / On his heart 'Nobody' / On his right arm, one word: 'Think'

The shrill cry of the Ouled-Nail women signals, before the hour of the minarets, that the men are returning to barracks, and sets off the melancholy sound of the sentry's bugle in front of the moon-blue wall of the 'clink'. / Be merry, pack your kitbag / Out of sight / Out of grasp / See it / Grab it / Foreign legion.

**pp. 148–9**

I'd thrust into your naked breast / Which they all fancy / the red and quivering blade / Of the first kitchen knife I could lay my hands on / And with little pinpricks I'd blind / Those eyes of yours with their caressing glances / So like a tart's calling passers-by / Down darkened alleyways …

**p. 157**

Behind the gang / The Foreign Legion / The cream of the Paris streets …

**p. 158**

In spite of all the gadgets / They may invent / They'll never come up with machines / Which can replace us … And to earn a living / On Sundays as well as during the week / We work on the assembly line / Just like they do at Citroën …

**p. 159**

Yet still dreamt that fate / Would bring him back to me one fine day / My legionnaire / That we'd go off together, far away / To some marvellous land / Flooded with sunlight.

Her beat was the Rue Pigalle, / She smelled of cheap vice / She was all black with sins, / With a pale pathetic face, / And yet deep down in her eyes there was / Something sort of miraculous / Which seemed to put a patch of blue / Into the smutty skies of Pigalle.

**pp. 160**

The tarts who offer themselves at night / on street corners / know some lovely tales / which they sometimes tell, / but in crude language, / cherished recollections preserved in their memories … They really have the worst and the saddest of parts to play / without ever once rebelling / and yet all of them / at the slightest promise of hope, / all of them still believe in love.

**pp. 166–7**

We were alone in the dunes / The wind was caressing the sea / In the sky, the moon was laughing / And he, he was biting into my flesh …

We went away on his ship / His beautiful white ship / he went away without telling me / One evening, at sunset. / I can still hear the siren / Of the ship that took him away. / Its voice screamed, dehumanised / 'You'll never see him again!'

**pp. 172**

Villon whom one might expect there within / Art there no longer, nor Verlaine, / In this dark and noisome cellar.

# Index

Writers and singers rather than book and song titles are indexed, but a few frequently referred to films are indexed by title. The illustrations and note on sources are not indexed; only substantive discussion in the notes is indexed

Chevalier, Louis, 12, 16-17, 22-3, 103, 204

Chevalier, Maurice, 4, 12, 25, 32, 34, 36, 49, 51, 57, 67, 70, 71, 74, 79-85, 143, 156, 172, 176, 185, 204, 206

*chiffoniers*, 18, 39, 44, 188

cinema, 4-6, 25-6, 133

City of the People, 4, 6, 48

city writer/poets, 2, 98, 105, 147, 160, 173

Clair, René, 5, 26, 28, 79, 191

Clément, Jean-Baptiste, 179, 183

Cocteau, Jean, 10, 142, 144, 153-4, 156, 166

Colette, 2, 9,16, 20, 24, 65-6, 79, 82, 107, 115, 118, 127, 135, 143, 156, 203

Commune of 1871, 4, 10, 12, 93, 46, 47, 49, 81, 92, 107, 180

Corbusier, Le, 9, 27

Corneau, André, 26

Coulonges, Georges, 180-1

Courbet, Gustave, 13

Crevel, René, 151

crime, 40, 65, 110, 11, 123-4, 125, 128, 138, 144, 147, 153

cross-dressing, drag, 143-7, 151

cultural industries, 15, 29, 50, 68-71, 73-4, 76-7, 90, 91, 100, 110, 165, 176-7, 179, 183, 198

Dabit, Eugène, 25, 107, 135, 182, 204

Daeninckx, Didier, 17, 208

Damia, Maryse, 185, 186

Daniderff, 148, 180, 184

Danjou, Henri, 123

Daudet, Léon, 47

Déat, Marcel 25

Dekobra, Maurice, 2, 58, 115

Delacroix, Eugène, 90

Delarue-Mardrus, Lucie, 107

Delvau, Alfred, 19, 72

Descaves, Lucien, 9, 13-16, 39, 104, 106-8, 173, 182, 187, 188, 190, 191, 195

Descaves, Pierre, 106-7

*Détective Magazine*, 8, 32, 62, 68, 74, 767 97, 114, 120-5, 182, 131, 132, 133, 136, 139-40, 142, 144, 147, 153, 162, 164, 168-9, 205

detective fiction, 20, 72

*différance*, 11, 21

Dignimont, 5, 18

Dognon, André du, 142, 150-5, 157, 169, 200

Doisneau, Robert, 36, 76, 120, 175-6, 209

Dorgelès, Roland 106

Dornain, Luc, 150

'Dossiers Banaux', 8, 18, 109, 134, 202

drag, *see* cross-dressing

Dubas, Marie, 68, 155, 185

Ducamp, Maxime, 44, 47

Dufrenne, Oskar. 113, 144, 149, 152

Duveau, Georges, 13, 22

Duvernois, Henri, 5, 6

D'Yverchen, M.-F., 115, 127

Emer, Michel, 174

*Enfants du Paradis, Les*, 15. 18, 24-9, 32-8, 43, 85, 108

*Enfer*, 20, 171

*Épuration*, 80, 84. 107

Fagus, Félicien, 67

*faits divers*, 16, 60, 61-2, 67, 68, 74, 80, 128, 150, 153, 179, 208

Faubourg Saint-Germain, 25, 131

*Faubourg Montmartre*, 6, 88-90, 106, 196

feminism, position of women, 9, 85, 118, 119

Ferny, Jacques, 183

Ferré, Léo, 183

flâneur, flânerie, 9, 20, 30, 34, 41, 50, 59, 67, 91-2, 100, 127, 131, 147, 198, 204, 205, 207

fleamarkets, 5, 6, 8, 28, 44, 53, 186-7, 190, 195

*France profonde*, 47, 173, 177

Fréhel, 28. 34, 81, 132, 149, 154, 157, 175, 186, 192, 196, 200-1

*fripier, fripière*, 38-40, 44, 52, 187

*Frou-Frou*, 95, 114, 138

Fuchs, Eduard, 109, 111

Gaboriau, Emile, 38, 72. 88, 90, 99

gallant, the, 9. 10, 93, 95